TEACHING KIT

A complete curriculum teaching kit is available to accompany this book. It is possible to teach the content of the resource in marriage seminars, Sunday School classes, retreats, small groups, etc. The kit contains the structure, outline, time sequence and learning activities, as well as many transparency patterns, that allow you to make professional level transparencies to use as you teach.

For information on ordering this unique teaching kit, either call Christian Marriage Enrichment at 1-800-875-7560 or write us at P.O. Box 2468, Orange, CA 92859-0468.

RAISING KIDS TO LOVE JESUS

A Biblical Guide for Parents

H. NORMAN
Wright & Oliver
GARY J.

Regal

A Division of Gospel Light
Ventura, California, U.S.A.

Published by Regal Books
A Division of Gospel Light
Ventura, California, U.S.A.
Printed in U.S.A.

Regal Books is a ministry of Gospel Light, an evangelical Christian publisher dedicated to serving the local church. We believe God's vision for Gospel Light is to provide church leaders with biblical, user-friendly materials that will help them evangelize, disciple and minister to children, youth and families.

It is our prayer that this Regal book will help you discover biblical truth for your own life and help you meet the needs of others. May God richly bless you.

For a free catalog of resources from Regal Books and Gospel Light please call your Christian supplier, or contact us at 1-800-4-GOSPEL or at www.gospellight.com.

Cover Design by Kevin Keller
Interior Design by Robert Williams
Edited by Karen Kaufman and Virginia Woodard

Library of Congress Cataloging-in-Publication Data
Wright, H. Norman.
    Raising kids to love Jesus / H. Norman Wright and Gary J. Oliver.
        p. cm.
    Includes bibliographical references.
    ISBN 0-8307-2153-3 (trade paper)
    1. Child rearing—Religious aspects—Christianity. 2. Christian education of children. I. Oliver, Gary J. II. Title.
    BV4529.W743 1999   98-43994
    248.8'45—dc21   CIP

1 2 3 4 5 6 7 8 9 10 11 12 13 14 15 16 17 18 19 20 / 05 04 03 02 01 00 99

Rights for publishing this book in other languages are contracted by Gospel Literature International (GLINT). GLINT also provides technical help for the adaptation, translation and publishing of Bible study resources and books in scores of languages worldwide. For further information, write to GLINT at P.O. Box 4060, Ontario, CA 91761-1003, U.S.A. You may also send e-mail to Glintint@aol.com, or visit their web site at www.glint.org.

CONTENTS

Section I

INTRODUCTION

1

THE BATTLE FOR YOUR CHILD'S HEART

By Gary J. Oliver

Fan into flame the gift of God, which is in you....
What you have heard from me, keep as the pattern of
sound teaching,...Guard the good deposit that was
entrusted to you—guard it with the help of the Holy
Spirit who lives in us.
—2 TIMOTHY 1:6,13,14

Hundreds of books have been written about parenting. We should know; we have written several of them. Some, including a couple of ours, are even worth reading. Now there is one more. Why one more? Why write another book about parenting? That is what our friends asked. That is what the publisher asked. In fact, when we first discussed this project, that is what we asked each other. So why did we take the time to write it? Why did Regal take the chance to publish it? Why should you invest your hard-earned dollars to purchase it and take your valuable time to read it?

Those are great questions. Let me answer them by sharing with you a phone call I received early in my counseling ministry.

DON AND MARGIE'S STORY

"Dr. Oliver," Don began, "you may not remember me, but Margie and I met you several years ago when you led the marriage enrichment conference at our church."

It didn't take long for me to place him. He was a lay leader in his local church, which was one of the largest in his community. He and his wife Margie were on the planning team that had brought me to their church. They were a lovely couple, and I could tell that he loved the Lord.

After a few minutes of small talk, he told me his reason for calling.

"I never dreamed I'd be making a call like this." Then after a long pause and a deep breath that I could hear on my end of the phone he continued, "but I need help." Here was a man who was a leader in his church and community and considered successful in everything he touched, but who was confused and brokenhearted.

Don went on to share that he had been struggling with deep bouts of depression for several months and that his oldest son had just been sentenced to nine months in prison for embezzlement.

"I've been a success in every area of my life except the one that counts the most, being a good dad."

Don planned to be traveling through my town on a business trip and asked if we could spend some concentrated time together. When we met, I learned about a man who grew up in a Christian home and as a young man gave his heart to the Lord. He had a sincere love for God and a deep desire to serve Him. After high school, he attended a strict Bible College that was so committed to helping students maintain purity that they made boys and girls sit on different sides of the chapel and take a chaperone with them on every date.

As a young man, Don committed himself to the spiritual disciplines of regular Bible study, Scripture memory, prayer, church attendance, tithing, etc. Every night before going to bed, he would set his Bible, notebook and Bible memory cards on the kitchen table. He would get up early each morning and start the day with his Lord.

When Margie and he had kids, Don was committed to raising them in the nurture and admonition of the Lord. He took them to church. He read the Bible to them. He made them read the Bible. He wouldn't let them listen to contemporary music, go to movies or attend dances. He didn't let them play with face cards or watch TV on Sundays.

When his children left home, however, they left the Lord behind them. Their young adult lives had been characterized by pregnancies out of wedlock, abortions, cheating, stealing and doing time in prison. In a tone of profound sadness Don reflected, "As I talk to you today, only one of my three children is even starting to become interested in spiritual things."

Don thought he was doing the right things. He had great intentions and good motives. He meant well. He had wanted to help his kids become more like Jesus. He prayed for his children every day. Don knew truth and he worked hard to expose his children to the truth.

So what went wrong? Given all the good intentions and good things he *did* do, some essential things he *did not* do. Don loved his children, but he didn't know his children. He didn't understand his children. Don didn't understand that the seeds of truth are planted most deeply in the soil of our children's hearts when they have been cultivated by understanding and intimate relationships.

THE CURRENT TREND

Is what happened to Don's kids uncommon in our Christian circles? I wish I could answer that question by saying no. I recently heard about a survey of roughly 8,000 Protestant kids from fifth through ninth grades. In this survey, 87 percent of the ninth graders said they believe Jesus Christ is the Son of God who died on the cross and rose again. That's wonderful news. My heart sank, however, when I went on to read that by the time those young people turn 18, only 20 percent of them will say they are committed to Christ or will in any way define themselves as Christians. A staggering 80 percent will turn their backs on the Church, the faith of their parents and their own faith.

Several years ago I had the opportunity to go on a speaking tour of southern England. I was awed by the many beautiful old majestic stone churches and cathedrals. Yet I was saddened to find that many of these places of worship were virtually empty on Sunday. My English host told me that today less than 10 percent of the population attend a Protestant church. The problem isn't that England has become less religious, because in the past five years the Muslim religion has grown 50 percent.

A close look at twentieth-century church history suggests that a major cause of this shocking decline was the way Christian parents did and didn't live their faith before their kids. Before World War II, the state of Christianity in Europe was similar to where it is in the United States today. It was only a few generations ago that their children were losing their way to Christ the same as many of our children are today.

THE DEEPER MESSAGE

How can this be? What is the problem? What is going on? Why is this happening? I agree with Dr. Ross Campbell when he writes, "I feel very strongly that the answer lies in the way we are raising our children. We don't really *know* our children."[1]

"You just don't understand me!" How many times have you heard that from one of your children? How many times have you heard that from your spouse? How many times have you wanted to say those words to someone you love? When someone says, "You just don't understand me," what is that person really saying? What is the deeper message?

Many of us get so busy working, worrying about our own personal problems, marriage and family relationships, health and financial concerns that, as long as our kids aren't causing major problems, we assume everything is fine. As they get older, it becomes easier to spend less time with them, to listen less and to understand them less.

At a time when they need us most, when they are going through some of the most dramatic changes people go through, when much of who they will become as adults is being formed, it is easy to allow circumstances to drive us to the sidelines having good intentions and sincere hearts. We allow ourselves, however, to be distracted by the tyranny of the urgent and lose touch with who our children are becoming.

When we don't make time to stop, listen, ask questions and experience intentional communication, our kids will get the sense that we don't understand, and when we don't understand, the underlying message is that we don't really care. If that happens enough times, our children will look elsewhere for the encouragement, validation and sense of significance that is so important to them.

On a recent talk show, I heard a guest say that the typical American family now works 1,000 more hours each year than it did 25 years ago. We live in a world where "busyness substitutes for meaning, efficiency substitutes for creativity, and functional relationships substitute for love...where communion with God is replaced by activity for God."[2]

PROVIDING THE MOST, BUT NOT THE BEST

All of us want the best for our kids. Many parents believe that if they can give their kids a nice place to live, a secure environment, good food, designer clothes, drive them to all their sporting events, provide them with adequate spending money, buy them a decent car and give them a good education, they will have done the best they could do.

Those things are good, but as Christian parents we know that the best isn't just providing things. The best involves leading our children into a personal relationship with Jesus Christ and giving them the tools they need to grow, deepen and mature. One of the most exciting times of my life was when each of my three boys asked Jesus into his heart. However, that is only the beginning. I don't merely want my kids to be saved; I want them to know what it means to "be conformed to the image of His Son" (Rom. 8:29, *NKJV*).

Salvation is the essential first step—but it is only the first step. I want to see my boys experience more than justification. I want them to know what it means to walk with the Lord. I want them to develop the intrinsic motivation to be in the Word, in prayer, active in church and to share their faith with clarity and boldness. I want them to develop emotional balance, the ability to love, the ability to face problems and handle conflict, and the ability to see the relevance of biblical truth for everyday life. How do we move our kids from decision to discipleship, from believing in Jesus to behaving like Jesus?

WHAT THIS BOOK IS ABOUT

That's what this book is about. We have prayerfully written this book to help you cultivate and communicate your own relationship with Christ in such a way that you will better understand your children and be much more likely to raise spiritually healthy and intelligent kids who love Jesus, look like Jesus, act like Jesus, reflect Jesus and want to spend time with Jesus. Children who understand the true basis for boasting heed the following words:

> "Let not the wise man boast of his wisdom
> or the strong man boast of his strength
> or the rich man boast of his riches,
> but let him who boasts boast about this:
> that he understands and knows me,
> that I am the Lord, who exercises kindness,
> justice and righteousness on earth,
> for in these I delight," declares the Lord (Jer. 9:23,24).

This book will help you discover what it means to be a wise and understanding parent. Proverbs 13:20 says, "He who walks with the wise grows wise, but a companion of fools suffers harm." Children who walk with wise parents, children who hear and see wisdom in action, are more likely to grow wise.

BEING AN UNDERSTANDING PARENT

It is true that understanding parents are concerned with the behavior of their children. Yet it is easy for parents to get distracted by a child's behavior. Our appropriate concern with performance can take priority over their person. What they do can become more important to us than what they are becoming.

AN UNDERSTANDING PARENT DOESN'T MERELY DISCUSS AND DISSECT TRUTH; HE OR SHE DEMONSTRATES THE POWER, FRESHNESS AND RELEVANCE OF TRUTH.

Understanding parents are much more concerned with the condition of the child's heart. Understanding parents are concerned with far more than imparting the correct information, or making sure their kids know from what kinds of activities they should abstain. An understanding parent doesn't merely discuss and dissect truth; he or she demonstrates the power, freshness and relevance of truth.

At the outset and in all fairness, we need to warn you that there is a high price to pay in making the choice to become an understanding parent. Every day you are presented with more challenges and opportunities than you will ever be able to take advantage of. There are always new things to hear, do, see, learn and accomplish. Day by day the list of options grows and grows. There are more opportunities than any of us have time to pursue. Therefore, we are forced to choose.

Either by intentional design or by default, we are making choices. To make wise choices, we must have some kind of grid through which we evaluate those things that are good, better and best. How do you decide what are those good and better things to which we can't say yes, because of the best things to which we cannot say no?

In God's economy, one of those "best" things involves our relationship with our children. If I choose to be a good and godly parent, it means that I may not have the time, money or energy to do many of the good and better things that I would enjoy doing. I could do well at many of them; they might bring some honor and glory to God, they would be a lot of fun and would help me become more self-actualized and maximize more of my potential.

Choosing to become an understanding parent will affect your career, leisure time, hobbies and friendships. You won't be able to read as much or play as much, your house won't be as big, your cars won't be as new, you won't have the money to ski or scuba dive as much, and your golf handicap will be higher.

We can spend our lives pursuing good things, or we can invest our lives pursuing the best. I have met with too many parents, who could buy me 10 times over, who own several homes, who with tears in their eyes coming from the deep, dark well of a shattered heart, tell me that if they could do it all over again, they truly would put first things first.

The Challenge

HANDLING THE ANACONDAS OF OUR LIVES

This past year a friend of mine pulled something off the Internet that is said to have come from the U.S. Government Peace Corps manual for its volunteers who work in the Amazon jungle. It tells volunteers what to do in case they are attacked by an anaconda, the largest snake in the world. An anaconda can grow up to 35 feet long and weigh between 300 and 400 pounds. Now, that is a big snake. Would you know what to do if you were attacked by an anaconda? The answer might surprise you. Here is what the volunteers are told:

1. If you are attacked by an anaconda, do not run. The snake is faster than you are.
2. Lie flat on the ground. Put your arms tight against your sides, your legs tight against one another.
3. Tuck your chin in.
4. The snake will come and begin to nudge and climb over your body.

5. Do not panic.
6. After the snake has examined you, it will begin to swallow you from the feet end—always from the feet end. Permit the snake to swallow your feet and ankles. Do not panic.
7. The snake will now begin to suck your legs into its body. You must lie perfectly still. This will take a long time.
8. When the snake has reached your knees, slowly, and with as little movement as possible, reach down, take your knife and very gently slide it into the side of the snake's mouth between the edge of its mouth and your leg. Then suddenly rip upwards, severing the snake's head.
   (The last two suggestions were the ones that really got to me!)
9. Be sure you have your knife.
10. Be sure your knife is sharp.

Today, many philosophical, relational, social and spiritual anacondas are out there seeking to devour our children. What do some of these anacondas look like? One of them is the fact that the only absolute our kids are taught today is that there are no absolutes. Nothing is certain. Kids are encouraged to question all values, especially the ones they acquire at church or in the home. Secular experts in child rearing tell us that we should treat our children as primitive savages in the area of values. Give them the freedom to select their own values from the slanted, distorted menu of situation ethics.

Another anaconda is that today's young people have few good models who demonstrate character and integrity. "Our society has replaced heroes with celebrities, the quest for a well-informed character with the search for a flat stomach, substance and depth with image and personality. In the political process, the makeup man is more important than the speech writer, and we approach the voting booth, not on the basis of a well-developed philosophy of what the state should be, but with a heart full of images, emotions, and slogans all packed into thirty-second sound bites."[3]

MEDIA INFLUENCES ON OUR CHILDREN

The majority of children today know much more about Barney, Beavis and Butthead than they do about the Bible. The media continue to make a blatant attack on traditional family values. The American Family Association revealed that 89 percent of all sex depicted on prime-time TV is outside marriage. Heavy exposure to prime-time television programming featuring intimacy between unmarried persons can clearly result in altered moral judgment, according to Dr. J. Bryant and S. C. Rockwell.[4]

> THE MEDIA HAVE NOT ONLY DESENSITIZED OUR CHILDREN IN THE AREA OF MORALS, BUT HAVE ALSO DESENSITIZED THEM TO THE DESTRUCTIVE EFFECTS OF VIOLENCE.

According to *The Parent's Guide to Current Movies*, the average PG movie contains a dozen four-letter words, 10 profanities and 6 sexual innuendoes, often explicit.[5] You can double that number for PG-13 movies. The pervasiveness of moral desensitization is well illustrated by the fact that McDonald's recently offered a mid-1990s PG movie to go along with a children's Happy Meal for an extra $5.95. The movie pokes fun at masturbation, alludes to satisfying oral sex and is laced with God-jeering profanity.

The media have not only desensitized our children in the area of morals, but have also desensitized them to the destructive effects of violence. Archie and Donald Duck have been replaced on almost every comic-book rack by drugs, sex and graphic superhero violence, all of which is packaged for young children. Television remotes allow kids to move from "South Park" to "Jerry Springer." At tender ages, kids become armed with joysticks that take them from "Mortal Kombat" to other blood sports. The most popular children's video games produced by the multibillion-dollar electronic game makers feature demons, witches and satanic-style violence.

It was interesting to observe the amazement of many people at the massacre of five people by 11- and 13-year-old boys, when studies I have read indicate that today's children watch about 43 hours of violent cartoons each week—48 acts of violence an hour. During the 10-year period between ages 5 to 15, children will witness an estimated 13,000 human deaths on television.

I agree with Joe White who has written that "history will record this period as the time when our family values were torched with a barrage of antifamily education, legislation, entertainment, and leadership. As always, the fire is the hottest and most lethal when it reaches the hearts of our kids, whose generation will close out this century with more promiscuity, suicides, abortions, drug addictions, and countless other examples of moral bankruptcy than any other generation of kids in any nation during any period of time since 'In the beginning'."[6]

The following is a great example of just how much family values have changed during the past four decades. "Roseanne" writer-coproducer Betsy Borns has compared some of the leading characters from the most highly rated TV family shows of the early '90s—the Conners—with their '50s counterparts, the "Leave It to Beaver" Cleavers.

June Cleaver	Roseanne Conner
· Full-time homemaker.	· Full-time waitress.
· Her house is tidy, her hair is perfect, and her meals are served on time.	· Her house is a war zone, her hair is a rat's nest, and her meals come from a box.
· Loves baking, washes pots.	· Loves bakeries, smoked pot.
· *Memorable romantic moment:* Goes to the door and kisses her husband.	· *Memorable romantic moment:* Goes to a gay bar and kisses a lesbian.
· *What she's proudest of:* She lives for her husband and children.	· *What she's proudest of:* She allows her husband and children to live.

Ward Cleaver

- Has a steady, white-collar job.
- Is often called Sir by his sons, Wally and the Beaver.
- Enjoys taking in news, via the newspaper.
- The children are punished when he comes home.
- *Sage advice to sons:* "Always follow the golden rule."

Dan Conner

- Fixes trucks. Has ring-around-the-collar.
- Was once called "the Fuhrer" by his daughter Darlene.
- Enjoys taking in beer, via the can.
- The children are punished when Roseanne feels like it.
- *Sage advice to sons:* "Stop peeing behind the garage; you're killing the tomatoes."

The Beaver

- Shy, adorable.
- Once hid money in his sock drawer to save up for a bike.
- *Memorable childhood moment:* Smashed Ward's car window with a baseball.
- *Charming boyish prank:* Got stuck trying to see if there was real soup in a billboard soup bowl.

D.J.

- Sly, incorrigible.
- Once hid women's magazines in his bedroom to read them...uh..."intimately."
- *Memorable childhood moment:* Went to a school party and "touched a boob."
- *Charming boyish prank:* Stole the family car one day and promptly proceeded to drive it into a ditch.

Wally

- *Shocking teen confession:* Admitted he lied to impress a girl; later apologized.
- *Dream date:* A quiet evening in a well-lit soda shop.
- *Taste in friends:* Brought his oily pal Eddie Haskell home after school.

Darlene

- *Shocking teen confession:* Admitted she tried cocaine; later tried it again.
- *Dream date:* A loud night in a cheap motel.
- *Taste in friends:* Brought her abused boyfriend David home to live.

- *A phase he went through*: Wore his hair in a ducktail; was reprimanded by June.
- *A phase she went through*: Dyed her hair black; sunk into a two-year depression.[7]

If you didn't believe it before, reading through this comparison will convince you that times have changed, priorities have changed and values have changed. The sad news is that those changes have not been good for our marriages, our families or our children. It might be tempting to allow our discouragement to turn into despair and to believe that the situation is hopeless. However, God is still on the throne; we have the promises of God's Word and the indwelling power of the Holy Spirit, so nothing could be further from the truth.

Yes, many powerful cultural influences shape our kids. By God's grace, though, we can still be the most powerful. Parenting is not just providing good input. It is not just creating a constructive home atmosphere and positive interaction between a child and his or her parent.

PARENTS ARE CALLED TO BE TEACHERS

The ultimate goal of Christian parenting is not kids who merely have a knowledge about God. It is kids who have a personal relationship with God. It is kids who really believe that God's Word is relevant for every aspect of their lives. It involves teaching our children the ways of God, helping them understand the character of God, helping them to become sensitive to the darkness of their own hearts and the danger of walking alone and trusting in themselves. It involves teaching them the power of the Cross and the provision of God's promises.

God has called us to lead, guide, nurture, correct and discipline our children. God has sovereignly placed us in authority over our children and we must be willing to assume that responsibility.

In Genesis 18:19, God speaks of Abraham when He says, "I have chosen him, so that he will direct his children and his household after him to keep the way of the Lord by doing what is right and just."

In Ephesians 6:4, we are commanded to bring up our children "in the training and instruction of the Lord." Children will be good decision makers as they observe faithful parents modeling and instructing wise direction and decision making on their behalf.

The core message of this book is that *the key to effectively accomplishing the task of helping our children become more like Christ is by understanding our children and making sure they know they are understood.* Do your children believe you care about what is going on inside them? What have you done in the past week that has given them this message? If we don't model the importance of understanding what they think and believe, why should they think it important to understand what we think and believe? Just because we are their parents? That didn't work a hundred years ago and, unfortunately, that's not how it works today!

If it is true that out of the abundance of the heart the mouth speaks, what is in our children's hearts? How do they learn to express what is in their hearts? What happens when they make awkward or crude attempts to express their hearts? Are they corrected, shamed and blamed? Are they humiliated? Are they pacified with the obligatory "uh-huh"?

Proverbs 20:5 says, "The purposes of a man's heart are deep waters, but a man of understanding draws them out." Today's Christian parents need to learn how to become *heart* monitors and draw out of their children who they are and what is most important to them. We have written this book to help you do just that.

Notes

1. Ross Campbell, *Kids Who Follow, Kids Who Don't* (Wheaton, Ill.: Victor Books, 1987), p. 15.
2. Brent Curtis and John Eldredge, *The Sacred Romance: Drawing Closer to the Heart of God* (Nashville: Thomas Nelson, 1997), p. 6.
3. J. P. Moreland, *Love Your God With All Your Mind: The Role of Reason in the Life of the Soul* (Colorado Springs: NavPress, 1997), p. 21.

4. *Facts About Pornography*, "Effects of Massive Exposure to Sexually Oriented Prime Time Television," American Family Association, Tupelo, Miss., brochure, n.d., n.p.
5. Dr. Tom and James Elkin, eds., *The Parent's Guide to Current Movies* (January-December 1988), n.p.
6. Joe White, *Faith Training: Raising Kids Who Love the Lord* (Colorado Springs: Focus on the Family Publishing, 1994), p. 3.
7. Betsy Borns, *Parenting Magazine*, Vol. 9, Issue 2, 1995, n.p.

2

WHAT DIFFERENCE CAN PARENTS MAKE?

By Gary J. Oliver

Choose for yourselves this day whom you will serve,
whether the gods your forefathers served...or the gods...in
whose land you are living. But as for me and my
household, we will serve the Lord.

— J O S H U A   2 4 : 1 5

The quality of family life influences every other part of our lives. Surveys have found that Americans' greatest source of happiness in life is the family. These surveys have also found that the greatest source of frustration and disappointment in people's lives is handling family problems.

People across the country have become alarmed at the decline and decay of the family. In unprecedented numbers our families are different from others': (1) fathers are working while mothers keep house; (2) both fathers and mothers are working away from home; (3) more parents are single; (4)second marriages are bringing children together from unrelated backgrounds; (5) couples are childless; (6) unmarried couples live together with and without children; (7) gays and lesbians are parents. Today we are witnessing a period of historic change in American family life, and the losers are our children.

This change is evident everywhere in our culture. Babies are having babies; kids are refusing to grow up and leave home; people casually move in with each other and out again; affluent yuppies spend more time with their BMWs than with their children; rich and poor children alike destroy their minds with drugs.

The divorce rate has doubled since 1965, and demographers project that half of all first marriages formed today will end in divorce. Six out of 10 second marriages will probably collapse. One-third of all children born in the past decade will probably live in a stepfamily before they are 18. One out of every four children today is being raised by a single parent. About 22 percent of children today were born to a teenage mother. One out of every five children lives in poverty; the rate is twice as high among Blacks and Hispanics.

Families who have a working father, a caretaking mother and one or more minor children now constitute only 9 percent of the households in the United States, in contrast to 60 percent in 1955. Fewer than 40 percent of the children born today will grow up in the traditional two-parent family. Twenty-seven percent of all families who have children are single-parent families—almost all have a female head of household.

The Bible tells us that in the beginning God created the family. In His infinite wisdom when He created humankind in His own image, He chose the family to serve as the cradle for personhood. In Deuteronomy 6, as well as in other biblical passages, it is clear that God designed the family as the crucible in which the reality of the Person of the living God is to be both taught (through formal education) and caught (by the example of the parents' lives).

Hear, O Israel! The Lord is our God, the Lord alone. And you must love the Lord your God with all your heart, all your soul, and all your strength. And you must commit yourselves wholeheartedly to these commands I am giving you today. Repeat them again and again to your children.

Talk about them when you are at home and when you are away on a journey, when you are lying down and when you are getting up again. Tie them to your hands as a reminder, and wear them on your forehead. Write them on the doorposts of your house and on your gates (Deut. 6:4-9, *NLT*).

From the beginning of time, God intended for the family to be the basic unit for all society. As goes the individual family so goes the church. As goes the church so goes the community. As goes the community so goes the nation. As go the nations so go civilizations.

How Healthy Families Should Function

In the past 10 years, much has been written about unhealthy and dysfunctional families. On a recent trip to California I saw an excellent illustration of how *healthy* families function. In the little seaside town of Cambria on the central California coast, I was shopping with my wife and came across a mobile made up of nine delicate seashells. Each one was a different size, shape and color. As I looked at the mobile suspended from the ceiling of the gift shop, I noticed each one of the separate shells hung suspended in delicate harmony and balance with the other eight.

I walked over to the mobile and gently blew on one of the shells. Do you know what happened? Of course you do. Because the shells were linked together, the energy from that gentle breath that touched the one shell was transmitted to the other eight. The entire mobile was affected and all the shells moved in different directions in a graceful dance.

This is similar to what happens in a family. In place of the seashells you can picture the members of your family. Your family "mobile" probably includes at least two sets of grandparents, your parents, your brothers and sisters, your spouse and your children. Regardless of the kind of structure your family has, what happens to one family member, or the decisions one member makes, can and does affect every other individual in the family as well as the entire family system.

Our relationships with our kids are the windows through which they get their first glimpse of God. It is also where they get their first glimpse of who they are and what they are worth. Our children discover their value and worth in the mirror of those closest to them, by how much they are looked at, listened to and touched, by what we say to them and about them in front of others and by how much time we make for them. Often this initial view will stay with them throughout their lifetime.

A Young Minister's Story—Enough Is Never Enough

Several years ago a discouraged pastor asked if he could meet with me. Paul was a young man who loved the Lord and had dedicated his life to serving Him through the local church. However, he was frustrated, defeated, guilty, burned-out and ready to quit his church and the ministry. He said he had come to realize that he had some serious problems that were handicapping his ministry and effectiveness as a witness for Jesus Christ.

In my initial interview I discovered that he was a compulsive workaholic who spent well more than 60 hours a week in church-related work and was gone from the home an average of four nights a week. His family got the leftovers. He said, "I'm working as hard as I can but I've decided that enough is never enough. What's wrong with me?"

As we talked, Paul told me the story of his childhood. He was reared in an evangelical Christian home and grew up in a solid Bible-teaching church. His parents were sincere, well-meaning and good-intentioned. They wanted each one of their children to grow up in the nurture and admonition of the Lord. They took him to church, they made him memorize Bible verses and they didn't watch TV on Sundays.

Paul was the second of three boys whose father frequently compared him to his handsome, intelligent and athletic brother. Tears came to his eyes as he recalled the many times his father said, "You're so lazy, you stink." These unfair comparisons, criticisms, put-downs and sarcastic remarks led him to believe that whatever he would do would never be good enough.

He tried harder and harder, first at home, then at school, then in seminary and then in his church. "Dr. Oliver," he said, "I have spent most of my life trying to please teachers, friends and parents and trying to shape my life by their expectations. I went through all of my schooling, including seminary, harboring these underlying motivations, apparently trying to find a deep sense of security and love."

His growing church was a testimony to his ability to teach the Word with conviction and clarity. In practice, however, Paul lived as if the principles and promises of Scripture applied to everyone but himself. He functioned as if his heavenly Father saw him the same way as his earthly father did. Do you think this is an extreme example? Trust me, it isn't! It was a joy for me to sit down with him, open God's Word, and share some familiar passages that helped him to see himself through God's eyes.

A Profile of the Christian Family

Isn't it enough for a child to grow up in a Christian family? Well, that depends on how you define a Christian family. In chapter 1 you met Don who raised his three kids in a "Christian" family. Pastor Paul grew up in what many would consider a strong "Christian" home. There is a difference between a family in which everyone is a Christian and a Christian family—a huge difference.

RELATIONSHIPS PATTERNED AFTER GOD
It takes more than the fact that every family member is a born-again Christian to make a Christian family. A Christian family is a family where relationships with each other are patterned after the way

God communicates and relates to them as His children. It is a place where costly grace is demonstrated, where truth is lived out and not merely talked about.

TRUTH IS TAUGHT
A healthy Christian family provides an atmosphere of support, encouragement and positive opportunities for growth, which includes helping each person to come to a knowledge, understanding and acceptance of God and Jesus Christ. It also provides a knowledge, understanding and acceptance to each family member as a unique person made in the image of God. It involves both a Bible-teaching and a Bible-living ministry. It is a family in which the truth is both taught and caught.

PARENTS MODEL BEING MADE IN GOD'S IMAGE
In a healthy Christian family, the parents function in a way that provides an observable model of what it means to be made in God's image. Family is where we learn the importance of a growing love relationship with Jesus Christ and the reality of sin and the need for salvation. We learn what it means to be a man or woman, how to relate intimately to another person and how to form strong lasting commitments. We learn how to acknowledge and express emotions and how to have constructive conflict. We also learn how to have physical, emotional and intellectual boundaries and how to communicate. We learn how to be self-disciplined, how to cope and survive life's unending problems and how to appreciate who God has made us to be and how to love others.

Parenting Approaches

PARENTING BY NEGATION
There are various ways to approach the ministry of parenting. Based on our desire to protect our children and keep them from the evil influences of the world, we can be like Don and emphasize what

they shouldn't do, where they shouldn't go and what they shouldn't listen to. This approach could be called parenting by negation, and it does have some value. We do need to protect our kids, to guard and guide them. However, there is more to it than that.

PARENTING BY INFORMATION

Another approach is seen in the many sincere Christian parents I have met who interpreted Proverbs 22:6 to mean that the most important task of parenting was to expose the children to as much sound biblical teaching as possible. I call this parenting by information.

The primary philosophy is that if you can just cram enough truth into their craniums as children, when they grow up they will turn out to be good kids with hearts for the Lord. Sadly, that in many cases simply doesn't happen. Chuck Swindoll has noted that biblical teaching is not like nuclear fallout. Exposure to it does not necessarily lead to absorption of it. Not all of those who are hearers become doers.

PARENTING BY COMBINING FORMAL AND INFORMAL INSTRUCTION

A third parenting approach combines the best of the first two, but is more consistent with the clear teaching of Scripture. In Deuteronomy 6:4-9, Moses reminds the people that they are to love the Lord with all of their heart, soul and might and focus on the things of God. He instructs the parents, "Repeat them again and again to your children. Talk about them when you are at home and when you are away on a journey, when you are lying down and when you are getting up again. Tie them to your hands as a reminder, and wear them on your forehead. Write them on the doorposts of your house and on your gates!" (NLT).

In this passage, Moses tells parents that there are two basic ways to teach their children. Instruction can be either formal or informal. In formal instruction we tell children the truth. In informal instruction we live or model the truth before them. Both are important, but in this passage Moses emphasizes the informal or lifestyle instruction.

In Andrew Murray's book *How to Raise Your Children for Christ*, he writes the following:

> Not in what we say and teach, but in what we *are* and *do*, lies the power of training. Not as we *think* of an ideal for training our children, but as we *live* do we train them. It is not our wishes or our theory, but our will and our practice that really train. It is by living the Christ-life that we prove that we love it, that we have it; and thus will influence the young mind to love it and to have it, too.[1]

Quality Parenting

The essential starting point in quality parenting is to realize that the greatest gift you can give your child is not only in what you *do*, but also in who you *are*. Don't get me wrong; what you do with and for your children is important. However, it is easy to focus on their performance to the exclusion of their person. It is easy to forget that some truths are better caught than taught. The lifestyle your children see you model day in and day out is much more powerful than what they are told. Both are important. However, there must be congruence between the talk and the walk.

AT AN EARLY AGE I DECIDED THAT MORNINGS WERE A RESULT OF ADAM AND EVE'S ORIGINAL SIN, SO I RARELY GOT UP EARLY!

MY PARENTS' EXAMPLE

As I was writing this, God brought to my mind the example of my own parents. Consistent with the clear teaching of Deuteronomy 6, my parents provided me with both formal and informal instruction. Yet when I think about what they did that was most helpful and meaningful to me, what stands out in my memory is their example.

They didn't merely tell me how important it was to have sound biblical teaching. They took me to church. They listened to Christian radio. Instead of giving me lectures about the evils of bad music and dwelling on what I shouldn't listen to, they listened to both secular and sacred music that was good.

My mom and dad didn't force me to get up early in the morning to read my Bible and pray. At an early age I decided that mornings were a result of Adam and Eve's original sin, so I rarely got up early! To this day, however, there is etched in my mind the vivid picture of when I did get up early, seeing my father in his bathrobe either reading the Bible or praying.

When I was wrong my parents corrected me. When I was disobedient they disciplined me. When I made a mistake they forgave me. When I sinned they reminded me of the need for repentance and the fact of God's grace. When I was overcome with discouragement they listened and encouraged me. When I was ashamed and felt like a total failure they didn't lecture or condemn. They loved me, accepted me and reminded me of God's promises.

No, they were not perfect. Yes, they did make mistakes; but that was yet another gift. They let me see their weaknesses as well as their strengths. They didn't try to model a false perfection. They were willing to admit when they were wrong and apologized. They acknowledged their limitations. They allowed me to see the process of sanctification and the ministry of the Holy Spirit in their lives.

One of the best illustrations of the importance of modeling comes from a saying printed on a refrigerator magnet I purchased for my wife several years ago. It is entitled "Children Learn What They Live":

> If a child lives with criticism, he learns to condemn.
> If a child lives with hostility, he learns to fight.
> If a child lives with shame, he learns to feel guilty.
> If a child lives with tolerance, he learns to be patient.

If a child lives with ridicule, he learns to be shy.
If a child lives with encouragement, he learns confidence.
If a child lives with fairness, he learns justice.
If a child lives with security, he learns to have faith.
If a child lives with approval, he learns to like himself.
If a child lives with acceptance and friendship,
he learns to find love in the world.

Striving to Be Model Parents

What do your children see when they look at you? What do you model? Do they see a Mom and Dad or single parent who has a visible love for God and for His Word and His people? Do they see 1 Corinthians 13 in action? Do they know that your love for them is not based on their performance? Do they have healthy examples of problem-solving and conflict-resolution skills? Are they getting a clear idea of what it means to be a male or female who is made in God's image? Do you appreciate and promote their uniqueness? Do you model and encourage a healthy experience and expression of emotions?

Let's get even more specific. What are some of the values and characteristics you would like your children to have when they become adults? Now for the hard part. At the present time, to what degree are you a model of those characteristics and values? In what specific way does your lifestyle reflect what you say is most important in life? Keep in mind the fact that I am not talking about big things. I am talking about little, simple, easy, practical things.

It doesn't take very much time or cost very much money to say I love you, to listen intently to what they are saying, to look them in the eyes when you talk to them, to apologize, to ask forgiveness, to touch, to call on the phone, to pray for or share a prayer request, to send a card, to compliment, encourage and nourish and build.

Our children live in a world of noise and busyness. Information and technology are increasing at such a fast pace that our everyday lives seem to be moving down a highway so fast that the telephone poles become a blur. Our kids are bored, bombarded, blinded, biased and bankrupt. They have more sound, brighter images, better graphics and faster action, and more despair, depression, cynicism and boredom. We must learn how to live before our children in ways that speak truth, that shine as beacons of hope to a generation growing up in a disintegrating culture characterized by sarcasm, despair and cynicism.

Understanding Our Children to Help Us Be Better-Equipped Parents

By now you have probably guessed that this isn't your typical parenting book. Our belief is that by the time you finish reading this book, you will never look at your children and the ministry of parenting the same. What lies in the chapters ahead is more than just a tool chest of parenting techniques. It is a fresh perspective about the purpose and process of better understanding your child and thus be better equipped to shepherd your child's heart.

If we don't understand our kids, if we haven't invested quantity time observing them, studying them, listening to them and knowing them, we won't understand them. If we don't understand them, we will miss what God is doing in their lives, and be unable to join with God in that process.

God has given ordinary parents like you and me everything we need to change our children's lives and to help them become extraordinary adults. Christian parenting involves more than instructing our kids in biblical principles, making sure they know what they shouldn't do and exhorting them to do what is right. Who we are in our walk with the Lord is what we will see in their walk with Him.

If some truths are better caught than taught, then what are our kids catching? What do our kids see when they look at us? Do our kids see us pray? How much time do we spend in the Word? Do we spend consistent time alone with God? What do they learn about knowing God's will? What kind of relationships/friendships do they observe?

We agree with Larry Crabb when he writes,

> The deepest urge in every human heart is to be in relationship with someone who absolutely delights in us, someone with resources we lack who has no greater joy than giving to us, someone who respects us enough to require us to use everything we receive for the good of others, and because he has given it to us, knows we have something to give.[2]

Whenever we speak at family conferences, the majority of parenting questions we are asked relate to correction, discipline and punishment. These are important concerns for every parent.

TODAY'S CHILDREN NEED MORE THAN GUIDELINES, GUARDRAILS AND DIRECTION. THEY NEED SHEPHERDS WHO UNDERSTAND THE TIMES AND UNDERSTAND THEIR HEARTS.

Proverbs 19:18 tells us, "Discipline your son, for in that there is hope." In Proverbs 15:32 we read, "He who ignores discipline despises himself, but whoever heeds correction gains understanding." Hebrews 12 tells us that God's discipline is a sign of His love; it is done for our good "that we may share in his holiness" (v. 10). In fact, "it produces a harvest of righteousness and peace for those who have been trained by it" (v. 11). Although we believe discipline is important, we are not going to talk a lot about it. Many other good books including *Dare To Discipline* by James Dobson provide sound, practical and biblically consistent counsel about discipline.

Parents as Good Shepherds

We have come to believe that the root of our parenting problems is a lack of togetherness, a failure to understand our children and connect with them in ways that allow our passion for Christ to spill over onto them and into their hearts. Today's children need more than guidelines, guardrails and direction. They need shepherds who understand the times and understand their hearts. The model for this kind of parenting is our Lord Jesus Christ. In the Gospel of John we are told that the Good Shepherd cares for the sheep:

> The watchman opens the gate for him, and the sheep listen to his voice. He calls his own sheep by name and leads them out. When he has brought out all his own, he goes on ahead of them, and his sheep follow him because they know his voice. But they will never follow a stranger; in fact, they will run away from him because they do not recognize a stranger's voice. I am the good shepherd. The good shepherd lays down his life for the sheep. The hired hand is not the shepherd who owns the sheep. So when he sees the wolf coming, he abandons the sheep and runs away....because he is a hired hand and cares nothing for the sheep. I am the good shepherd; I know my sheep and my sheep know me—just as the Father knows me and I know the Father—and I lay down my life for the sheep. My sheep listen to my voice; I know them, and they follow me (John 10:3-5,11-15,27).

Any shepherd will tell you that sheep aren't likely to follow a voice they don't know. They won't follow a stranger. Christ said His sheep hear His voice and they know His voice. Do your kids know your voice or have you become a stranger to them? Do they know that, like their heavenly Father, you are a good shepherd who knows them, understands them and truly cares for them?

Simple observation and personal experience will tell you that kids won't follow the voice of parents who don't know them. It is obvious that you can't guide children you don't know, and they aren't likely to follow a parent who they believe doesn't know them. Children are much more likely to trust a parent who delights in them, believes in them, assumes the best about them and is quick to forgive them.

Kids who are listened to tend to listen. Kids who know they are understood usually want to understand. Kids who have parents that assume the best about them are more likely to assume the best about others.

A strong, consistent, Christ-centered, love-based relationship with our kids that helps them know they are loved, accepted and understood is the environment in which the "Good News" of the gospel will be caught and not just taught. This is the environment that will make the difference between kids who follow Christ as adults and those who don't.

> The key to successful parenting is not found in complex theories, elaborate family rules, or convoluted formulas for behavior. It is based on your deepest feelings of love and affection for your child, and is demonstrated simply through empathy and understanding. Good parenting begins in your heart, and then continues on a moment-to-moment basis by engaging your children when feelings run high, when they are sad, angry, or scared. The heart of parenting is being there in a particular way when it really counts.[3]

Guidelines for Being a Successful Parent

The fact that you are reading this book says you care about your kids. What is your goal for them? How will you know you have been a successful parent? How do you measure success? What will your children be doing, saying, etc., when they are young adults who will tell you that you did a good job? Is your goal well-behaved kids, manageable kids, kids who don't embarrass you, or kids who are "becoming conformed to the image of His Son"?

If you have read the Bible very much you have discovered that truth has the unique ability to annoy, to frustrate, to destabilize and to make people feel uncomfortable. It sure has had those effects on me. If you don't want to change and grow, if you merely want a few new discipline techniques, you may regret having spent your time and money on this book.

We can't give our kids what we don't have; we can't take them where we haven't been and aren't willing to go. If we aren't willing to let God parent our hearts, if we aren't willing to trust Him as our Good Shepherd, if we don't listen to His voice and follow Him, why should our children be willing to let Him, through us, parent their hearts? If our kids aren't observing us becoming more like Christ, why should they want to become more like Him?

Before you turn the page and go to the next chapter ask yourself: Am I prepared to set myself apart for the work of the Holy Spirit in me to become a good shepherd? Am I willing to allow God's spirit to work in my life in ways that lead others to see more of Christ in me? Do I really want to become more like Jesus?

Notes

1. Andrew Murray, *How to Raise Your Children for Christ* (Minneapolis, Minn.: Bethany House Publishers, 1975), p. 12.
2. Larry Crabb, *Connecting: A Radical New Vision* (Nashville: Word Publishing, 1997), p. 45.
3. John Gottman, *The Heart of Parenting* (New York: Simon & Schuster, 1997), p. 18.

DO YOU *REALLY* WANT YOUR CHILD TO BE LIKE JESUS?

By H. Norman Wright

*If anyone would come after me, he must deny himself
and take up his cross and follow me.*

—MATTHEW 16:24

To train your child to become more like Jesus is a noble step. It is probably what we think we ought to be doing. Christians are those who are following Christ and proclaiming that He is the Lord of their lives. He called us to follow Him.

But do we really want our children to become like Him? Think about it when you read about the life of Christ.

Who felt comfortable around Jesus? His lifestyle really wasn't the respectable type of that time. The Pharisees saw Him as a worldly person and a rule breaker. A rich young ruler walked away from his encounter with Jesus feeling puzzled. Nicodemus was an open-minded man, but he thought it better to meet with Jesus at night than let others see the two of them together. The respected elite of society weren't drawn to Him. The so-called misfits, however, seemed to be comfortable around Him.

A social outcast, a military officer of the hated army, a tax collector, a person who was filled with demons and a prostitute made up those who responded to Jesus. That's a curious group of people.

If Jesus were here today, who would His followers be? We may not want to consider them. They would probably dress differently from those with whom we worship in church. They could be the gay, the HIV positive or the homeless disturbed who live under bridges and in alleys. They would be outspoken and either to the left or the right of society. Is this the group we really want our children to be around or to attract?

Do you know what you are asking your son or daughter to become? You are saying, "Don't fit in! Be different to the extent that others question you, wonder about you, shake their heads about you, aren't sure whether you'll make it in their group, their clique or their organization." You are asking your child to be a nonconformist to the status quo.

You may be uncomfortable reading this right now. Jesus was a man who looked at what was going on in the world—the society, everyday life around Him—and said, "This isn't good." He looked at the way people were living and essentially said, "That's the easy way to live. But it's not good." He confronted the destructiveness of people's lifestyles, which wasn't very popular with the establishment. He encouraged people to live a life that would be different and contrary to the establishment. He also claimed that only a few would be willing to live that kind of life. Jesus called people to live a risky, different kind of life—one that promised peace, but a peace different from that which the world around us gives.

Do you know what Jesus preached? *Nonconformity*. He was different. Do you want your child to be seen the same way He was? Others saw Him as an eccentric, which is contrary to our desire for popularity and comfort. He was also seen as a heretic by the religious leaders of that time.

When Jesus was tempted by Satan in the wilderness, the message of the temptations had one theme: Fit in, Jesus. Conform. Today, the world's message is the same: Go along with everything and you'll get along.

Paul echoed the message of Jesus by declaring the words, "Do not be conformed to this world" (Rom. 12:2, *NKJV*). This is the message to be taught by parents who want their children to be like Jesus: nonconformity.

So do you want your child to be like Jesus? I'm sure you want your child to behave in a Christlike manner. We all do. But Jesus wants more than that. He wants us to have His mind in all of its fullness. We may be satisfied with behavioral change, but God wants a mind change. The mind has always been more important to God than our behavior. The emphasis in the Old Testament is the heart. At times, the Bible uses the word "heart" where you and I would use the word "mind." Jesus did the same: "And Jesus knowing their thoughts said, 'Why are you thinking evil in your hearts?'" (Matt. 9:4, *NASB*).

We Are to Imitate Christ

One of the themes in the New Testament is to imitate Christ or to be like Him. We are to be like God. Paul said, "Put on the new self, *created to be like God* in true righteousness and holiness" (Eph. 4:24, italics added). What is the purpose of the new self? It's Godlikeness. Paul told the Colossians, "[You] have put on the new self, which is being renewed in knowledge *in the image of its Creator*" (Col. 3:10, italics added).

Now, you and I and each of your children are to be like Jesus. He was God made human. Isn't it interesting and amazing that He became like us so we might become like Him. "For whom He foreknew, He also predestined to become conformed to the image of His Son, that He might be the first-born among many brethren" (Rom. 8:29, *NASB*).

Jesus taught in many ways, directly and indirectly, by what He did and what He said. He gave Himself as our example. Remember the time He washed the disciples' feet? When He was done, He said, "For I gave you an example that you also should do as I did to you" (John 13:15, *NASB*).

THE WORD OF GOD TELLS EACH OF US TO PARTICIPATE IN THE PROCESS OF BECOMING LIKE HIM [JESUS].

Then we come to the verse that is our focal point: "Let this mind be in you" (Phil. 2:5, *NKJV*). His mind is to be in us. The wording actually means "to think or be minded in a certain way." Like every other aspect of the Christian life, the mind of Christ in a person is a growth process. I wonder how it would affect parents when they look at a newborn baby and realize that God wants that little infant to have the mind of His Son! Would that give a direction for parenting? The Word of God tells each of us to participate in the process of becoming like Him.

What is God's plan for your child's mind? What is His desire for your mind? Did you know that the New Testament describes six times directly or by implication what our minds are to be? Let's consider each and the implications for your children.

Characteristics of a Godly Mind

ALIVE

God says our minds are to be *alive*. Now, it appears obvious that you don't want a dead mind. Consider, though, what is said: "For the mind set in the flesh is death, but the mind set on the Spirit is life and peace" (Rom. 8:6, *NASB*). If we have the mind of Christ, we will have a new attitude toward sin and in the choices we make. Many of these choices are going to be counterculture responses. This means it is possible to choose a different lifestyle because of being alive. I wonder how many parents have ever shared with their child, "You are a child with the power to say no to bad things, to say words that will help others, to control your anger and to be different. Why? Because your mind has strength because it is alive. And it's alive because Jesus is in your life." It is something to think about.

PEACEFUL

Second, the Christian mind is one that is *peaceful.* "The mind set on the Spirit is life and peace" (Rom. 8:6, *NASB*). Notice the word "set." You and I *set* our minds. God gives us the peace.

SINGLE MINDED

Third, we find another adjective to describe the mind of the Christian: to be *single minded.* "But I am afraid, lest as the serpent deceived Eve by his craftiness, your minds should be led astray from the simplicity and purity of devotion to Christ" (2 Cor. 11:3, *NASB*).

If you want another model of Jesus' life to follow, we can find one in James 3:13,17. It is based on wisdom that comes from God rather than what our culture has to offer. "Who among you is wise and understanding? Let him show by his good behavior his deeds in the gentleness of wisdom. But the wisdom from above is first pure, then peaceable, gentle, reasonable, full of mercy and good fruits, unwavering, without hypocrisy" *(NASB).* This is a partial picture of the virtues of Jesus' life. Wouldn't you like to see these character qualities developing in your child's life?

Distractions! They are all around us. They entice us. Why not? They are attractive. The competition for your child's mind is fierce. It is a constant struggle and these distractions lead us astray, as Paul says. Even when we pray, read the Word and sit in churches our minds go off on vacation. They take detours and struggle to stay focused. We are called to be single minded. We're not to be distracted.

HUMBLE

The fourth characteristic of a godly mind is found in Philippians 2:3. "Let nothing be done through strife or vainglory; but in lowliness of mind let each esteem others better than themselves" *(KJV)*. A state of mind leads to *humility*. The *Phillips* version says, "Live together in harmony, live together in love, as though you had only one mind and one spirit between you. Never act from motives of rivalry or personal vanity, but in humility think more of one another than you do of yourselves."

PURE

Another characteristic of a godly mind is having a *pure mind*. "To the pure, all things are pure; but to those who are defiled and unbelieving, nothing is pure, but both their mind and their conscience are defiled" (Titus 1:15, *NASB*).

HANDLING THE TEMPTATIONS OF LIFE IS NOT AN ACT THAT OCCURS AT THE MOMENT OF TEMPTATION; IT IS DECIDED AND PLANNED FOR BEFOREHAND.

One of the struggles your children will face is the problem of lust for things that shouldn't be a part of their lives. They will have constant temptations to drift into activities that are not part of a Christian life. A child or an adult can't just wait until the temptation hits to decide what to do. Children whose parents teach them in advance how to say no to drugs, sex, alcohol, gang activity, etc., and how to counter persistent conformity pressures have a greater opportunity to survive. I know; I've been there.

In high school, our church group worked on The Navigator's Bible memorization program. One of the passages I memorized was 1 Corinthians 10:13: "No temptation has overtaken you but such as is common to man; and God is faithful, who will not allow you to be tempted beyond what you are able, but with the temptation will provide the way of escape also, that you may be able to endure it" *(NASB)*. I don't know how many times that passage came to mind (and not by accident either!) when faced with the choice of doing something right or wrong. I must admit that I didn't always appreciate having it come to mind, but it was a life saver. Handling the temptations of life is not an act that occurs at the moment of temptation; it is decided and planned beforehand.

SENSITIVE AND RESPONSIVE

The sixth characteristic of a godly mind is one that is *sensitive* and *responsive*. On the night of the resurrection, Jesus opened the disciples' minds to understand the Scriptures. The disciples were responsive to learning what Jesus had to say.

Being responsive to God creates spiritual sensitivity which is the only way to make progress. The model for this is Jesus being sensitive to God. He said, "I do nothing on My own initiative, but I speak these things as the Father taught Me" (John 8:28, *NASB*). Jesus saw what His Father was doing, heard Him and did nothing independent of Him.[1]

T. W. Hunt describes our response this way:

> As the Father is to the Son, so Christ is to us. He imitated the Father; we imitate Christ. He saw the activity of the Father; we pay close attention to the known earthly activity of Jesus (and for that matter, also His present activity). He heard from the Father; we must hear from Him. The Father taught Him; He teaches us. He could do nothing independently of the Father; we cannot function independently of Him. He was very close to the Father; we must remain close to Him.[2]

Learning to Think Like Jesus

How do we learn to think and use our minds the same way Jesus did? Three commands are given in the Scriptures for us to follow. Let's consider it as though it were a three-stage process.

WILL

The place to start is with the will. We find this in "Set your mind on the things above, not on the things that are on earth" (Col. 3:2, *NASB*). Setting your mind is a definite step. It takes initiative on your part. When this is done, your will can override your instincts or feelings. When Jesus was in the garden, His soul was troubled. The *Amplified Version* states, "He began to show grief and distress of mind and was deeply depressed. Then He said to them, 'My soul is very sad and deeply grieved, so that I am almost dying of sorrow'" (Matt. 26:37,38, *Amp.*).

Then we read, "Yet not what I will, but what Thou wilt" (Mark 14:36, *NASB*). He set His will to what God desired. Helping a child to say no, to not give in to impulses and to delay gratification are examples of strengthening the will.

Years ago, I read a suggestion in a family magazine of a way to help become more discerning about what the family watches on television. The suggestion was to write Colossians 3:2 on a small placard and place it on top of the television. Having this verse there could have an effect on the choice of program selection. How would you respond if you read "Set your mind on the things above" as you watched your favorite sitcom?

The second principle comes from Romans 12:2, "Be transformed by the renewing of your mind" *(NASB)*. T. W. Hunt said the following:

In the command to be transformed by the renewing of our mind we have another principle—the River Principle. Our growth is like the flow of a river, Jesus said, "He who believes in Me, as the Scripture said, 'From his innermost being shall flow rivers of living water'" (John 7:38). Our problem is that most of us do not work on the River Principle, we work on the Pond Principle. Ponds stagnate, but rivers flow. Ponds become puddles, but rivers become oceans. We are to grow, and our growth is to be God-sized. Even Jesus grew: "And Jesus kept increasing in wisdom and stature, and in favor with God and men" (Luke 2:52).[3]

The word "renewal" literally means to make new, or freshness or vigor. Is your child learning something new each day? Or is there a waiting from Sunday to Sunday for renewal to occur? Several years ago, a group of teenage superheroes captured the interest of the six-year-olds in the United States. They were called *The Mighty Morphin Power Rangers*. The television shows were a low-budget production from Japan and dubbed into English. What appealed to the children was the Rangers' ability to "morph." These teens were typical everyday adolescents, but when necessary they used a power beyond their own ability to become martial-arts heroes who fought against evil. At a time of crisis their cry was, "It's morphing time!" and they were transformed into teens who had tremendous abilities. The phrase "it's morphing time" has caught on. Most of us would like the ability to transform.

The little word "morph" comes from a Greek word in the New Testament. *Morphoo* means, "The inward and real formation of the essential nature of a person": It's a term to describe the formation and growth of an embryo in a mother's body.

Do you remember where Paul used this word? It was in Galatians: "until Christ is *formed* in you" (Gal. 4:19, *NASB*, italics added).

We are all in a process of spiritual gestation.

Paul also told us to be "conformed to the image of His Son" (Rom. 8:29, *NASB*). The word used here means to have the same form as another. We all are to be like Jesus as an image is to the original.

The word "transformed" in Romans 12 comes from an English word "metamorphosis." Our change is to be noticeable.[4]

John Ortberg in his book *The Life You've Always Wanted* offers the best definition of morphing:

When morphing happens, I don't just *do* the things Jesus would have done; I find myself *wanting* to do them. They appeal to me. They make sense. I don't just go around trying to do right things; I *become* the right sort of person.[5]

God's Word teaches us how to morph. That is why it is so important to memorize *and* understand the Scriptures. The purpose of knowing Scripture is to become equipped for good works. Now our model looks like this:

WILL

Renewal

The final principle reflects the way people dressed in the first century. Back then people wore long flowing robes. When someone had to run or move quickly, these robes got in the way. So they turned the robe into more of a pantaloon by "girding up" the robe.

In 1 Peter 1:13 it tell us to gird up our minds. "Gird" literally means strengthen or put out of our minds anything that would hinder our Christian walk. It means that we need to keep our minds on the alert, ready for action. So the three stages look like this:

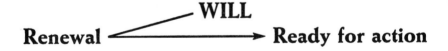

WILL

Renewal ← → **Ready for action**

As your child learns to have the thoughts of Christ, what would your child's outlook be like if these qualities were developing?

· If your child's mind is *alive*, you will notice:

> Your child's conscience responding more quickly to the prompting of the Holy Spirit.

Your child becoming more conscious of God throughout the day and not just at devotions or when praying at meals.

· If your child's mind is experiencing *peace* you will notice:

Your child learning to rely on the truth of Scripture and the joy and peace of Christ helping to overcome the mental struggles of everyday life.

Your child beginning to understand how to learn from the experiences and difficulties of life.

· If your child is learning to be *single minded* you will begin to notice:

Your child learning to pray and asking God when a decision needs to be made.

Your child's knowledge of the Lord increasing in both content and application.

· If your child is learning to be *lowly* you will begin to notice:

Your child developing a sense of humility instead of constantly drawing attention to him or herself or striving to be number one.

Your child becoming more willing to live the Christian life and do for others.

· If your child is learning the concept of *purity* you will begin to notice:

Your child learning to resist the standards of others in terms of attitude, language, standards, stating the truth and becoming selective in selecting activities and viewing.

- If your child is learning to be *sensitive* and *responsive* you will begin to notice:

  Your child having a greater desire to study about God, read and learn His Word and center his or her life on the Church.[6]

If you want your child to be more like Jesus, you are asking him or her to live His lifestyle. This is essentially what Philippians 2:5 is saying: "Have this attitude in yourselves which was also in Christ Jesus" *(NASB)*. Several more admonitions need to be mentioned. Scripture tells all of us to "Consider Jesus, the Apostle and High Priest of our confession" (Heb. 3:1, *NASB*). "Consider" means using the mind. It is saying, "Think about Him."

Have you ever thought about the fact that Jesus came to show us what God really had in mind when He created humankind? Think about it—God created us. We sinned. We messed up the way we were supposed to be. We spoiled it. So God decided to give us a real flesh-and-blood model of a perfect man. *Jesus became like us* (see Heb. 2:14,17) so *in turn we could become like Him.* Hebrews tells us to "fix our eyes on Him" (12:2). We do this so we can see how Jesus lived and thus how our children (and us) are supposed to live our everyday lives.

So what was Jesus like? He was *pure.* He didn't talk about it, but He was. He also had many adoring women who thronged about Him. Did Jesus notice women? Of course. Did you ever think that in His humanity He may have wanted to be married? Why not? He was a complete human, a man.

He remained pure, however. Peter described Jesus as a "lamb unblemished and spotless" (1 Pet. 1:19, *NASB*). John said, "in Him there is no sin" (1 John 3:5, *NASB*).

Lust wasn't part of His life, as it is in ours. However, Jesus wasn't a prude either. Have you ever talked with a prostitute or had one visit in your home or have a meal with one? Jesus did, but it didn't drag Him down. Have you ever shared a meal with a well-known crook? Jesus did with a tax collector, but He wasn't corrupted. He remained pure. It was a simple purity. He didn't go around flaunting it.

Your child will struggle with this. The world has another standard called "get what you can, even if you have to deceive to do so." Purity doesn't limit itself just to sex, but extends to thoughts, motives and intentions. Purity is a valued commodity, but the standards for purity vary. Just as an example look at some of the standards for the Food and Drug Administration (FDA). It monitors and protects the purity of what we eat. Consider these two examples:

Apple butter: If the mold count is 12 percent or more or if it averages four rodent hairs per 100 grams or more or if it averages five or more whole insects per 100 grams, the FDA will pull it from the shelves. Otherwise you will end up using it on your toast or muffins.

Coffee beans: Coffee beans will get withdrawn from the market if an average of 10 percent or more are insect-infested or if there is one live insect in each of two or more immediate containers.[7]

Is this really purity? You and I and our children are called to a "pure purity." Not somewhat.

Teaching Good Qualities to Our Children

Jesus was a person of peace as well as being peaceable. Did He encourage competition? No. In our culture, however, we place a high value on being competitive to get ahead. We use the word "competition" and place an overemphasis on being number one. We teach children how to win, but not how to lose. Winning is everything—even if we create bad feelings, step on someone else or cheat to get there. What about striving for excellence and enjoying the process of getting there?

What about teaching your child to encourage others?

Does your child know how to accept and enjoy coming in second? Some children learn to be agitators or to pit one person against another. Jesus didn't.

Is your child gentle? This is a quality most of us would like to have in our lives. The opposite is harsh or a "heavy hand." A delicate tenderness is expressed in how we talk or the way we treat another. Have you ever run your hand lightly over the back of a puppy or a kitten, just barely stroking it? That is a gentle touch. Harshness cuts, hurts, limits, is abrupt, usually angry and insensitive.

In what way would you like to have your child become more gentle?

Are your children reasonable or approachable? This quality helps them listen to you, hear you and be receptive to what is said. Such people don't mind having someone ask them to do something or to consider some things differently. It doesn't mean they are pushovers or can be walked on. They exercise discernment. They are available, but not wimpy. They have a willingness to serve others. I also think they would not be concerned about always winning.

Another quality we would like to develop in our children is that of being merciful. They are able to forgive, to give others another chance. A merciful person is not a harsh taskmaster. His or her heart responds to others. Certain people said to Jesus, "Have mercy on me." It is a person asking to be given a break when it is not deserved, and then receiving it. Mercy also means being able to forgive. Does your child have a forgiving spirit or is he or she a reservoir of resentment?

Exercising the Fruits of the Spirit

What does it mean for a person to have "good fruits" or to be fruitful? When a tree is fruitful, it produces what it is supposed to produce. In this case, it could be either sharing the fruits of the Spirit in Galatians 5 or it could be leading others to the Lord. Does your child give increasing evidence of a desire to have others come to Christ as growth in the fruit of the Spirit? Evaluate each of your children, based on this chart, to find out where each one was last year, and is presently, in exercising the fruits of the Spirit.

Place an *X* in the appropriate categories:

LOVE	LAST YEAR	NOW
Very Low	_____	____
Needs Work	_____	____
Good Some of the time	_____	____
Good	_____	____
Quite Consistent	_____	____

JOY	LAST YEAR	NOW
Very Low	_____	____
Needs Work	_____	____
Good Some of the time	_____	____
Good	_____	____
Quite Consistent	_____	____

PEACE	LAST YEAR	NOW
Very Low	_____	____
Needs Work	_____	____
Good Some of the time	_____	____
Good	_____	____
Quite Consistent	_____	____

LONG-SUFFERING	LAST YEAR	NOW
Very Low	_____	_____
Needs Work	_____	_____
Good Some of the time	_____	_____
Good	_____	_____
Quite Consistent	_____	_____

GENTLENESS	LAST YEAR	NOW
Very Low	_____	_____
Needs Work	_____	_____
Good Some of the time	_____	_____
Good	_____	_____
Quite Consistent	_____	_____

GOODNESS	LAST YEAR	NOW
Very Low	_____	_____
Needs Work	_____	_____
Good Some of the time	_____	_____
Good	_____	_____
Quite Consistent	_____	_____

FAITH	LAST YEAR	NOW
Very Low	_____	_____
Needs Work	_____	_____
Good Some of the time	_____	_____
Good	_____	_____
Quite Consistent	_____	_____

MEEKNESS	LAST YEAR	NOW
Very Low	_____	_____
Needs Work	_____	_____
Good Some of the time	_____	_____
Good	_____	_____
Quite Consistent	_____	_____

TEMPERANCE (SELF-CONTROL)	LAST YEAR	NOW
Very Low	_____	____
Needs Work	_____	____
Good Some of the time	_____	____
Good	_____	____
Quite Consistent	_____	____

Another quality of Jesus' lifestyle is steadfastness. It means "without wavering." It is a sense of balanced determination or pursuing something. It is also not allowing yourself to get off track or be detoured. It includes the discernment not to be stubborn or inflexible.

The last quality is being honest or sincere. The word "sincere" comes from a Latin word that means "without wax." In ancient times, fine expensive porcelain often developed tiny cracks when it was fired in the kiln. Dishonest merchants smeared pearly white wax over the cracks until the cracks disappeared. Then they claimed the porcelain was unblemished, but when the porcelain was held up to the sun, the light revealed the cracks filled in with wax. So honest merchants marked their porcelain using the word "Sincere"—without wax. That is what is meant by genuine sincerity: no hidden cracks, no ulterior motives, no hidden agendas, no attempts to con or deceive others.[8]

Why We Should Follow Jesus

What has been presented here are some goals for you to think about as you watch your child or children grow and develop.

If anyone ever asked why your children should follow Jesus, you could answer this way:

Because everything He said and did was in our best interest.
Christ said to follow Him because following anyone or anything else gets us lost.

Christ said to know who we look like because drawing our self-image from any other source but God poisons our souls and spirits.

Christ said to love our neighbor as ourselves because we grow the most when committed to fostering another's growth, not just our own.

Christ said to clean the inside of the cup because that is the only way to develop true character and avoid a shallow existence.

Christ said to stop fitting in with our culture because our culture is sick, and adapting to it will make us sick too.

Christ said to *get real* because wearing masks makes our lives empty and our relationships unfulfilling.

Christ said to stop blaming others because taking responsibility for our own problems is essential for true maturity and health.

Christ said to forgive others because unforgiveness is arrogant and hurts others as well as ourselves.

Christ said to live like an heir because to live like an orphan leads to settling for far too little in life.

Christ said to solve paradoxes because it is often that which seems contrary to common sense that is the healthiest route of all.

Christ said to stop worrying because worry only drains us of the energy we need to work on the things that we can do something about.

Christ said to persevere because the fruit of our labor won't ever show up if we grow tired of doing what it takes to bear it.

Everything Christ tells us is in our best interest, and it is critically important to understand that. His counsel wasn't designed to burden us, but to set us free. When He gave His counsel to us, it was aimed at meeting our deepest needs and it will if we follow it.[9]

Jesus said, "Come, follow me" (Matt. 4:19).

Notes

1. T. W. Hunt, *The Mind of Christ* (Nashville: Broadman & Holman Publishers, 1995), pp. 7-12, adapted.
2. Ibid., p. 12.
3. Ibid., p. 14.
4. John Ortberg, *The Life You've Always Wanted* (Grand Rapids: Zondervan Publishers, 1997), pp. 23, adapted.
5. Ibid.
6. Hunt, *The Mind of Christ*, pp. 8-15, adapted.
7. Ortberg, *The Life You've Always Wanted*, pp. 168, 169, adapted.
8. Hunt, *The Mind of Christ*, pp. 42-48, adapted.
9. Dr. Chris Thurman, *If Christ Were Your Counselor* (Nashville: Thomas Nelson, 1993), p. 134.

$$\boxed{4}$$

CULTIVATING A CLIMATE FOR GROWTH

By Gary J. Oliver

Apply your heart to instruction and your ears to words
of knowledge. My son, give me your heart
and let your eyes keep to my ways.

—PROVERBS 23:12,26

In the mid-70s, I moved from Southern California to central Nebraska. I didn't have much furniture so the large old farmhouse I rented seemed rather empty. A friend suggested I go to a nursery and purchase some plants. Plants enrich the air, add warmth and character, are attractive and are cheaper than furniture. It sounded like a good idea.

I went to the nearest nursery and selected about 10 different plants. As I picked out each plant, the clerk explained to me its uniqueness—things such as when to prune, fertilize, how much water and the amount of light each plant preferred. It seemed as if each plant had its own unique personality.

Unfortunately for me and the plants, I didn't listen to her. I had other more important things on my mind and, besides, everyone knows that plants are plants. To nourish them and help them grow, all you need to do is give them some water and light, fertilize them once in a while, and they will grow. Right? Wrong!

On my way out the door, I picked up some fertilizer spikes and took my plants home. The package said you should use one spike for an eight-inch pot. I decided to really nourish my plants, so I put in three spikes rather than one. Knowing that plants need water, I gave those plants more water than any plant deserved. One of my favorite hymns is "Like a River Glorious," and that is the way I watered those plants. I knew that in no time those plants would be growing and I would be seeing new buds and leaves.

You can guess what happened. In several weeks all my plants were dead. I couldn't believe it. I gave them what I thought they needed—and a lot of it! I had faithfully nourished each one of those plants—or so I thought. Obviously I hadn't nourished them. I had killed them. What had I done wrong?

I returned to the nursery and told the clerk what I had done. At first she thought I was kidding and started laughing. I let her know that I wasn't kidding and that I didn't think it was funny—especially considering the price of plants.

She explained to me that I had treated all the plants as if they were the same. I had not given the plants what they needed. I gave them what I *thought* they needed. She repeated that each plant is different. What may nourish one plant can kill another. It is important to learn the unique needs of each plant and treat it accordingly.

I purchased more plants, but this time I wrote down everything the clerk said about each plant. I followed the instructions on the fertilizer spike package carefully. Guess what? My plants grew and blossomed and flourished. Why? Because this time I had truly nourished them.

Many parents are the same way I was when I went to the nursery for the first time. One of my mistakes was that I thought I knew more about plants than I really did. In parenting, many tend to think they know and understand their children better than they really do.

We believe we can nourish our spouses or our children by giving them what we think they need. Often this involves us giving them what we would like, assuming that if we would like it so should they. We give them more, we give them bigger and we give them better. It doesn't seem to work. We become frustrated, disappointed and discouraged. The desire of our heart is to nourish, but that isn't the result.

"Nourish" does not mean giving your child what you *think* he or she needs and wants. Intentional nourishment involves stopping, looking, listening and studying that special little gal or guy. Taking the time to do this will help you to know what they truly need and want. "Nourish" means investing the time to learn the love language of those you love and to love them in ways that are meaningful to them. Often what says love to you, what excites you, what brings you great joy is different from what says love to your spouse or your child.

Most parents have good intentions. We want our children to become healthy, mature adults. However, good intentions aren't enough. If we want to grow healthy children, we must go beyond good intentions. We must learn how to create the kind of environment that can help children grow. In this chapter we will look at *seven keys* for growing healthy children.

Seven Keys for Cultivating Growth in Your Children

1. CULTIVATE AN ENCOURAGING ENVIRONMENT

If you knew me, there would probably be several things you would like. At least I hope so. Unfortunately, there would also be several things you wouldn't like. To be quite honest, there are several things about myself that I don't like. One of them is the way I talk to my kids.

Sometimes I discipline my boys in ways that make them feel bad about themselves rather than about what they have done. Sometimes I speak to their character rather than the issue at hand. Sometimes I continue to ramble on even after I know I have made my point. I have thought of starting a support group for parents like me. I might call it "On and On." Without fail, this kind of parenting produces frustration and discouragement in my kids.

One of the most powerful things we can do for our kids is to catch them being healthy and seize every opportunity we can get to encourage them. John Gottman and his colleagues have studied more than 2,000 marriages, and we believe the results of his research about marriages extend to the family. His groundbreaking research demonstrated that in virtually all satisfying and enduring marriages, there are five or more positive interactions for every negative one. These relationships are characterized by high levels of mutual satisfaction, positive feelings, thoughtful behaviors that build and strengthen the partner.

However, when the ratio of positive-to-negative interactions **drops** below five-to-one, the level of marital satisfaction significantly decreases. These marriages are characterized by dissatisfaction, defensiveness, stonewalling and emotional withdrawal.[1]

First Thessalonians 5:14 states, "And we urge you, brothers, *warn* those who are idle, *encourage* the timid, *help* the weak, be *patient* with everyone" (italics added). It is clear from Scripture as it as clear from our life experiences that different needs, conditions, circumstances, personality types, etc. require different approaches to communication.

What is an encouraging environment? It is one in which our kids know they are of value and worth to God and to us. It is one in which we spend more time building and encouraging them than we do scolding and correcting them. It is one in which we honor them by speaking respectfully to them.

An encouraging environment is one where our emphasis is on catching them doing good rather than catching them doing bad. We invest more energy in praising them for being responsible than in criticizing and castigating them for falling short of our expectations.

An encouraging environment is one in which we respond to our children's pleasant as well as painful emotions. Without intending to, many parents primarily respond to their children when their emotions are inappropriate or out of control. What many kids learn is that if they want any attention, the only way they will get it is by being in a crisis or creating a crisis.

Several years ago, I saw an advertisement for a course that could help students get better grades. Several television celebrities were interviewed and shared how it helped their children significantly increase their school performance. As I read through the parents' manual, I found a tool I have found helpful for evaluating my performance as a parent.

A Report Card for Parents

A B C D F   1. Do I praise my child at least once a day?

A B C D F   2. Do I treat my child as a worthwhile member of our family?

A B C D F   3. Am I available when my child wishes to talk to me?

A B C D F   4. Do I include my child in family plans and decisions?

A B C D F   5. Do I set reasonable guidelines and insist that my child follow them?

A B C D F   6. Do I treat my child the way I treat my best friends?

A B C D F   7. Do I treat my children equally?

A B C D F   8. If I tell my children to do something, do I frequently take the time to help them understand why instead of saying: "because I said so!"?

A B C D F   9. Do I set a good example for my child?

A B C D F   10. Do I think positive thoughts about my child and encourage achievements?

A B C D F   11. Do I take an interest in my child's education and attend PTA meetings?

A B C D F   12. Do I occasionally give my child a hug or friendly pat on the back?

A B C D F   13. Do I encourage attendance at weekly religious services?

A B C D F   14. Do I spend time each day looking over my child's school work with him?

A B C D F   15. Do I send my child off to school each day with a kind word of encouragement?

A B C D F   16. Does my child see me pray?

A B C D F   17. Does my child see me reading the Bible?

A B C D F   18. Does my child hear me apologize when I am wrong?

A B C D F   19. Do I talk to my child about my emotions?[2]

2. BE OPEN ABOUT YOUR OWN MISTAKES AND WEAKNESSES

An encouraging environment is one where it is safe to make mistakes. In fact, it is not only safe, but our kids also begin to learn that God can use their failures to help them grow. They learn that Romans 8:28 is really true. They learn that one of the best questions to ask after making a mistake is, "What can I learn from this?"

One of the best ways to accomplish this is to model it. A couple I have been seeing for several months recently had an opportunity to put this principle into practice.

"Dr. Oliver," the female voice on the other end of the line started, "this is Joan Nauman. I'm concerned about Mel. I've never seen him so depressed. I know that we have an appointment tomorrow afternoon but I wonder if there is anything I could do now to help him?"

Mel had been raised in a family where men didn't express emotions. Real men were strong, self-sufficient and stable. A Christian man expressing any emotion that might reflect weakness or need was a sure sign of spiritual immaturity, carnality or a massive lack of faith.

Mel remembered his dad saying, "Son, God has promised to supply all of our needs and if you're not happy it must be because you aren't trusting God to be faithful to what He has promised." It didn't take long for Mel to get the message.

Unfortunately, the 42 years of stuffing, repressing, suppressing, denying and ignoring his emotions had produced an emotional Mt. Saint Helens. The pressure continued to build and build. Finally some marital and financial difficulties combined to become the straw that broke the proverbial camel's back.

When I saw them at the next session, both Joan and Mel were doing better. He was still depressed, but the depression was no longer in control of him. Toward the end of the session I turned to Mel and asked, "Are you going to talk to your kids about what happened and why your behavior has been so different this past week?" Their two early-adolescent children had noticed the dramatic difference in their dad and were frightened by it. They had asked Joan what was going on, but she hadn't known what to say.

"Are you serious?" Mel asked, and then he paused. "Why would I want to do that?"

In our previous work together we had talked about the legacy of being raised in a dysfunctional family and the effect it had on him. Mel volunteered that from his perspective he was an emotional preadolescent. In previous sessions he had stated that he didn't want his kids to grow up as emotionally impaired as he was.

"What better way to teach your children about the specific ways that God can help us through difficult times than to share with them what you are currently going through? What better way to teach them the reality of Romans 8:28 than by letting them see it working first-hand?" I asked.

"I just never would have thought of doing something like that," Mel replied. "What would I say to them?"

"You could talk about what happened to you, what depression is, what can cause it, what some of the symptoms are and how you are starting to not only work through it but actually learn from it." I shared how they could do some reading and listening to some tapes together. "One of the most powerful things you could do for them, and for yourself, is to ask them to pray for you, and then share with them the progress you have made."

Joan jumped in, "What a great idea! We can teach them about prayer, trusting God's promises and dealing with painful emotions without lecturing them. They can better understand Mel and at the same time learn what fear and depression are and what they can do about it."

We worked out a plan together and Mel and Joan implemented it. That incident became a turning point in the family's communication pattern. Through Mel's courage in being honest with his kids and letting them work through his depression with him, they received an invaluable education about the power of prayer, the practicality of God's promises and how God can give us victory over painful emotions.

Because Mel had modeled being responsibly open and transparent, it became easier for his children to be open and honest about some of their problems and concerns. Mel and Joan were surprised to discover that both of their kids had also struggled with depression, but, because of the covert "we don't have any emotional problems in this family" rule, they didn't understand what they were experiencing and didn't feel safe sharing it.

Learning from our own mistakes is easier said than done. I recently found in my file a faded photocopy of the one-way conversation of a father who realized he had blown it with his son that day. There was no name or date on it and I have no idea where it came from. Yet it illustrates many of the factors that go into cultivating an encouraging environment.

3. BE AVAILABLE

This key is the simplest of the seven, but it is also the most difficult. Of all seven it is clearly the most important because, to a great degree, the other six steps depend on this one. Why is it simple? Because it doesn't involve any reading or special training. It only involves being available to our kids. Anybody who is living and conscious can be available.

What makes it so difficult? All of us are busy. We have demands and pressures that we place on ourselves and that others place on us. There is almost always more we can do and more we would like to do. Few of us can sit down at the end of the day and say we accomplished all we wanted.

In the midst of this busyness, children can easily be an interruption. It is unrealistic for us to always drop everything and cater to the demands of our children. At the same time, we need to remember that children don't have the same sense of time we do. Children have poorly developed abstraction skills, and for most of them the present is all there is.

We can be available for our children in two ways.

First of all, we can set aside special times for them. We can acknowledge them when they get up in the morning, when they get home from school, on weekends or any other event.

As you study your children, you may discover certain times during the day when he or she is more open to chatting. It would be wise to periodically "set aside" your schedule during these times and just "happen" to be available to talk about their day, read with them, play with them or share your day with them.

Second, we can learn how to "make" time when needed. We can develop the ability to look for "teachable moments." In Luke 5:17-20, Christ was teaching a distinguished group of Pharisees and teachers of the law. They had come from miles to hear His message.

Right in the middle of Christ's message, the tiles above His head began to move. Well, not only did the tiles move, but they were also pulled off and a paralyzed man on a stretcher was lowered down in front of Him.

What a lousy time for an interruption. Can you think of a better way to blow a good message? We don't know if Christ was on His second or third point, or if He was doing the wrap-up for a powerful close. His flow must have been ruined.

Yet what most of us would view as an interruption, Christ viewed as a unique opportunity. Christ saw the need, He recognized their faith and it was clear that this was more important than His talk. He immediately saw this as a teachable moment and took advantage of it.

We can make time to help our children handle their concerns. Sometimes they want to solve them immediately. Sometimes they need to think about them and can talk about them before going to sleep. Kids don't always forget painful emotional experiences. They need to process them. They need to learn, however, how to process with someone who will help them "get it out" but not try to "solve" it for them. Through trial and error we as parents can make time and provide a safe place for them to process their problems.

LACK OF TIME MIGHT BE THE MOST PERVASIVE ENEMY

THE HEALTHY FAMILY HAS.

I don't know of very many families today who aren't overcommitted. This is especially true of the Christian family. In addition to the normal demands of work and the kids' schedules, we also have to attend board and committee meetings, Bible studies, fellowship groups and children's programs. In her excellent book *Traits of a Healthy Family*, Dolores Curran says that lack of time might be the most pervasive enemy the healthy family has.[3]

That may sound a bit strong, but in many ways it is true. This is because virtually every other aspect of building strong relationships is dependent on making time to be together. Only as we are together are we able to communicate, resolve conflict, build, nourish, cherish, love and encourage each other.

When 1,500 school children were asked the question, "What do you think makes a happy family?" the most frequent answer was "doing things together." Through the years I have learned that in life it is not so much what we do *for* people that influences them as what we do *with* them.

Jesus said, "For where your treasure is, there will your heart be also" (Matt. 6:21). One of the best ways to measure what is important to people, or what they treasure, is where and how they spend their time. From the four Gospels it is easy to understand what Christ treasured. Relationships were one of our Lord's highest priorities. If we look at Christ's life, it is impossible to ignore the value

He placed on people. While He was on earth, He invested His life in people. He came, lived, died, rose and has promised to come again for people.

Christ knew the importance of modeling. He didn't just give His disciples lectures and tell them to read scrolls, but He also spent a lot of time with them. Quantity time. Because of my parents' example, it has been easier for me to invest time and money in my family time. We play games, enjoy going to parks and taking short and long trips.

During these times together, my sons are able to observe our strengths and weaknesses. They have the opportunity to observe what biblical values and truth look like in action. They are able to observe if what we believe makes any difference in how we handle the real issues and situations of life. I believe it is almost impossible to overestimate the effect of quality time invested with your children. Remember, you don't have quality time without some quantity time.

When you think back to the happy times of your childhood, what kinds of memories come to mind? When you get together with family or childhood friends and recall the "good old days," what is it that made those days good?

Several years ago, I heard about a middle-class family in the 1940s who had set a family goal of remodeling their old bathroom. After a year of financial sacrifices, they finally had enough cash for the project. At the family conference held to select the colors and finalize the plans, one of the children suggested, "Why don't we use the money for a trip and fix the bathroom next year?" Although it involved a change in plans, everyone liked the suggestion and that summer they took the money and went to Yellowstone National Park.

The money spent, the saving started all over to do the postponed remodeling. When it came time to hire the contractor, the family's conversation drifted to how much they had enjoyed the trip to Yellowstone and the inevitable suggestion surfaced: "Why not put off the bathroom for just one more year and take another family trip?" They all agreed.

This scene was repeated every year from 1940 until 1950 when the youngest son was killed in Korea. On the night before his final battle he wrote a letter to his parents. The letter arrived months after the family had been notified of his death. There was a special emotion as Mom and Dad sat in their living room to read to each other their son's last words.

It was a touching letter in which the young soldier expressed a premonition that he might soon die. He thanked his folks for their love and the many happy experiences of growing up, especially recalling the annual family trips they all shared. Long silence followed the reading as both quietly wept. The silence was broken when Dad asked, "Honey, could you imagine a son writing home on the night before he died and saying how glad he was for a fancy new bathroom?"

4. LOOK, LISTEN AND THEN TALK

When it comes to good communication, many of us get the formula backward. We tend to talk and talk and talk, and then maybe look and listen. When most people think about communication, they tend to emphasize the verbal aspect. To them communication is the words that one person says to another. Many are surprised to learn that the actual words we use only account for 7 percent of a message. Tone of voice contributes 38 percent and other nonverbal factors account for 55 percent.[4]

When your child is speaking, it is important to develop the habit of listening attentively to what he or she has to say. Notice I said develop the *habit*. It is not easy to be a good listener. It is not something that comes naturally. Yet the Bible has a lot to say about the importance of listening. In Proverbs 18:13 we are told, "He who gives an answer before he hears, it is folly and shame to him" *(NASB)*. In James 1:19 we are told, "But let everyone be quick to hear, slow to speak and slow to anger" *(NASB)*.

Norm Wright has written that people tend to listen five times as fast as another person can speak. If your child speaks at one hundred words a minute, and you can listen at five hundred words a minute, what do you do with the rest of the time? It is easy for us to get bored and daydream. While maintaining eye contact with our child, we can work on the next day's schedule, compose that letter or plan the weekend fishing trip—or we can focus on what he is saying and how he is saying it.

Do you remember the last time you had something really important to tell someone and the person took the time to listen to you? What did it feel like? How did it make you feel about yourself? How did you feel about the person? What did it say to you about the person's commitment to your relationship? How did it affect your willingness to listen to what that person might have to say?

One of the many unique things about our Lord Jesus Christ is that He really cared about people. No one was too uneducated, too young, too old, too slow or too anything else for Him not to take the time for people. Common, ordinary people are the reason He came, the reason He died and the reason He rose again. If ordinary people were that important to Christ, how much more important should our sons and daughters be to us?

You can let your son or daughter know you care about them through something as simple as good eye contact, smiling, nodding and allowing them to talk uninterrupted. Sometimes your child may have more to say than you have the time, at that moment, to listen to. Clearly communicate your interest in hearing more, explain why you cannot and promise to get back to him or her. Then, be sure to keep your promise.

When you listen to your children, don't merely listen to their words. Learn to read their nonverbals. Remember that they are reading yours! They can tell whether you are really interested or merely faking it. Look at the facial expression, posture and gesture.

If your child is a slow talker, do you get impatient and try to help him express his feelings rather than taking the time to listen beyond the words to what he really means? That is a mistake I have made with my sons more times than I care to admit. I love my boys, but there are times when my rational mind tries to solve the problem or make sense of something that doesn't make sense.

Remember what we discussed in the first chapter? Emotions aren't always rational. Sometimes there isn't a logical reason for what a child did or is feeling. You don't need to figure it out; you only have to listen and try to understand. If we only listen to the words or "what" is said we could miss up to 93 percent of the real meaning our child is trying to communicate.

Listen to her voice. What are the differences in her tone, tempo, texture, pace and volume? Sometimes a change in a person's tone is due to emotional changes. At other times it is a reflection of tiredness or trying to cram a lot into a little bit of time. Children are especially prone to do this if they sense we are in a hurry and getting impatient with them. Learn to read your child's tone of voice. Reflect your interpretation back to her. This lets her know how she is coming across and it allows you to check out the accuracy of your interpretation.

What does your tempo mean? When you talk more quickly, do your children interpret that to mean you are busy? Does it mean that what you are doing is more important than they are? Does it mean you are frustrated with them or disappointed with them? Or does it mean you have had a rough day and are exhausted?

Do we give our kids the message that if they don't see things our way something must be wrong with them? Do we encourage our kids to think? Do we help them verbalize their plans, ask questions and then learn to make their own decisions? If our kids think just like us, then one of us is totally unnecessary.

When you have developed good looking and listening skills, you will understand your child better. You will be better equipped to notice when something is going wrong. When we listen to our kids and let them empty themselves of negative, painful and confusing emotions, they are free to discover some positive feelings and may be more open to hearing us talk about some solutions.

5. WHEN YOU DO TALK, ASK QUESTIONS

The sixth key to cultivating a healthy environment is to learn the art of asking good questions. A question says, "I've been listening to you; I'm with you; you are worth taking the time to understand better; your ideas and opinions are important to me; you are important to me."

There are two kinds of questions: closed questions and open questions. A closed question is one that can be answered in one word such as, "Did you have a nice day today?" An open-ended question is one that requires more than a one-word response such as, "What was your favorite part of the day today?" It is usually better to ask several open-ended questions than several closed questions.

Timing can also be important. When possible, pick a time that is unhurried for both you and your child. If you hear yourself finishing a sentence for your child, or saying, "Yeah," "Uh-huh," "I get it" or "That's enough," you have most likely picked a bad time.

When asking a question, be sure to give your child enough time to respond. Often we ask questions we have thought about but our children haven't. If you ask a question and push for a response too quickly, it can put pressure on your child and send the wrong message. Although you intended to communicate "You are important," the message they receive can be, "What you have to say is important as long as you can say it quickly. I have a lot of other important things to do."

When your child responds to your question, remember to listen carefully to what he says and how he says it. Both the content and the tone of his reply are important. If he responds in an enthusiastic, energetic way, and if he volunteers even more information, you have hit on a key. Either you asked a great question, hit on a topic that is important to him or you found a time during the day when he is open to conversation.

6. GIVE CHILDREN PERMISSION TO EXPRESS THEIR EMOTIONS

Tedd Tripp writes that communication doesn't just discipline, it also disciples. Good communication can shepherd our children in the ways of God. Consistent with Deuteronomy 6:4-9, this biblically faithful kind of communication occurs while lying down, waking, rising, walking or sitting. "Parents are often too busy to talk unless something is wrong. A regular habit of talking together prepares the way for talking in strained situations. You will never have the hearts of your children if you talk with them only when something has gone wrong."[5]

Through lack of education or through misinformation, many of us, especially males, have been educated not knowing when we are feeling something or what we are feeling. When we were depressed, we were told it was only discouragement. When we were sad, we were told to cheer up. When we were angry, we were told to keep our cool. When we felt pain, we were told to be brave and smile. Dr. Haim G. Ginot says, "Emotions are part of our genetic heritage."

> Fish swim, birds fly, and people feel. Sometimes we are happy, sometimes we are not; but sometimes in our life we are sure to feel anger and fear, sadness and joy, greed and guilt, lust and scorn, delight and disgust. While we are not free to choose the emotions that arise in us, we are free to choose how and when to express them, provided we know what they are.[6]

So what is the solution? It is emotional education that can help children be aware of what they feel and when they feel it. I agree with Dr. Ginot when he says, "It is more important for a child to know what he feels than why he feels it. When he knows clearly what his feelings are, he is less likely to feel 'all mixed-up' inside."[7]

If our children are going to have a solid foundation for their later emotional life, they need to be encouraged to both experience and express a wide range of emotions. Their emotional experience must not just be limited to the pleasant emotions. If they are allowed to only experience one side of their emotions, they will have a limited awareness of who God has made them to be and a distorted perspective of others. They will be severely limited in their ability to learn the important lessons our emotions can teach us, and they will be more vulnerable to being controlled by their emotions.

> REAL LEARNING CAN'T TAKE PLACE IN THE ABSENCE OF
> THE FULL RANGE OF EMOTIONS. THAT INCLUDES BOTH
> PLEASANT AND PAINFUL EMOTIONS.

Children must not only be allowed, but also rather enthusiastically encouraged to experience happiness and sadness, hope and fear, joy and depression, jealousy and compassion. Real learning can't take place in the absence of the full range of emotions. That includes both pleasant and painful emotions.

Part of what it means to be made in the image of God is that we have emotions. Healthy parents give their children permission to express a wide range of emotions in appropriate kinds of ways. Like us, our kids may not always do it right, but they need to know that in this home, their honest expression of emotion will be acknowledged and that they will be given opportunities to understand those feelings and handle whatever issues are there.

Watch your children. Look for the emotions that might be registered on their faces. Take stock of the emotional stresses affecting them. Whenever possible, encourage your children to talk about any and all their worries and feelings. Encourage them to share whatever they are feeling, positive or negative, pleasant or painful. If it is hard for them to open up, you can "prime the pump" by sharing some of your own feelings.

Invite your children to interact with you. Encourage them to elaborate on what they are saying. "Would you like to help?" "I'd like to hear about how your day went." "Tell me more about that." "Then what happened?" "You look upset. If you'd like to talk about it, I'd like to listen."

It is easy for parents to only notice and talk about "problem" emotions. If that is all we focus on, our kids will learn that those are the only ones worth expressing. Take time to notice all their emotions.

Simple phrases such as, "You look like you are really angry," "It sounds as if your feelings are hurt" or "It seems like you are afraid that you won't do well on the test" help a child better understand what he or she is communicating.

7. UNDERSTAND THAT THE QUALITIES NEEDED TO SUCCEED IN BUSINESS AND PARENTING ARE NOT THE SAME

I have met many parents, especially fathers, who thought that the qualities needed to succeed in business could simply be transferred to the home front. If it worked well at the office, it should work well at home. After all, I am preparing my child for the "real" world, am I not? I don't know where that silly idea came from, but in the "real" world of being a parent it just isn't true. Here is a partial comparison of the qualities needed to succeed in a chosen career and the qualities needed to be a successful parent.

Qualities Needed to Succeed in a Chosen Career	Qualities Needed to Meet the Needs of a Growing Child
1. A constant striving for perfection	A tolerance for repeated errors
2. Mobility	Stability
3. A need to be free from time constraints to pursue an independent life	Plenty of time for family activities
4. Impatience	Patience
5. A goal-oriented attitude toward the project at hand	Emphasis on process, surprises, and change as the child matures
6. A total commitment to yourself	A total commitment to others
7. A stubborn self-will	A softness and willingness to bend

8. Efficiency	A tolerance for chaos
9. A belief that succeeding must always be the top priority	An understanding that failure promotes growth
10. A controlling nature that enjoys others	A desire to promote directing in dependence in others even if their ways are not your ways
11. A concern about image	A relaxed acceptance of embarrassment
12. Firmness	Gentleness
13. A feeling that nobody is as smart as you	A true respect for your child's activities, free from comparison with your own
14. A preference for concise information	Ability to listen patiently while children talk
15. An exploration of others	Ability to put another's needs ahead of one's own[8]

Conclusion

An absolutely essential ingredient for cultivating kids who love Jesus is choosing to become parents who make time to provide a climate in which Christlike characteristics can grow. This climate moves beyond a focus on rituals and rules to the sometimes time-consuming and energy-draining activities of building relationships.

In this chapter we've shared seven keys for a growth-enhancing environment. All of the keys we've discussed are so simple and basic that you could easily underestimate their significance. I should know, since in my early years as a parent, that is exactly what I did. You might even be tempted to move right on to the next chapter and ignore some of these very basic insights. Hold on; don't turn that page quite yet.

One of the *best* ways you can avoid passing over these practical pearls is to do the following simple exercise. I want to encourage you to review the seven keys and with a prayerful heart, pick one to focus on and practice every day for the next seven days. After you've made your selection, pick three friends to share your project with and ask them to pray for you daily. Then, at the end of the seven days, call them back and let them know what you learned from your exercise.

1. Seven Keys for Cultivating Growth in Your Children

   a. Cultivate an encouraging environment.
   b. Be open about your own mistakes and weaknesses.
   c. Be available.
   d. Look, listen, and then talk.
   e. When you do talk, ask questions.
   f. Give children permission to express their feelings.
   g. Understand that the qualities needed to succeed in business and parenting are not the same.

2. This is the one key that I have chosen to practice for the next seven days:

3. These are the three friends I have asked to pray for me:

   a.
   b.
   c.

4. Here is what I learned from my exercise:

Notes
1. J. M. Gottman, *Why Marriages Succeed or Fail* (New York: Simon & Schuster, 1994), pp. 13-32.
2. Claude W. Olney, *Where There's a Will There's an A: How to Get Better Grades in Grade School* (Scottsdale, Ariz.: Olney Seminars, 1989), p. 21. Used by permission.

3. Dolores Curran, *Traits of a Healthy Family* (San Francisco, Calif., HarperSanFrancisco, 1984), n.p.

4. Albert Metowbian, *Silent Messages* (Belmont, Calif.: Wadsworth Publishing Co., 1971), pp. 42-44.

5. Tedd Tripp, *Shepherding a Child's Heart* (Amityville, N.Y.: Calvary Press, 1995), p. 114.

6. Haim G. Ginot, *Between Parent and Child: New Solutions to Old Problems* (New York: Macmillan Company, 1965), pp. 34,35.

7. Ibid., p. 35.

8. Andree A. Brooks, *Children of Fast-Track Parents* (New York: Viking, 1989), p. 29.

Section II

UNDERSTANDING
YOUR CHILD

UNIQUE BY GOD'S DESIGN

By Gary J. Oliver

*Your eyes saw my unformed body. All the days
ordained for me were written in your book
before one of them came to be.*

—PSALM 139:16

Have you ever been frustrated with your child because he or she is just too particular and nit-picky? Have you ever been confused by that child because he or she almost always seems preoccupied with "heaven only knows" what?

Does your son start the day with great intentions to get a few specific things done when the many distractions that greet him around every corner turn into opportunities that entice him away from his goals? Does that tendency ever discourage you or make you want to scream?

Do you have one child who always seems to be calm and relaxed with ample time to play while the other one looks like a hamster on a treadmill—and always has at least three more things on his or her list to accomplish?

Why do some children love to sit and play alone for hours on end while others go crazy if other children aren't around?

Why is one child always coming up with new ideas and inventing things while another child is content to play with toys the way kids are "supposed to"?

Why do some children like to talk things out while others prefer to work it all out inside and then talk about it?

Why does one child welcome a new baby-sitter and another act as if it's the end of the world?

How can some children read a book for an hour without being bored or distracted while others start climbing the walls after only 10 minutes?

Why do some children take pride in having a clean, neat room while other kids' rooms appear as if they had been used for nuclear testing?

Nowhere is the breadth of God's creativity and sense of humor more evident than in the pinnacle of His creation, children. If you've had more than one child, you know that no two children are exactly alike. I've seen identical twins who had opposite personalities. God has designed each of us with a combination of gifts, talents, attitudes, beliefs, needs and wants that are different from anyone else's. Uniqueness is part of what makes parenting so exciting, and at times frustrating.

If you've ever observed families with more than one child, you've probably at some point been amazed that children from the same gene pool, raised by the same parents, in the same neighborhood, eating the same diet and going to the same school and church can be totally different. What accounts for these differences?

Born to Be Different

In Psalm 139:14 we read King David's words, "I will give thanks to Thee, for I am fearfully and wonderfully made; wonderful are Thy works" (*NASB*). Christians believe that every person is made in the image of God and is of infinite worth and value. We acknowledge that every person is unique. Yet as parents, most of us find it much easier to value the aspects of our children that are similar to our own. I've heard parents remark, "Tommy is just like me, but I'm not sure where Jill came from. She is so different from the rest of us."

What is the first thing that comes to mind when you hear the word "different"? Are the meanings you associate with "different" primarily positive or negative? If I were to approach you on the street and say, "You sure look different today," would you think I was giving you a compliment and reply, "Well, thank you very much?" Or would you think that perhaps I was being critical?

"Different" suggests a deviation from some kind of standard or norm. It suggests that something is not quite the way it usually is or the way it should be. Many people interpret "different" to mean "unusual, inappropriate, inferior or wrong." Now if I were to say to you, "You sure look like a deviate," you would know that I was being negative and critical.

On the other hand, what do you think of when you hear the words "unique" or "special"? Do you tend to have a more positive response to those terms? Every person is different. Yet often those differences are not understood or valued.

Replicated scientific research has shown that infants show significant individual differences from birth. We know that infants are born with unique temperamental characteristics, behavioral traits and ways of responding to external stimuli. Some distinguishing characteristics include their activity levels, responsiveness, irritability, curiosity, soothability and their abilities to signal their needs and feelings. Because every infant has a unique way of interacting with his or her environment, every parent must understand and relate to the infant's uniqueness.

Know Your Child

In the busyness of being parents, it's easy to forget that our children are not adults; they're "only" children. And when we have more than one child in the house, it's easy to forget that each child is unique. I've talked with many parents who have, without ever intending to, lumped all of their kids into the "children" category and forgotten that not only is each child unique but each one is also facing different developmental tasks at different ages.

We believe one of the most important aspects of parenting to be *knowing your child*. Your effectiveness as a parent will be in direct proportion to the extent your child believes you know and understand him or her. Notice I didn't say you agree with the child, but that you understand your child.

In Proverbs 22:6 we read, "Train up a child in the way he should go [and in keeping with his individual gift or bent], and when he is old he will not depart from it" (*Amp.*). For years, many well-meaning Christian parents interpreted that verse to mean that they should decide what kind of person their child *should* become and then work as hard as possible to cram the child into that mold. This kind of parenting is also known as the cookie-cutter approach.

An in-depth study of the words used in Proverbs 22:6 suggests that, rather than using the cookie-cutter approach, God is instructing parents to take the time to discover the God-given uniqueness of each child. God isn't telling us to rear our children to become what we think they should become. He is saying, "If you want your training to be godly and wise, observe your child, be sensitive and alert in order to discover his way, and adapt your training accordingly."

Don't Straighten Your Child's God-Given Bent

Charles Swindoll says:

> In every child God places in our arms, there is a bent, a set of characteristics already established. The bent is fixed and determined before he is given over to our care. The child is not, in fact, a pliable piece of clay. He has been set; he has been bent. And the parent who wants to train this child correctly will discover that bent![1]

In the last chapter we talked about the importance of understanding God's unique design for each of our children. How can I discover the God-given design of my child? In what way is he or she unique? We saw that Proverbs 22:6 encourages us to discover the unique aspects of each child's personality and to raise him or her accordingly. We are exhorted to approach each child differently because each is divinely different. But how can we understand and make sense of the differences?

After years of working with families, I have discovered that while few parents will dare to fight the law of gravity, many attempt to fight the law of differences. Even when the differences are recognized, rarely are they appreciated or understood. Think about it. When was the last time you complimented your child on an aspect of his or her personality, an opinion, or a way of doing something that differs from the way you would have done it? When was the last time you let that child know you appreciate those differences? Is there a way to understand and make sense of some of those differences?

Celebrate the Differences

First, we must acknowledge the value of individual differences. There is tremendous value in learning to appreciate our differences. In 1 Corinthians 12–14, we learn that *diversity does not necessitate division.* We can learn to maximize the value of our differences.

Second, it is impossible to understand and appreciate who your children are without understanding their God-given uniqueness.

> If I do not want what you want, please try not to tell me
>   that my want is wrong.
> Or if I believe other than you,
>   at least pause before you correct my view.
> Or if my emotion is less than yours, or more,
>   given the same circumstances,
>   try not to ask me to feel more strongly or weakly.

Or yet if I act, or fail to act, in the manner of your
  design for action, let me be.
I do not, for the moment at least, ask you to understand me.
That will come only when you are willing to give up changing
  me into a copy of you.
I may be your spouse, your parent, your offspring, your
  friend, or your colleague. If you will allow me any of
  my own wants, or emotions, or beliefs, or actions, then
  you open yourself, so that some day these ways of mine
  might not seem so wrong, and might finally appear to you
  as right—for me.
To put up with me is the first step to understanding me. Not
  that you embrace my ways as right for you, but that you
  are no longer irritated or disappointed with me for my
  seeming waywardness.
And in understanding me you might come to prize my
  differences from you, and, far from seeking to change
  me, preserve and even nurture those differences.[2]

While the first two steps are important, the third one is critical. Not only do we need to acknowledge our differences and be willing to value them, but we also need to have a way to understand or make sense of those differences. Just as there are different routes we can take to get to the same destination, there are different ways to understand personality and individual differences.

In his book *Standing Out*, Chuck Swindoll beautifully illustrates the importance of understanding and valuing individual differences. He quotes the following article, printed in the Springfield, Oregon, *Public Schools Newsletter*:

Once upon a time, the animals decided they should do something meaningful to meet the problems of the new world. So they organized a school.

They adopted an activity curriculum of running, climbing, swimming and flying. To make it easier to administer the curriculum, all the animals took all the subjects.

The duck was excellent in swimming; in fact, better than his instructor. But he made only passing grades in flying, and was very poor in running. Since he was slow in running, he had to drop swimming and stay after school to practice running. This caused his web feet to be badly worn, so that he was only average in swimming. But average was quite acceptable, so nobody worried about that—except the duck.

The rabbit started at the top of his class in running, but developed a nervous twitch in his leg muscles because of so much make-up work in swimming.

The squirrel was excellent in climbing, but he encountered constant frustration in flying class because his teacher made him start from the ground up instead of from the treetop down. He developed "charley horses" from overexertion, and so only got a C in climbing and a D in running.

The eagle was a problem child and was severely disciplined for being a nonconformist. In climbing classes, he beat all the others to the top of the tree, but insisted on using his own way to get there...

Swindoll comments that this story has an obvious moral. Each creature has its own unique characteristics in which it will naturally excel—unless it is expected or forced into a mold that doesn't fit.

When that happens, frustration, discouragement, and even guilt bring overall mediocrity or complete defeat. A duck is a duck—and only a duck. It is built to swim, not to run or fly and certainly not to climb. A squirrel is a squirrel—and only that. To move it out of its forte, climbing, and then expect it to swim or fly will drive a squirrel nuts. Eagles are beautiful creatures in the air but not in a foot race. The rabbit will win every time unless, of course, the eagle gets hungry.[3]

Your Child Is Unique, Not a
Chip off the Old Block

Several years ago I heard a story about Michelangelo, the great Renaissance sculptor, painter, architect and poet. "I've read that one day Michelangelo was looking at a free-standing mass of rough Carrara marble and exclaimed, 'There's an angel in that stone and I am going to liberate him!'"

I think that's a great way to look at our children—as people we can encourage, influence, help "liberate" to be and become all God has gifted them to be. But first we need to recognize that God has already given them a certain design. It's true that due both to maturity and the effects of sin in their lives, the design may be quite rough. Nevertheless, it is there!

> WHEN SOME PARENTS THINK OF CHANGING
> THEIR CHILDREN, THEY OVERLOOK THE FACT THAT GOD
> IS THE CREATOR; PARENTS ARE ONLY, AT BEST, A TOOL
> IN THE CREATOR'S HANDS.

The problem occurs when we get confused about our role in the process. Some parents see themselves as the Michelangelo whose job it is to determine what needs to be "liberated," what the child "should" be and become. (Those are the same people who are patiently waiting for a vacancy in the Trinity.) That's not our job. God has already started the work of art. He has already determined what He wants it to be. He is the Master Craftsman whose job it is to select the marble, create the design and determine where to start and how to progress.

Parents are the primary tools God will use in children's lives to help "release" and shape and polish who, in eternity past, He designed them to be. As parents, He may need us to help chip off some of the larger pieces, or to help polish them to add life, luster and beauty. Our job is to be available as tools in His hands and to understand His will and design for them. Then we can be available to be His assistant in completing the final work.

When some parents think of changing their children, they overlook the fact that God is the Creator; parents are only, at best, a tool in the Creator's hands. One of the first and most important steps in helping someone to change is to discover their unique "design." This takes time and patience; you can't do it overnight. During this process, you will not only gain a new sense of appreciation for your child, but you will also become better equipped to meet that child's real needs.

The Blueprint of Personality

In our more than 60 years of combined ministry, we've found that one of the most helpful tools for understanding and appreciating some of the natural personality differences in people is discovering a person's psychological type. While everyone is different, some of the most important ways in which people differ can be grouped into a few basic patterns. People can be more easily understood when we know

- how they perceive or take in information;
- the kinds of information that are important to them;
- how they use that information to make decisions;
- whether they are energized by focusing their attention on their inner world or by being actively involved with other individuals in their outer world; and
- how they prefer to organize their worlds.

Psychological or personality type provides a kind of map to help us understand some of the most important parts of a person's personality. Keep in mind that while a map doesn't give us all of the information we need, it does point us in the right direction. It provides markers along the way to let us know if we are going in the right direction. Some of the most important things we need to know about people to better understand them can be found by identifying their personality types.

Personality type consists of several inborn preferences or tendencies that have a strong impact on how we develop as individuals. We all begin life with a small number of inherited personality traits that make us a little different from everyone else. Do you know what some of yours are? What about you makes you a little bit (or a lot) different from your mom and dad, brother or sister? Each trait is a fundamental building block of personality. These basic inborn traits determine many individual differences in personality.

While these core traits are present at birth, they are influenced and modified by environment and how we are raised. There is an interaction between how God has designed each child and the ways the child interacts with the world around him or her. Every child is an *initiator* who in part creates his or her own environment. The child is a *reinforcer* who selectively rewards or punishes people for the way they treat him or her, and also a *responder* who interacts with the effects of the environment based on his or her personality.[4]

Presently, the best tool for identifying personality types is the Myers-Briggs Type Indicator. We've used the MBTI for many years as one way to help parents and family members see each other through different eyes. The MBTI identifies four sets of contrasting personality traits or preferences: extrovert and introvert, sensor and intuitive, thinker and feeler, judger and perceiver. Each trait can be identified by its complete name or by the single letter assigned to it.

Extroversion (E)_____(I) Introversion
Sensing (S) _____(N) Intuition
Thinking (T)_____(F) Feeling
Judging (J)_____(P) Perceiving

A "preference" is the conscious or unconscious choice a person makes in a designated realm. All eight preferences are found within each person, but with varying amounts of expertise and intensity. However, in each pairing, one preference is more prominent than its opposite.

According to type theory, everyone uses all eight of the traits, but one out of each of the four is preferred and better developed. It's similar to the fact that while we have two hands and use both of them, we tend to prefer one hand or the other. Most people are either right-handed or left-handed. When using your most-preferred hand, tasks are usually easier, take less time and are less frustrating, and the end result is usually better.

Here's a simple way to experience what I mean. Take a pen or pencil and put it in your less-preferred hand. Now on line #1 write your full name as quickly as you would if you were using your preferred hand. Now place your pen or pencil in your preferred hand and write your full name on line #2.

#1_____   #2_____

Did you notice any difference? Of course you did! When most people do this simple exercise, they say that using their less-preferred hand is more awkward, frustrating, takes more time and concentration, and has an inferior result.

That's the way it is with personality type. When we or our children are forced to face certain life tasks with one of the less-preferred and thus less-developed traits, the activity feels more awkward, frustrating, takes more time and concentration and often produces an inferior result.

Your daughter might be an introvert and your son an extrovert. She likes to solve problems by going off by herself and thinking about them; he likes to solve problems by getting them out in the open and talking about them. For her to problem-solve by immediately talking about it, or for him to problem-solve by going off by himself to think about it, is at best difficult and at worst impossible.

Maturity and healthy relationships involve not only being able to see things from our own perspective, but also being able to look through the eyes of others. Someone once said, "If the only tool you have in your tool chest is a hammer, you will tend to see every problem as a nail." If the only language you speak is your own, if you are only able to see things from your point of view, if your way almost always seems like the "right" way, then you are in for some difficult times.

> A VERY NORMAL PART OF BEING IN A FAMILY IS DEALING
> WITH EACH OTHER'S DIFFERENCES.

As you can see from the previous diagram, each of the eight traits has a letter associated with it. Your preference on each one of the four categories is indicated by a letter and your four letters are considered your personality type.

When you put together the possible combinations on each one of the four levels, you end up with the possibility of 16 different personality types. Each type is represented by four letters. The first letter is always either an E or an I. The second letter is always either an S or an N. The third letter is always either a T or an F. The fourth letter is always either a J or a P.

ISTJ	ISFJ	INFJ	INTJ
ISTP	ISFP	INFP	INTP
ESTP	ESFP	ENFP	ENTP
ESTJ	ESFJ	ENFJ	ENTJ

Throughout the years we've discovered two other personality types that have yet to be added to the 16. The sports-lovers type is ESPN and the farmers type is EIEIO!

You can better understand your own personality and the personalities of those you love when you consider how all four preferences work together, how they modify each other and how they interact to create the unique people God made you and your child to be.

A very normal part of being in a family is dealing with each other's differences. Some degree of frustration resulting in conflict is inevitable in any relationship. Clashes between different personality types are to be expected. But when we understand personality type and the different relational languages God has given each of us, we can significantly decrease the unnecessary conflicts and misunderstandings that plague many families.

When I first came across the concept of personality type, I discounted it. But as I've used these insights for the past 20 years, I have been amazed at how helpful they can be. With the insights of personality type, you are less likely to spend time trying to squeeze your children into your own mold. Instead, you will be more likely to understand their unique design and help them become the special individuals that God intends them to become.

Insights about our children's personality type "can contribute to the intelligent rearing, teaching, counseling and overall understanding of children; it can help children to better understand themselves and to improve their relationships with teachers, parents, and friends; and by identifying individual strengths, it can help children to strengthen self-esteem, enhance achievement, and build social interaction."[5]

Conclusion

In this chapter we've only been able to scratch the surface in introducing the important insights of personality type as identified by the Myers-Briggs Type Indicator. However, even with this brief overview, I'm sure you can see how invaluable these insights can be—not only in understanding your child, but also in communicating more meaningfully to him or her.

In the next two chapters you're going to get better acquainted with your children through the eyes of personality type. You will learn how personality type indicators can be an invaluable aid in navigating the mine field of parenting. You'll discover how understanding God-given personality preferences can help you better understand your children, communicate your love as well as God's love to them, and help them become godly men and women.

As you understand your child's unique design, it will become easier for you to know what can be changed, accept what can't or shouldn't be changed and be available to God in helping your child become all he or she can be.

As parents, we have the greatest influence on how our younger children learn, how they understand themselves and others and how well they grow according to the God-designed "bent" in each of them. The differences in personality type appear to profoundly affect a child's learning style and developmental pattern.

You can become aware of how your own personality preferences and expectations either blend or clash with those of your children. You can learn how to speak your child's language and thus increase the probability of clear communication. If you understand some of the most important personality differences between you and your children, you are likely to be more successful in nurturing their growth.

I strongly encourage you to do additional reading on personality type. At the end of the chapter I've included some of the most helpful resources available. They are packed with practical illustrations of how to apply these insights in your family.

Now that you have a clearer understanding of the basic categories of personality type, it might be helpful to take a look at what your child's preferences might be. Keep in mind that because a child's personality is still developing, some children's preferences might be perfectly clear on some scales while there still might be a lot of ambiguity on others.

The following questions are not a substitute for and do not have the validity or reliability of the MBTI or MMTIC, but they may help you better understand what your child's preferences might be. Based on your observation of your children, what do you see?

1. Does your child...
_____ act quickly, sometimes without thinking?
_____ get tired of long, slow jobs or games?
_____ enjoy learning by doing?
_____ chatter?
_____ enjoy new activities?
_____ want to do things with others?
_____ care what other children think?
_____ unload emotions as they occur?

These are all characteristics of extroverts. Thus when your child does these things, he or she might be extroverting.

2. Does your child...
_____ think before acting?
_____ work or play patiently for long periods of time?
_____ enjoy learning by reading?
_____ keep things to himself or herself?
_____ hesitate to try something new?
_____ have a few close friends?
_____ want a quiet space to work or play in?
_____ set his or her own standards despite others' opinions?
_____ bottle up emotions?

These are all characteristics of introverts. Thus when your child does these things, he or she might be introverting.

3. Does your child...
_____ enjoy familiar activities and routine?
_____ want to know the right way to do things?
_____ observe carefully and remember lots of details?

_____ memorize easily?
_____ ask, "Did it really happen?"
_____ like coloring books?
_____ enjoy collecting things?
_____ enjoy working with his or her hands?
_____ seem steady and patient?

These are all characteristics of sensing types. Thus when your child does these things, he or she might be perceiving through the senses.

4. Does your child...
_____ enjoy learning new things?
_____ enjoy being different?
_____ learn quickly but forget details?
_____ have a vivid imagination?
_____ enjoy imaginative stories?
_____ use toys in new and original ways?
_____ often lose things?
_____ quickly go from one new interest to another?
_____ work and play in fits and starts?

These are all characteristics of intuitive types. Thus when your child does these things, he or she might be perceiving through intuition.

5. Does your child...
_____ ask "Why?" a lot?
_____ insist on logical explanations?
_____ get alarmed if someone is treated unfairly.
_____ like to arrange things in orderly patterns?
_____ show more interest in ideas than in people?
_____ hold firmly to his or her beliefs?
_____ seem uncomfortable with affection?
_____ want rules in games established and kept?
_____ like to be praised for doing something competently?

These are all characteristics of thinking types. Thus when your child does these things, he or she might be making thinking judgments.

6. Does your child...

_____ like to talk or read about people?

_____ want to be praised for caring for others?

_____ get alarmed if someone is unhappy?

_____ tell stories expressively, in great detail?

_____ try to be tactful, even if that means lying?

_____ show more interest in people than in ideas?

_____ generally agree with his or her friends' opinions?

_____ want to be told you love him or her?

_____ relate well to other children, teachers, relatives?

These are all characteristics of feeling types. Thus when your child does these things, he or she might be making feeling judgments.

7. Does your child...

_____ like to know what is going to happen?

_____ know how things "ought to be"?

_____ enjoy making choices?

_____ usually work before playing?

_____ discipline himself or herself?

_____ have definite goals?

_____ have strong opinions?

_____ keep a well-ordered room?

_____ want to be in charge?

These are all characteristics of judging types. Thus when your child does these things, he or she might be relating to the world through his or her judging function.

8. Does your child...

_____ enjoy spontaneity?

_____ show a lot of curiosity?

_____ enjoy sampling new experiences and ideas?

_____ turn work into play?

_____ overextend himself or herself?

_____ adapt well to changing circumstances?

_____ keep an open mind?

_____ not object to having things out of place?

_____ want to understand whatever's happening?

These are all characteristics of perceiving types. Thus when your child does these things, he or she might be relating to the world through his or her perceiving function.[6]

Please note: The best way to determine your personality is to take the MBTI from a qualified professional. You can start by contacting your pastor, a local Christian counseling center or the Association for Psychological Type (APT), P.O. Box 5099, Gainesville, FL 32602. If you would like to receive training in the MBTI or sponsor a parenting or marriage seminar based on these insights, please contact Dr. Gary J. Oliver at The Center for Marriage and Family Studies, John Brown University, 2000 W. University, Siloam Springs, AR 72761; phone: (501) 524-7105.

Notes

1. Charles R. Swindoll, *You and Your Child* (Nashville: Thomas Nelson, 1977), pp. 20,21.
2. David Keirsey and Marilyn Bates, *Please Understand Me* (Del Mar, Calif.: Prometheus Nemesis Books, 1978), p. 1.
3. Charles R. Swindoll, *Standing Out* (Portland, Oreg.: Multnomah Press, 1979), n.p.
4. Adapted from A. H. Buss and R. Plomin, *A Temperament Theory of Personality Development* (New York: John Wiley & Sons, 1975), p. 237.
5. Charles Meisgeier, Elizabeth Murphy and Constance Meisgeier, *A Teacher's Guide to Type: A New Perspective on Individual Differences in the Classroom* (Palo Alto: Consulting Psychologists Press, 1989), p. 1.

6. Adapted from LaVonne Neff, *One of a Kind* (Portland: Multnomah Press, 1988), pp. 24-26

Suggested Readings

If you would like to learn more about the MBTI, you will find the following books to be helpful. Those with the * are especially helpful in applying the insights of type to children.

Harbaugh, Gary L. *God's Gifted People, Discovering and Using Your Spiritual and Personal Gifts*. Minneapolis: Augsburg Publishing House, 1988.

Keirsey, David, and Marilyn Bates. *Please Understand Me*. Del Mar, Calif.: Prometheus Nemesis Books, 1978.

Kroeger, Otto, and Janet M. Thuesen. *Type Talk*. New York: Delacorte Press, 1988.

Mayhall, Jack and Carole. *Opposites Attack: Turning Your Differences into Opportunities*. Colorado Springs: NavPress, 1990.

*Neff, LaVonne. *One of a Kind*. Portland: Multnomah Press, 1988.

Pearson, Mark. *Why Can't I Be Me?* Grand Rapids: Baker Book House, 1992.

Stoop, Dave and Jan. *The Intimacy Factor*. Nashville: Thomas Nelson Publishers, 1992.

Ward, Ruth McRoberts. *Self-Esteem: Gift from God*. Grand Rapids: Baker Book House, 1984.

*Wright, H. Norman. *The Power of a Parent's Words*. Ventura, Calif: Regal Books, 1991 (especially chapters 12 and 13).

*Wright, H. Norman, and Gary J. Oliver. *Raising Emotionally Healthy Kids*. Colorado Springs: ChariotVictor Books, 1992.

6

UNIQUE IN PROCESSING INFORMATION: DETAILED OR DREAMER?

By Gary J. Oliver

The plans of the righteous are just.
— P R O V E R B S   1 2 : 5

Kelsey is a positive, outgoing and energetic 16-year-old who is active in school and church activities. Her brother Carl has just become a teenager. While he isn't as outgoing as Kelsey, he is very active and very much a boy. Kelsey and Carl are basically good kids. The only problem is that they are both teenagers and they are related—a potentially dangerous combination.

When Paul and Kathy called me and asked for an appointment to discuss some "parenting issues," they told me that they weren't having major problems with the kids. They were, however, frustrated by the frequent miscommunication and the growing sense that they didn't understand their children as well as they could have. With a sober tone of voice Paul said, "Dr. Oliver, we aren't going to have many more years with our kids at home and we want to make these last years count."

Kathy added, "Dr. Oliver, I know that our kids love us and we love them, but we just don't connect like we used to." Paul concluded, "At times it seems like we just endure each other."

Within a few minutes it became clear that they felt stuck and were becoming discouraged. Kathy and Paul sensed that the frustrations they were experiencing in parenting Kelsey and Carl involved more than gender and age. As we continued to talk, I realized that much of their miscommunication and resulting frustration was occurring simply because they didn't understand some of their children's most basic personality differences.

> UNDERSTAND THE UNIQUENESS OF THE OTHER PERSON
> AND SPEAK TO THAT PERSON IN WAYS MEANINGFUL
> TO THAT INDIVIDUAL.

The Bible gives numerous passages for understanding healthy marriage and family relationships. One of my favorites is 1 Corinthians 12:4-26. In this passage Paul lays out what I refer to as a theology of differences. He talks about the fact that God has made each person unique and given them different spiritual gifts. The clear teaching of Scripture is that the same differences that so often frustrate and divide can, in God's hands, produce strength and harmony.

A key to effective parenting, or to any other relationship, is the ability to understand the uniqueness of the other person and to speak to that person in ways meaningful to that individual. When you look at Christ's interactions in the four Gospels, you quickly discover that He started where people *were* and not where He thought they *should be*. He took the time to appreciate their uniqueness and spoke to them in ways they were most likely to understand.

It Starts with You

One of the most practical tools to help people put shoe leather on this biblical concept of individual differences is the Myers-Briggs Type Indicator. This simple tool helps us identify and understand some of the most basic differences between people. Throughout the past 20 years, we've seen God use the simple insights of the MBTI to give literally thousands of family members a new way of looking at, listening to and talking with those they love.

The first step in using type to communicate with our children is to identify our own type; then identify what their preferences might be. When Paul and Kathy took the MBTI, Paul's results indicated preferences for introversion, sensing, thinking and perceiving (ISTP). Kathy's results indicated her preference for extroversion, intuition, feeling and judging (ENFJ). It didn't take long for them to notice that they preferred exact opposites in all four categories.

"Well, that sure explains it," Kathy said with a dejected resignation. "I guess there's not much hope for us."

After a brief pause I replied, "On the contrary. There is a lot of hope. You and Paul have great potential to complement each other, to balance each other out The very differences that seem to contradict can be used by God to complement. It's just a matter of both of you taking the time to understand your differences and to learn how to speak each other's language."

Over the next several sessions Paul and Kathy began to better understand some of their own differences, the unique personality preferences of Kelsey and Carl and the implications of those differences to better understand and parent their children. Paul and Kathy learned how the differences in their own personalities affected their interpretation of their children's behavior and their communication with them. Understanding each child's unique design allowed them to more fully understand the child's heart and thus more effectively model truth for that child.

In the next four chapters we'll take you through each of the four personality preferences. We'll look at them through the eyes of real parents, real children and real family situations. While we will illustrate a two-parent family, all of the principles apply to those of you who are single parents. As you read through the various preferences, we would encourage you to look not only at the distinctives of each preference, but also at the ways in which the opposites can actually complement and balance each other.

The Sensing and Intuition Functions

At any given time we are either taking in information or making decisions based upon the information we have received. Sensing and intuition are two different ways of perceiving or gathering information. This preference influences how we listen, what we hear and what we remember.

Detail people (sensors) are influenced more by what they actually see, hear, touch, taste and smell than by the possibilities of what might be. They are not necessarily more sensible or sensitive. Kelsey prefers sensing (S). Although she uses her intuitive function, she prefers or is better at sensing. She has a here-and-now orientation, is very observant and pays attention to detail. She stays focused on the task at hand and prefers to deal with things that are practical. She is the kind of person who, as a young child, always colored within the lines and was proud of it.

The intuiting function (N) processes information by way of a sixth sense or hunch. Carl prefers intuition. Although he uses his sensing function, he prefers or is better at intuition. He has more of a future orientation. In school Carl sometimes finds it hard to concentrate on what the teacher is saying because he is thinking about the possibilities and options of a previous statement. He can get bored with details or mundane tasks. He loves to create.

When he would color as a child, Carl wasn't too concerned about staying within the lines. He is much more of a dreamer. He looks at what is and imagines what might be.

The difference between sensing and intuition is critical to parenting because the ways in which we gather information and the kinds of information we pick up on provide the raw material for how we look at life, the issues we need to address and how we address those issues. It is the starting point for almost everything else that we do.

SENSORS VERSUS INTUITIVES

Failure to understand and appreciate the differences between sensing and intuition can negatively affect a family. Why? Because parents who don't understand and value this critical difference will have a difficult time understanding their child. Poor communication leads to miscommunication and is one of the most basic barriers to understanding.

How do sensors and intuitives differ in their communication? Sensors and intuitives can go to the same social event, talk to the same people, participate in the same conversation and come away with two different recollections of what was said.

Another difference is how they respond to questions. When Kelsey is asked a question, she usually gives a specific answer. When asked the same question, Carl will usually give a more general answer and tends to answer several other questions at the same time.

Here is a common sensing-intuitive (S/N) conversation based on a relatively simple request:

S: (simple question) "Can you tell me what time it is?"

N: (simple answer) "It's getting late!"

S: (a bit frustrated): "What time is it?"

N: (matter-of-fact): "It's almost time to go!"

S: (clearly impatient): "Hey, read my lips! I'd like to know what time it is!"

N: (equally impatient): "I think it's a bit past three but I'm not sure."

S: (exasperated): "Close, but no cigar! I shouldn't have to ask
a simple question four times to get an accurate answer."

N: (perturbed, because he believes he answered correctly
the first time): "You shouldn't be so picky."

Those who prefer sensing tend to be much more literal in their communication. They stick with the topic. They answer what they've been asked. It's not too difficult to stay on track in a conversation between two sensors. Dave and Jan Stoop observe that while sensors end their sentences with a period, intuitives are more likely to end their sentences with a comma. There's always room for one more thought.[1]

As Paul began to understand some of their basic personality differences, he realized his preference for the sensing function causes him to automatically listen for the facts, the details, in the conversation. In fact, he thrives on them. "Now I know that my son Carl is an intuitive," Paul said. "When he is involved in a discussion, he automatically listens for the big picture."

Kathy jumped in, "Carl may not remember all of the specifics, but he can tell you where the person is coming from, what some of their values are and if they can be trusted."

Another important difference is that many intuitives have a difficult time finishing their sentences. There are so many ideas running through their minds that a lot of energy is needed to focus on one thing. Before they finish one sentence, their minds are already on to a new thought. Two intuitives can have a conversation and a listener may think that neither of them ever completes a thought. However, the two intuitives understand each other perfectly.

Several years ago, I was leading a workshop for pastors and church counselors on the Myers-Briggs Type Indicator (MBTI) in Denver. In the audience was a carload of six people who drove down from a small town in Wyoming. As I was finishing my discussion on the differences between sensors and intuitives, one of them started laughing. In fact, she was laughing so loud everyone turned around to look at her.

"Now I know why I thought I was going crazy," she blurted out. "I prefer sensing, but I spent four hours riding in a car with five intuitives. They jumped from topic to topic, didn't complete their sentences, brought in information that seemed to me to be totally irrelevant to the topic—whatever it was—that was being discussed." The rest of the grouped cracked up and the others who preferred sensing began nodding their heads.

"What was the most frustrating part of it?" I asked her.

"Well," she paused, "it seemed as though it all made sense to them, like the pieces fit. It seemed as if they all thought that this was the normal way to communicate."

Like the good intuitive that I am, I paused, looked her straight in the eyes, smiled and said, "Well, isn't it?"

The answer from the intuitive is yes. The equally valid answer from the sensor is a resounding no. Before I could move on to the next part of the workshop, the woman added, "Well, now that I understand this, the trip home won't be nearly as frustrating or painful as the trip down here."

Frustrating. Painful. Confusing. Those are apt descriptions (I've heard even more colorful ones) describing what it can be like to try to communicate with a child who has an opposite preference—especially if you don't understand the differences. I hope it's becoming clearer to you that if you want to be effective in understanding your children and communicating truth to them, you've got to understand how to speak their language.

One of the easiest ways to determine if a person prefers sensing or intuition is to ask directions. If you ask a sensor for directions, he or she will give you specific details. "Go four miles north, make a right turn on Hampden Avenue, go seven blocks east and make a right on University (it's the second stop light); and it's the fourth house on your right."

If you ask directions of people who have a strong preference for intuition, they first have to stop and try to remember where they are. Once they get their bearings, they will give you their version of how to get there. For example: "Go north towards the mall, and then after you pass Wendy's you'll want to make a right; I think it's the fourth or fifth street. Anyway, after you make a right, you'll go past an elementary school, or maybe it's a junior high school. Anyway, you'll go over two speed bumps, and watch out for the second one. I scraped the bottom of my car on it the last time I drove over it. Anyway, let's see, where are we? OK, after you've gone past the second speed bump, look on the right-hand side of the street for a kind of Cape Cod-looking house, make a right on the street after the one with the Cape Cod on the corner and their home is in the middle of that block. I'm pretty sure it's on the right-hand side. They have a huge oak tree in the middle of their front yard, so you can't miss it."

There's a huge difference between those two descriptions. If a sensor gives a sensor directions, he or she will usually get there. If an intuitive gives a sensor directions and doesn't take into account that person's need for the specifics, the sensor may end up lost for hours.

Another important difference between a sensor and an intuitive is that when an intuitive describes something, the person often experiences what he or she is describing. Many intuitives enjoy planning a trip as much as actually going on the trip. I discovered this principle in my own marriage. I prefer intuition and my wife, Carrie, prefers sensing. Early in our marriage, I described to her a fantasy I had held for many years. Now as you read this conversation, remember that Carrie had never been out of the United States, but I had traveled and studied in Europe, the Middle East and the Far East on several occasions.

I described my dream of getting together with two or three other couples, flying to Amsterdam, buying two used camper vans and driving around the world. I described what it would be like to drive along the Rhine river, to visit Paris, to see the beauty of northern Italy, to lay on the beaches of the Greek islands, to visit Israel, and on and on. The more I talked, the more excited I got describing the beauty of the places we could visit. As I was talking, I could visualize Carrie and myself walking along the beaches together or standing by the garden tomb in Jerusalem.

When I had finished, I turned to Carrie, eager to see her equally enthusiastic response, and said, "Well honey, isn't that exciting? What do you think?" As soon as those words came out of my mouth, I knew I had asked the wrong question. Carrie's face was pale and she looked panicked.

"Well, that's interesting," she responded, "but we will never be able to afford it. And how will we communicate in all of those different languages? And what if someone gets sick? And what if one of the vans breaks down? You don't know how to fix anything."

As you might have already guessed, her response didn' t just rain on my parade; a sinkhole opened up and sucked my entire parade down into it. I couldn't believe it. From my perspective, she had missed the main point. From her perspective, there *was* no main point.

Do you see what happened here? I had shared my dream in a typical intuitive fashion. If Carrie had understood my language, she would have known that she didn't need to take what I was saying too seriously, and that all I wanted to do was to share my dream with her. However, if I had understood Carrie's language, I might have prefaced my story by saying, "This is probably pretty unrealistic and I don't know how we will ever do it; but, if we could, this is something I think would be a real adventure."

At the end of the conversation I felt frustrated and discouraged. Carrie felt overwhelmed. Why? Simply because we didn't understand each other's language and didn't know how to communicate and listen in ways consistent with our spouse's preferences.

As I shared this story with Paul and Kathy I saw Paul's face light up. "If this is the only thing I learn out of our time together, it has already been worthwhile." He went on to share the frequent frustrations he experiences with Carl. "It's obvious that Carl prefers intuition and I prefer sensing. We speak two different languages! I knew that was the case with Kathy, but I just didn't see it in Carl."

At our next session, Paul explained how he had applied his new insight. "One of things that has frustrated me about Carl is that during our family devotions he can ask questions that seem totally unrelated to the lesson." He continued to tell me that his goal was to get through the lesson and make sure everyone understood the point for the day. When Carl would ask questions that didn't seem "on track," he would interpret this as his not paying attention or just trying to sidetrack the devotional. There were times he had become angry at him for what he interpreted as a lack of commitment and cooperation.

Paul concluded, "Now I understand that Carl was doing what a normal intuitive does. What I had interpreted as something negative was actually a sign that he was engaging in the devotional and really thinking about what I was saying and how to apply it."

To help you better understand the differences between these two different yet equally valuable ways to taking in information, I've prepared two lists. As you read through the lists, you can note some of the important differences. Which of these describe you? Which ones describe your spouse? Which ones describe your child?

Sensor	Intuitive
Looks at specific parts and pieces.	Looks at the broad overall relationships between the specific parts and pieces.
Focuses on the immediate, enjoying what's there.	Focuses on the future, anticipating all the exciting and important things that might be.
Prefers handling practical matters.	Prefers imagining all of the potential possibilities for himself, his family, friends, his world and even other worlds.

Asks "Will it work?"	Asks "Is it possible? If so, what do we need to do? If not, why not? And who says why not?"
Likes things that are definite and measurable.	Likes opportunities for being inventive and if not given the opportunity will go ahead and do it anyway.
Starts at the beginning and takes one step at a time.	Isn't sure where the beginning is, doesn't think it's important, jumps in anywhere, leaps over steps, and doesn't usually know that he's skipped anything.
Enjoys reading instructions and notices details.	Skips instructions and follows hunches, until he's tried two or three times and can't figure it out. Then he either calls an S friend for help or, as a last-gasp effort, looks at the instructions, if he can find them.
Can't see the forest for the trees.	Can't see the trees for the forest. In fact, he may not even be looking at the forest that is in front of him because no matter where his body is, his mind is probably elsewhere.
Likes set procedures, established routine.	Likes frequent change and may have come up with three or four different ways to come home from work because it's too boring to come home the same way every day.

Looks for the evidence.	Looks for the potential, the possibilities, the options, the way to take what isn't and bring it to pass, the way to find new solutions to old problems.
They may seem too practical, boring and literal minded to N's.	They may seem like fickle and impractical dreamers to S's.

What differences did you notice between these two lists? An S would love the list on the left. It is precise, concise and specific. No rambling, no nonsense, no wasted words. An N would appreciate the list on the right. It was written by an intuitive for intuitives. It is much more creative and expansive, and may wander a bit but that makes it even better for an N.

Now reread each of these two lists and imagine what it would be like to have one preference but to be raised in a home where you were expected to be the total opposite. Imagine what it would be like to be an intuitive child who was talked to and expected to act like a sensor. What would the message be? Would there tend to be more miscommunication and conflict? Would you tend to feel misunderstood and out of place? Would you be more likely to think that something was wrong with you? Would you wonder if God had made a mistake?

KEYS TO PARENTING A SENSOR

Start with the details; then move to the big picture. Intuitives start with the forest and then maybe get to talking about the trees. Sensors work best when they have the specifics; then it's much easier for them to make sense of the big picture. Start with what they can see, then move to what they can't see. When it comes to sharing prayer requests, sensors prefer to have the details of the request first and then (maybe) an elaboration of why the request is important.

Be factual and specific. Don't ramble. Show an appreciation for their love of details, but don't overwhelm them with too much information. Remember that sensors tend to communicate with a period rather than a comma. If you want to increase the likelihood that your sensing child will both hear you and understand what you want to say, learn how to end your sentences with a period. If you want something done, tell them the why, when, where, who and how of the task. And be sure to let them know when you are changing subjects.

Let them know how you want them to listen. Do you remember the frustration that Carrie and I experienced when I shared my dream of driving around the world with her? I would have been much more successful, and she would have been much less frustrated, if I had started by saying something like, "Carrie, I've had this dream for a long time. I know it may not be very practical and I don't know if or when we would ever be able to do it, but I'd love to share it with you."

Do you see how helpful that would be? Carrie knows how to listen. She doesn't need to be concerned about all of the details and specifics. She doesn't need to wonder if I want to leave on this trip within the next month. She knows that to a great degree I am simply thinking out loud with her. And because she loves me, she wants me to share my dreams with her. Even outrageous ones like this.

Show them specific ways in which what you are talking about is realistic and workable. One of the most frustrating differences between a sensor and an intuitive is that it's easy for the intuitive to forget that the sensor doesn't get excited about possibilities. In fact, sensors can feel overwhelmed by them. What energizes an intuitive can overwhelm a sensor. Sensors are more interested in and more secure with that which is practical. If you want to communicate your dream, do it in such a way that the sensor can identify with how it might work.

Use concrete examples. Sometimes an intuitive parent can paint a picture with such a broad stroke that the sensing child isn't sure what the parent means. By giving concrete examples, you ensure that the message you intended to send is the same message your child receives. When sharing a biblical principle, make sure you use simple, clear and relevant examples.

Now that you intuitives have some hints on how to parent a sensor, we'll give you sensors some helpful helpful hints on how to parent an intuitive.

KEYS TO PARENTING AN INTUITIVE

Start with the big picture. Remember that the intuitives' language is enthusiastic and imaginative. Feed their imagination. Remember, they like to see the forest and not just the trees. Try to show how the specifics relate to the big picture. If you discover that the intuitive has forgotten some of the facts, don't assume it's because that person has intentionally disregarded them. Intuitives are more likely to remember the facts when they are tied to the big picture.

If you want to get their attention, point out an interesting possibility or ask some questions. Asking questions taps into the intuitives' possibility bank. When they are into their possibility mode, don't constantly correct them with the exact details unless that information is critical for the discussion. If you are sharing a biblical principle with them, start with the gist or the main idea and then, if they're still with you, fill in the details.

When they ask you to do something, make sure to clarify exactly what they want. Don't assume that what they really want to communicate is contained in the exact words they have used. It's common for intuitives to think they've given you more specifics than they really have. If *you* need more specific information (and if you prefer sensing you almost always will), just ask for it. Don't criticize or shame intuitive children because they don't think like you do.

Don't overwhelm them with details. When intuitives ask, "What did you do today?" they're not asking for a precise breakdown of everything you did in 15-minute intervals. They more likely want to get a general sense of what you did. When you discipline an intuitive, don't move into an annotated lecture. Share your concern, make sure the child knows what the more appropriate behavior would look like, have the child repeat it in his or her own words and move on.

Don't be afraid to let intuitives jump into the future. In fact one way you can love intuitives is to dream with them. Dreaming or possibility thinking is the framework for the details that are so valued by the sensor. This dimension of the intuitive preference can be utilized in helping them consider ways for applying truth in other areas of their lives. Many sensors see themselves as the string that keeps the intuitive kite attached to the ground. If you understand how God has made intuitives and how their minds work, you will be able to give them a lot of string.

Note

1. David and Jan Stoop, *The Intimacy Factor* (Nashville, Tenn.: Thomas Nelson Publishers, 1993), p. 77.

7

UNIQUE IN MAKING DECISIONS: MORE HEAD OR MORE HEART?

By Gary J. Oliver

We ask God to give you a complete understanding of what he wants to do in your lives, and we ask him to make you wise.

—COLOSSIANS 1:9 (*NLT*)

"I know he's a boy, and boys are not supposed to be as sensitive as girls, but sometimes Carl seems so overly hard and cold in how he responds to people that it worries me." During a previous session Kathy had expressed concern for what seemed to be Carl's lack of social skills, and now some events of the previous week had caused her concern to resurface.

As we talked, Kathy and Paul both shared several examples of times Carl's matter-of-fact response had seemed to alienate some of his friends. Paul was quick to add that this wasn't some new phenomenon. "Our son Carl has never had a problem disagreeing with anyone, especially us."

Head-Driven Carl

When making decisions or coming to a conclusion, Carl prefers the thinking function. When asked to do something, he's likely to ask why. It's not that he's being rebellious or that he's cold and unemotional; he simply prefers to make decisions based on logical reasons. Carl wants to know why, and "just because" is not an acceptable answer for him.

At times Carl wonders why his sister Kelsey gets "so emotional about everything." If someone disagrees with Carl, he's likely to want to know the reason. Sometimes Carl can be so straightforward that he comes across as cold and uncaring. But that's not true. Underneath his matter-of-fact exterior, Carl is a tender and sensitive young man.

Honesty and fairness, however, are very important to Carl. He tends to see things as black or white, right or wrong; there aren't a lot of gray areas in his thinking. As a Christian the ability to take what could be an unpopular stand can be a strength. And yet, if not understood and properly developed, it can also communicate an insensitivity, arrogance and lack of caring that might drive people away.

Heart-Driven Kelsey

Kelsey's preferred decision-making function is feeling. Feeling refers to a person who is more value-centered in the decision-making process, which doesn't necessarily mean the person is more emotional or illogical. While Carl tends to approach problems in an objective manner, Kelsey's preferred approach is more subjective. Kelsey "thinks" as well as Carl does, but as a person preferring F (feeling), she simply incorporates different values into her decision-making process. If someone disagrees with Kelsey, she will often overlook the problem because of her desire to maintain harmony.

When asked to do something she doesn't understand, Kelsey is more likely to do what is asked because of her strong desire to please. Children who prefer the feeling process can be especially sensitive to the emotional climate in the home. Constant conflict in the home can lead to emotional and even physical problems for those who prefer feeling.

This Is What I Think Versus This Is What I Feel

When it comes to making decisions, your child prefers either the thinking function or the feeling function. Whenever we make decisions, we utilize both the thinking and feeling functions, but we prefer or are better at one than the other. Those who prefer the thinking function tend to decide on the basis of linear logic and objective considerations. Those who prefer the feeling function decide more on the basis of personal subjective values.

It's a person's preference in the thinking/feeling dimension, not whether they are male or female, that largely determines whether they will be seen as tough-minded or tender-hearted. These are the only personality-type preferences where a difference between male and female exists. Approximately 60 percent of the males prefer thinking with 40 percent preferring feeling, and about 60 percent of the women prefer feeling while 40 percent prefer thinking.

Dr. David Stoop describes the difference as follows:

The thinking person uses pro-and-con lists of acts in order to arrive at the best decision. The feeling person will probably make a bad decision if he or she relies only on factual information. The feeling person needs to look at the values and emotions involved in order to make a good decision.

The way we handle our emotions is related to our preference on this trait, even though the trait has nothing directly to do with emotions. Those who score on the thinking side are often uncomfortable talking about the area of feelings. They may also not be as comfortable in the area of aesthetics and the cultivation of relationships. To others, they appear cool and aloof; sometimes they are accused of having ice in their veins, even though they are very sensitive.

Feeling persons, on the other hand, can be quite comfortable in the area of emotions. They are usually aware of what they are feeling and can tune in to what others around them are feeling as well. When they make a decision, they are concerned about how it will affect the others involved.[1]

Kathy and Paul experienced the effects of their differences in decision making when Kathy suggested going on a weekend retreat to get away from their home-life pressures in order to focus on their relationship. Paul didn't hear the "why" behind Kathy's suggestion; he didn't hear her concern for him, his health and their relationship.

The first thing Paul did was to consult their budget and checkbook balance. Based on what he saw there, he made a unilateral decision that they couldn't really afford it, so the retreat was out of the question.

What started out as a simple request for some special time together suddenly became another all-too-common standoff between two frustrated and misunderstood people. Here were two people who loved each other but were divided by two different ways of making a decision. They were so focused on wanting to be understood themselves that they didn't try to understand each other.

"What might these different preferences look like in your roles as parents?" I asked. It didn't take long for them to respond. Paul shared that Kelsey had recently started to drive. Let's look at how these important differences might affect a thinker (Paul) and a feeler (Kathy) as they try to make a decision about their teenage daughter using the family car.

Early in the week they had promised Kelsey that she could take the car to a party on Friday night. However, an unexpected snowstorm developed and the roads became dangerous. This new data meant that their earlier decision had to be reevaluated. Otto

Kroeger and Janet M. Thuesen illustrate how the thinking dad (Paul) and feeling mom (Kathy) might arrive at the same conclusion using their different decision-making preferences.

ARGUMENTS FOR KELSEY GETTING THE CAR:

> **Thinker:** "We can each learn a lesson from this. Parenting involves learning how to take risks and growing up requires learning how to take responsibility. Parenting involves training yourself to let go and this will be good practice for letting go when she is no longer under this roof. According to my calculations, the risks here are outweighed by the benefits of the learning experience."

> **Feeler:** "How would I feel if the car was indiscriminately snatched out from under me without any regard for my personal feelings? She will feel embarrassed if she has to call her friends and ask for a ride when she was going to be one of the drivers. If I were she, I would be crushed and understandably so. There is no way that I could be so insensitive."

ARGUMENTS AGAINST KELSEY GETTING THE CAR:

> **Thinker:** "Parenting is a *tough role* and *difficult decisions* must be made. They are *not always decisions liked by everyone* and sometimes they lead to temporary unhappiness. However, *I am not called upon as a parent to be liked* or to make others happy. As a parent I must make *responsible decisions* that reflect *a competent role model* and that are in the *best interest* of everyone."

> **Feeler:** *"I remember when I was a teenager,* one of the ways my parents told me they *loved* me was to *not always give me* what I wanted. Even though *I felt crushed* and *wounded* at the time, when I got over it I really felt as though *they cared about* me

enough to look out for my best interests. *The only loving thing to do* is not to let her use the car."[2]

Do any parts of those conversations sound familiar? Let's look at some of the differences between the thinking preference and the feeling preference.

Thinker	Feeler
Decides with the head.	Decides with the heart.
Decides by linear logic.	Decides by personal convictions.
Concerned for truth and justice.	Concerned with relationships and harmony.
Needs to understand emotions before experiencing them.	Needs to experience emotions before understanding them.
More firm-minded.	More gentle-hearted.
Experiences life as onlooker, from outside a situation.	Experiences life as from inside a situation.
Takes a long view.	Takes an immediate and personal view.
Spontaneously finds flaws and criticizes.	Spontaneously appreciates praises.
Can speak the truth but not always in love.	Can have difficulty speaking truth if it might hurt someone's feelings.

Thinker	Feeler
Wants to understand intimacy.	Wants to experience intimacy.
Can be a "romantic," yet not be very romantic.	Loves courtship and romance.
A natural at analyzing plans.	A natural at understanding people.
May have the gift of justice.	May have the gift of mercy.
Sees things in black and white.	Sees a lot of gray areas.
May seem cold and condescending to F's.	May seem fuzzy-minded and emotional to T's.

What are some of the benefits of understanding your own and your child's decision-making preferences? What are some possible consequences of not understanding your preferences or your child's preferences?

Review each of these word lists and imagine what it would be like to have one preference while living in a home where your parents expected you to be the total opposite. Imagine what it would be like to be a feeling person who was talked to and expected to act like a thinker. What would the message be? Would there tend to be more miscommunication and conflict? Would you tend to feel misunderstood and out of place? Would you be more likely to think something was wrong with you? Would you wonder if God had made a mistake?

KEYS TO PARENTING A THINKER

Listen for what the thinker is saying before attempting to interpret how it was said. I've led workshops on the MBTI for more than 15 years. When I ask T's to list some of the things that frustrate them about communicating with F's, the same issue is always in the top two or three. One man summarized his frustration by saying, "If we are in the middle of an intense discussion, she will frequently ignore what I was talking about and take a detour to how I was talking. Most of the time we get sidetracked and never finish dealing with the initial issue."

This same frustration was expressed by Paul in one of our sessions. He was starting to open up and share some of his concerns. After a few minutes, Kathy jumped in and criticized him for how he had made a certain statement. "I don't know how you can talk about something so sensitive in such a callous way." As soon as the words came out of her mouth, I knew Paul would respond.

Paul asked with a great deal of intensity, "Can we ever have a discussion without you commenting on *how* I said something?" He looked directly at Kathy and continued, "For once I'd like you to try to understand *what* I'm saying before you jump into trying to interpret what I might have meant by *how* I said it!"

Explain yourself clearly, logically and concisely. T's often want to know the *why*. Give them the reasons before they ask. As Kelsey began to better understand her dad's preference for the thinking function, she gradually learned more effective ways to ask him for things.

Rather than asking for "some extra money for this afternoon," she learned it was more helpful to Paul to list two or three of the items she wanted to purchase and why she needed them. Paul said, "I really appreciated it when Kelsey told me, 'Dad, my soccer practice is this afternoon and I've grown out of the shoes I used the last two years. I need to buy some new shoes and socks.'" Paul continued, "Kelsey doesn't need to justify her purchases. I just appreciate the specific information." Most T's would say the same thing.

Don't personalize what T's say or how they say it. Do you remember the illustration at the beginning of this chapter? Because they make decisions based on reason and logic, T's may not always be aware of how their communication may affect people. That doesn't mean they don't care about people. It's just that the care and compassion may be expressed in other ways.

Don't automatically personalize their criticism and assume they are trying to be cold, cruel or unkind. The fact is that T's are the most critical of all the types. Many F's are surprised to learn that T's can express affection by caring enough to make a critical observation that will help the other person be more accurate and effective.

Encourage their feeling side. Help T's find labels for what they're feeling. Paul and Kathy found that this was a most effective insight with Carl. Because competence is a highly valued commodity for T's, Paul and Kathy encouraged Carl to express his emotions with greater clarity. Most T's value precision, so if you help them become more accurate in *what* they say, they will be grateful. Don't forget that, in many ways, T's and F's have a different relational vocabulary. It's not a matter of eliminating your vocabulary. It's more a matter of expanding your vocabulary and helping your children to expand theirs.

Try to be calm and objective. As we were discussing some of the differences between those who prefer feeling and those who prefer thinking, Paul said, "Kathy complains that I don't share very much. I'm afraid to talk about things with Kathy because I'm afraid she'll become so emotional that I'll then have to deal with the emotional response as well as the original problem. Sometimes I don't have the energy to deal with my own emotions, let alone somebody else's."

If a subject becomes emotionally intense, it may be hard for you to keep your cool. But if the conversation becomes too emotionally charged, or if you start using overgeneralizations, such as "you always" or "you never," most T's will "check out" of the conversation. They'll be looking at you, but you'll know they're not really there with you.

By this time it's easy to see how helpful these practical suggestions can be. Now let's turn to some ways in which those who prefer the thinking function can influence those whose decision-making preference favors the feeling function.

KEYS TO PARENTING THE FEELER

Provide plenty of verbal affirmation. Most F's thrive on praise and encouragement. Take the time to notice and comment on little things that tell them they're important and valuable to you. Be sure to compliment them for who they are, not just what they do.

WHAT MAY BE NOTHING MORE THAN AN INTELLECTUALLY AEROBIC DEBATE TO A T MAY FEEL WOUNDING AND DISCOURAGING TO AN F.

Remember that the language of an F is different from the language of a T. Attempt to be more animated, warm, real. Put a bit more of yourself into the conversation. Begin some sentences with the words "I feel" or "I was really excited when."

Paul described it this way: "As a T, I usually communicate in black and white. My F child, Kelsey, is more likely to communicate in color." What is the color? It's the passion, the intensity, the emotion, the personal, the sharing of self, the moving beyond abstract ideas to how they might affect the people involved.

Also be sensitive about your use of criticism. What may be nothing more than an intellectually aerobic debate to a T may feel wounding and discouraging to an F. Most T's view criticism as an important step in finding the best solution. They often subject their plans to an uncompromising examination that uncovers all flaws in their data or logic. What may work great with data and logic may lay an egg with relationships. Many T's are naturals at sarcasm and put-downs. In fact I know many male T's who express affection by saving their best put-downs for those they care about the most. Trust me! This is not the love language of feelers.

Never underestimate the value of "small talk." To most F's there's no such thing as small talk. When they share their day with you, they aren't just downloading a list of data; they are giving you a part of themselves. If you appear bored with what they're saying, your appearance may be unconsciously translated to mean that you are bored with them. Kelsey likes to chat when she comes home from school, but Paul usually has a long list of things he needs to do and can get bored with what seems like some of the mundane details she shares.

I turned to Paul and said, "When you take the time to listen and share some of the events in Kelsey's day, it may seem boring and insignificant to you but it tells your daughter that you care about her—that she is important to you. Active listening also helps you understand what she's going through and how you can better pray for and support her. It's not as much the things she did or what happened as it is that she did them, how it affected her and that Dad cared enough to listen."

Ask F's how they feel; then listen, not to how logical their reasons are for what they are saying, but for what they are feeling. Ask questions that draw them out. Ask open questions that require more than a one-word response. A closed question asks "Did you have a nice day?" An open question asks "What happened today?" After you've listened, follow it up with another open question. When you think you've understood, ask one more question and end with your response.

Listen for the message behind the message. This can be very frustrating for T's. Learn to listen for what F's mean, not just what they say. For feelers, a conversation is more than merely an exchange of information; it's sharing lives and hearts; it's giving a part of the self. I've worked with countless families who are stuck in the rut of misunderstanding caused by misinterpretation. For example, have you ever heard the statement, "I know you think you understand what I said, but what you think you heard is not what I meant"? If the parent prefers thinking and the child prefers feeling, it's common for the feeling child to express the frustration: "They just don't seem to care. They never really listen to what I'm saying."

I'm sure you won't be surprised to know that Kelsey and Paul experienced this common problem. Paul shared a recent example: "Kelsey will be talking to me, and I am working hard to listen and pay attention to her. If she misuses a word or gets a fact wrong, I often jump in and correct her. At times Kelsey will respond by saying something a bit different from what she originally said. I then respond by saying, 'But honey, that's not what you said.' And Kelsey will immediately reply, 'Well Dad, that's what I meant.'"

LOOKING AT THE COMBINATIONS

As parents, it's important for us to understand that who we are affects how we worship, what energizes and inspires us and how we pray. There are certain ways of praying that help us feel closer to God and other ways that can leave us cold.

Different people experience God's presence and sense his leading in different ways. Our kids won't experience God the same way we do. That's not just because of generational differences, although those differences are significant. It's also because of personality differences.

In Luke 10:27, Christ summarized the Ten Commandments by saying, "You shall love the Lord your God with all your heart, and with all your soul, and with all your strength, and with all your mind; and your neighbor as yourself" (*NASB*). Grant, Thompson and Clarke in their helpful book, *From Image to Likeness*, contend that this passage calls us to love God with all four core functions.

Loving God with all of our heart involves the feeling (F) function. Loving God with all of our soul involves the intuitive (N) function. Loving God with all of our strength involves the sensing (S) function. Loving God with all of our mind involves the thinking (T) function.[3]

As Paul and Kathy went through the descriptions of each of the categories, I could see lights coming on, illuminating their understanding of themselves and their children. Though understanding each of the individual traits is important, it is also valuable to understand how they interact with each other when combined. What happens when your preference for sensing or intuition and thinking or feeling are combined?

In the last chapter we talked about the value of understanding how our various preferences work together to influence who we are, what we do, and how we interact with each other. Before looking at the final two personality-preference categories, it will be helpful to look at the ways in which our preferences in the perceiving and deciding functions combine to affect who we are and how we come across.

So far we've been introduced to the two perceiving functions, sensing and intuition, and the two deciding functions, thinking and feeling. That means that at this point we have the possibility for four different personality patterns:

1. sensing and thinking (ST)
2. sensing and feeling (SF)
3. intuition and thinking (NT)
4. intuition and feeling (NF)

Dr. Gary Harbaugh has written a practical little book entitled *God's Gifted People* that many parents have found helpful in understanding and appreciating these four different combinations. In the book, Dr. Harbaugh observes that each of the four types have a special "gift" to give to others.[4]

Paul is the ST person who prefers sensing and thinking. Dr. Harbaugh says that these folks have the gift of practicality. They are well equipped to live in the here and now, to make decisions based on specific facts and to handle technical tasks. They are often the ones who will stand firm for traditional values. In a marriage relationship the ST has the skills to keep the marriage on track.

Kelsey is the SF person who prefers sensing and feeling. SF's have the gift of personal helpfulness. They have great potential for noticing the details and specifics of everyday life and applying them to build and encourage people. I've worked with some SF's who can intellectualize their emotions.

Carl is the NT person who prefers intuition and thinking. These people have the gift of looking ahead. They are inquisitive, ask a lot of questions, are open to new ideas, help others see the possibilities and the big picture and can face changes logically. They have an insatiable quest for competence and can be the most critical of the four combinations. Some NT's may spend more time thinking about how much they love someone and too little time actually showing them.

Kathy is the NF who prefers intuition and feeling. These folks have the gift of possibilities for people. They often have the gift of encouragement. These are the teddy bears of life. They are always good for an individual or a group hug. They are insightful, thoughtful, look for the possibilities in people and relationships, value harmony and work hard to create it, and have an intense desire to grow. At times their need for harmony can keep them from making the tough decisions.

Remember that nothing is wrong with any one of these combinations. No one of them is better or more valuable than the others. Each one has some unique strengths or gifts to give to each of the others. But when that uniqueness is not understood or appreciated, what has the potential to provide balance and harmony can also produce a frustrating dissonance.

Can you imagine what it would be like for an ST to parent an NT child? That's what happened with Paul and Carl. Before he understood these important differences and the implications of the combinations, Paul's ST kept bumping into Carl's NT. It was when we began discussing personality type that Paul was able to acknowledge Carl's gift of looking ahead. From that point, Paul became better skilled at helping Carl understand his gift of practicality.

In the next chapter we're going to look at the attitudes of extroversion and introversion. If you've gained some insights in this chapter, you'll find even more "lights coming on" in the next.

Notes

1. David and Jan Stoop, *The Intimacy Factor* (Nashville, Tenn.: Thomas Nelson Publishers, 1993), p. 77.
2. Otto Kroeger and Janet M. Thuesen, *Type Talk* (New York: Delacorte Press, 1988), p. 26.
3. Harold W. Grant, Magdala Thompson and Thomas E. Clarke, *From Image to Likeness* (Ramsey, N.J.: Paulist Press, 1983).
4. Gary L. Harbaugh, *God's Gifted People* (Minneapolis, Minn.: Augsburg Publishing House, 1988), n.p.

8

UNIQUE IN FOCUSING ENERGY AND RELATING: MORE SOCIAL OR MORE SOLITARY?

By Gary J. Oliver

The pleasantness of one's friend springs from his earnest counsel.

— PROVERBS 27:9

You are the owner of an orchard. You prepare the soil. You plant the tree. You nurture, water, you shape and prune. You know your orchard—every tree is different. Some grow straight and tall and naturally open their branches to the sun. Other trees need support. As children begin to bend to the elements, they need you to train them: to straighten their trunks, to prune damaging growth, to spread their branches.[1]

God has a unique mission for the heart of each of your children. Our most important task as Christian parents is to identify that mission and encourage them in their growth process. If we want to speak the truth of historic Christianity into the lives of our sons and daughters, we must find ways to remain connected to their growing and changing needs. In a generation of tattoos, died hair and earrings for boys, this can be easier said than done.

If we want to guide, encourage and gently direct our children into healthy patterns, we need to understand who they are, how they see themselves and how to speak to them in ways they will be able to hear and understand. If we want to be used of God to shepherd their hearts, they need to believe that we understand their hearts.

In the two previous chapters, you gained a new understanding of how your child takes in information and prefers making decisions. These activities are two of the core building blocks of personality. If we stopped with these two personality preferences, you would have some powerful insights into becoming a more effective parent. In this chapter we'll introduce you to another valuable dimension of personality type.

Remember, a key to your raising sons and daughters who have a love for the Lord and a heart for spiritual things is knowing them, understanding them and communicating to them in ways that let them know you care. The better you understand their God-given uniqueness, the more likely you are to be able to communicate in ways that are meaningful to them. When the shepherd speaks the sheeps' language, the sheep are much more likely to hear and understand what the shepherd has to say. If they know that the shepherd is a good shepherd who really cares for them, they will be more likely to follow.

Extroversion Versus Introversion

Extroversion and introversion are two different ways of relating to the world around us. They identify where we are most comfortable focusing our attention and where we are energized. Everyone uses extroversion and introversion, but each person prefers or is more comfortable with one more than the other.

It's safe to say that the terms "extrovert" and "introvert" are two of the most misunderstood words in our vocabulary. What do you think of when you hear the word "introvert"? Is your first response positive or negative? For most people (including introverts), their first response is usually more negative than positive. The truth is that neither preference is positive or negative. Introverts have been described as loners, wallflowers, etc. On the other hand, extroverts have been described as loud, overbearing and obnoxious.

Children who are extroverts are energized by people, action and the things going on around them. They not only focus on the outer world but are also energized by contact with it. They don't necessarily talk more than introverts, and not all extroverts are party animals. They simply draw energy and inspiration from the outer world of people and things.

Introverts are more likely to be energized by their inner worlds of thought and reflection. It's not that they like people any less than extroverts. They may enjoy people and have the same communication skills as extroverts. However, they recharge their batteries when they are away from large groups of people. It's not even that they talk less than extroverts. The introverted child simply feels uncomfortable spending a disproportionate amount of time "socializing" in the outer world.

Extroverts can view introverts as being unfriendly or cold, but this isn't necessarily true. The natural God-given design of introverts leads them to be energized by time alone. Thus, when introverts have to deal with people who may not be close or familiar to them, they may well feel like fish out of water.

Taming the Fox

In the popular children's story *The Little Prince*, Antoine de Saint-Exupéry describes how to tame a fox. This process was also illustrated in the movie *Dances With Wolves*. For example, Kelsey prefers extroversion. If she were the first to see the fox, she would say to herself, *Oh boy, a fox! Wouldn't he make a great pet. I'd love to be his friend,* and run right up to the fox. The fox, being wily yet cautious, would likely immediately disappear into his hole. After all, he's never seen this girl before. How does he know what her intentions are?

Saint-Exupéry explains that the way to tame a fox is to start by going to a place a good way off from the fox where you can just sit and wait. This gives the fox time to size you up from a safe distance. The next day, go back and move a little closer. Sit there quietly and let the fox study you some more. If you patiently continue the process, each day sitting a bit closer, the fox will eventually have studied you enough to know and trust you. After some time you will have tamed the fox. Introverts are different than extroverts and can be 'tamed' in the same way.

Remember, this preference isn't a measure of how much a person talks but what the person talks about. While a hard-core extrovert may self-disclose every one of his or her indiscretions in the first five minutes of a conversation, most introverts will need to know someone for years before they will share what is most important to them.

Kelsey: Born to Know and Be Known

Kelsey is a typical extrovert with an outgoing and bubbly personality. She has a lot of friends at school and prefers being with several friends rather than being alone. She is stimulated by being with and doing things with people. When she is introduced to a new person, Kelsey will immediately share her name, the name of her brother, and ask the new acquaintance a personal question.

Her preferred way to process information is to talk about it. When Kelsey comes home from school, she immediately wants to talk to someone in the family or have some friends over. If she can't do that, she finds someone to talk with on the phone. For an extreme extrovert, it can be painful not to talk.

Though Kelsey has a difficult time being alone, Carl loves to spend time by himself reading, thinking or working on his computer. He is energized by being alone. Carl is friendly, likes people and is a good communicator, but he doesn't seek people out in large groups. He has a couple of "best" friends and that is enough for him.

Carl: Born to Be Private

When Carl comes home from school, he often goes to his room to read or work on his homework. During these private times, he doesn't like to be interrupted. He tends to say very little until he has known a person for a while. Even then, he doesn't share much personal information until he knows the person quite well.

When you ask Kelsey a question, she responds immediately. In fact, she may start to respond before you have even finished your question. When you ask Carl a question, he prefers to take some time to think about it.

Mom Kathy and sister Kelsey, the two extroverts in his family, try to engage him in conversation. But Carl has found this tendency to be a real source of frustration. "Whenever I start to talk, they want to finish the conversation for me." At times both Carl and Paul would tell you that they have felt like an unnecessary part of the conversation.

Learning to Love Our Differences

As I spoke with Paul and Kathy about the natural bent of introverts and extroverts, Kathy said, "I wish I had understood that years ago. I can now see that for most of my life, I have viewed extroversion as normal and Carl as a bit abnormal. I thought I was trying to change him for his own good when really I was trying to make an extrovert out of an introvert. I was trying to change him into someone God hadn't designed him to be." I complimented Kathy on her valuable insight.

Lack of understanding about this personality difference had been another source of significant frustration in the family. Kathy would often interpret Carl as avoidant and closed. Carl would interpret his mom as pushy, demanding and not respecting of his need for space. We talked about the fact that, though God had made Carl and Paul introverts and Kelsey and Kathy extroverts, they all had things they could learn from each other.

Most introverts think before speaking. When they speak, they have usually spent some time processing what they will say. This skill would be helpful for many extroverts to put into their relational tool chests. I have heard countless stories from extroverts who have regretted times when they "put their foot in their mouth" or, as one person described it, "opened my mouth only to change feet."

Because introverts and extroverts are energized and share information in different ways, it's easy for them to "miss" each other. As an extrovert, Kelsey wants to talk as soon as she comes home. As an introvert, Paul likes to get alone and recharge his battery before jumping into a conversation. At times Kelsey thought her dad was ignoring her or didn't care about what she had to say. And Paul thought Kelsey was being pushy and insensitive by ignoring his need for space.

As Dad and daughter began to understand these differences, Paul was able to work out a different approach. He decided that if Kelsey wanted to talk with him, he should seize that moment and spend a limited amount of time with her. He realized that, while he needed some alone time, it was better to postpone his "time-out" and take advantage of the opportunity to share his daughter's heart.

Paul said, "On the way home from work I turn the radio off and ask God to prepare my heart for whatever I'm going to find when I walk in the door."

If he has had an especially draining day, Paul will pull the car over a few blocks from home, listen to some praise music and pray for each family member and for the evening. "It doesn't take more than 5 or 10 minutes, but I've found that these mini-charges can reenergize me. I walk in the door prepared for conversation and don't feel nearly as put upon and drained as I used to."

Introverts need some extroversion skills for balance. Extroverts need some introversion skills for balance. Paul and Kathy finally recognized that the differences which had frustrated many of their past attempts at good communication with their children were actually a gift from God and a source of potential blessing and balance to their family.

A Closer Look at the Differences

The following is a list of some of the differences between introverts and extroverts. Like most people, you will probably find some things in both descriptions that sound like you. However, you will also have a pretty clear sense that you prefer, or are better at, one or the other. The first time you read through the list, look for yourself. Then read through the list again and see which one best describes your child.

Extrovert	Introvert
Feels drawn outward by external requests and opportunities.	Feels pushed inward by external requests and intrusions.
Energized by other people and external experiences.	Energized by inner resources and internal experiences.
An interruption is an opportunity.	An interruption is an intrusion.
Enjoys people.	Enjoys pondering.
The unlived life is not worth examining.	The unexamined life is not worth living.
Acts and then (maybe) reflects.	Reflects and then (maybe) acts.

Extrovert	Introvert
Seeks activity.	Seeks solitude.
Is often friendly, talkative, easy to know.	Is often reserved, quiet, hard to know.
Expresses emotions.	Keeps emotions to self.
Problem solves externally	Problem solves internally.
Values relationships.	Values privacy.
Gives breadth to life.	Gives depth to life.
May seem shallow to I's.	May seem withdrawn to E's.[2]

What are some of the benefits of understanding your child's preference for extroversion or introversion? What are some possible consequences for not understanding his or her preference?

Review each of these word lists and imagine what it would be like to have one preference but be in a family where you were expected to be the total opposite. Imagine what it would be like to be an introverted child who was talked to and expected to act like an extrovert. What would the message be? Would there tend to be more miscommunication and conflict? Would you tend to feel somewhat misunderstood and out of place? Would you be more likely to think something was wrong with you? Would you wonder if God had made a mistake?

KEYS TO PARENTING AN EXTROVERT
Let your extroverts be extroverts. Let them know that you appreciate

their social skills. Be patient with what may, at times, appear to you to be pointless rambling. Remember that extroverts think while speaking or after speaking. Don't interpret their chatty nature as being shallow or superficial. Think out loud with them. Often what may appear to be pointless rambling can be directed into a meaningful discussion that integrates some important biblical principles.

When extroverts say something, don't assume that they have thought about it. Remember that extroverts prefer to process information externally. Find out whether they are merely thinking out loud or have given the idea/suggestion some thought in order to be sure it is something they really want to do. It's common for an introvert to take seriously what an extrovert is merely tossing around as an idea. It's equally common for an extrovert to interpret as a casual idea something the introvert has spent days or weeks thinking about.

> EXTROVERTS RECHARGE THEIR EMOTIONAL BATTERIES BY BEING WITH PEOPLE. INTROVERTS RECHARGE THEIR EMOTIONAL BATTERIES BY GETTING AWAY AND BEING ALONE.

Be a ready listener. Proverbs and numerous other passages have a lot to say about the importance of listening. Since extroverts love to talk, they will give you ample opportunity to apply the biblical teaching on listening. Sometimes it's good to encourage them to think out loud and to do some of your thinking out loud with them. When talking to an extrovert, make sure your pauses aren't too long. A hard-core extrovert may mistake your taking a breath as a sign that you have completed your thoughts and are ready for him or her to jump in.

If something is important to you, let the extrovert know it. Because extroverts think out loud, they tend not to assume something is as important as it may be to an introvert. Paul and Kathy shared numerous examples of times when they experienced major (and frustrating) miscommunication with Kelsey and Carl because they either under- or overestimated the importance of what one of them had communicated.

Encourage their time with friends. I've read that men and women differ in the frequency with which they contact friends during a week. In my experience, it's not as much a male/female issue as it is an extroversion/introversion issue. I heard a speaker who had surveyed 600 people and found that the frequency of contacting friends was as much a function of their preference for introversion or extroversion as it was being male or female.

Kelsey is an extroverted-feeler. The extroverted-feeling women were only slightly ahead of the extroverted-feeling men in their frequency of talking with friends. Carl is an introverted-thinker. The introverted-thinking men and women were at the bottom of the list. Extroverts recharge their emotional batteries by being with people. Introverts recharge their emotional batteries by getting away and being alone. One is not better or healthier than the other. Both are equally valid and valuable.

As you get to know your extroverted child, you will discover new opportunities for parenting his or her heart. Several years ago when my son Matt came home from school, I asked, "Matt, how did your day go today?"

"Fine," he replied.

Because of what Matt said, I could have assumed that everything was "fine." But by listening to his tone of voice and noticing his one-word response, I immediately had reason to think something might be wrong. Why?

Like most extroverts, Matt rarely gives a one-word response to that kind of question. He is energetic, extroverted, enthusiastic and usually very positive. I once heard about a little boy whose teacher asked the class to write a story about cowboys. This little guy ended his story by saying, "And the cowboy jumped on his horse and rode off in all directions." That describes Matt.

Because I had studied Matt, I knew he was an extrovert and I was aware of his usual communication patterns. Therefore, I was alerted to the fact that something might be wrong—either he was tired and had a hard day or he was experiencing some emotions he didn't know how to deal with. With these insights, I chose to check out my impression with him. Sure enough, something had happened at school to discourage him. We were able to talk about it. I basically just listened and asked a few open questions. Matt learned something about his emotions that day, and I learned more about him.

KEYS TO PARENTING AN INTROVERT

Let your introverts be introverts. Don't assume that something is wrong with them or that they need to be changed. Remember, they can be as lonely in a crowd as you can be when you are alone. Someone said, "Introversion isn't a disease that needs to be surgically removed." He was right. In the United States approximately 75 percent of the population prefers extroversion and only 25 percent prefers introversion. However, in Japan the percentages are reversed. The majority of the population prefers introversion, and introversion is what is viewed as "normal."

When Paul and Kathy took the MBTI, Paul—like his son Carl—showed a clear preference for introversion. For most of their married life, however, Kathy had tried to turn Paul into an extrovert. Her intentions were great. She sincerely thought that she was doing him a favor. She looked Paul straight in the eyes and said, "I'm sorry, Honey." He reached over and took her hand.

Kathy continued, "While there are times when I wish you would share more of yourself with me and the kids, I want to learn how to understand and honor your need for solitude and reflection."

Paul acknowledged how helpful that would be and added, "Now I better understand both of our needs and that crawling into my cave when I first get home can keep me from being the kind of husband and father I want to be."

Armed with these insights Paul and Kathy were able to make some small changes that made a big difference in their home.

Be patient with introverts. Their initial response to new ideas can appear to be a bit negative, and they tend to be more resistant to change. Be careful not to jump to conclusions (something introverts are rarely accused of doing), assuming that they are stubborn, unwilling to bend or uninvolved. Because of their preferred way of processing information, introverts may take longer to come to a conclusion, but when they do make a decision, it is likely to have been well thought out.

Give introverts time and space. Remember it often takes many introverts a little longer to "warm up." Researchers have done time studies on how long it takes extroverts and introverts to respond to a question. The results indicate that the average response time for an extrovert is under two seconds. That's no surprise! Keep in mind that their initial response may not be very profound, but at least they do start talking.

The same research showed that introverts wait an average of more than seven seconds—a lifetime to extroverts—before they say anything at all. Many extroverts jump to the erroneous conclusion that if introverts aren't saying something, it must mean that they are bored, confused, asleep, want the extrovert to say more or are playing passive-aggressive power games.[3]

Ask introverts for their opinion; then when they give it, listen, ask a few more questions and look into their eyes. Introverts may take more time to communicate a thought than extroverts do. Don't assume that when they stop speaking to take a breath, they are finished. For introverts, a three-minute pause is a short period of time; for extroverts the same three minutes can seem like an eternity. I don't know of anyone who likes to be interrupted. Introverts are no exception. Taking time says that you value them and that what they have to say is important to you.

Kathy realized that, with the best of intentions, she has a tendency to cut Paul or Carl off before they have finished their thoughts. When this happens, the introverts get the message that what they have to say isn't important. Giving them a bit more time to respond can result in more communication and greater understanding.

Don't assume that introverts don't have an opinion or don't want to talk. Encourage them to think out loud. Invite them to share where they are in the process of thinking about an issue. Remind them that they don't have to have everything thought out before they share it with you. This can help them develop the skill of thinking out loud and help you develop the skill of thinking before you speak.

Give introverts time to work through their emotions. My son Nathan stormed into the house, stomped up the steps and slammed the door. This isn't how Nathan usually comes home, so I knew something was wrong. I was also frustrated by his slamming his door. We've trained our boys to know that experiencing anger is okay, but it should be expressed in healthy ways—and slamming a door isn't one of them.

I had a choice. I could walk into Nathan's room, criticize him for slamming his door and let him know in no uncertain terms that I didn't want it to happen again, or I could choose to understand his pain and help him work through it. Because Nathan is an introvert, he needs to process emotions and events internally before he is ready and able to talk about them. Therefore, I knew that if I wanted to understand him and if I wanted him to feel understood, I would need to give him some alone time.

After waiting half an hour, I went up to his room and sat down on the floor next to him. "Sounds like you had a rough day," I said quietly.

After a few moments of silence (keep in mind that if you are an extrovert, this may seem like hours), he said, "Yeah."

"Well," I continued, "I came up so you could talk to me about it. You don't have to, but in the past you've told me that it helped." After another pause I concluded, "I'll just sit here with you for a few minutes and you can share whenever you want."

After a few minutes, Nathan started to open up. I listened, and then I listened some more. I asked a few open questions. I didn't offer a solution or give advice. As it turned out, one of his best friends at school had cracked a joke at Nathan's expense and all of his friends had laughed. On the outside he had laughed with them, but inside he felt a hurt and humiliation that quickly led to anger. Of course, like a good introvert, he kept all of these feelings inside, so none of his friends had any idea that he had been offended.

When Nathan finished sharing his heart with me, I had the opportunity to explore some other responses with him. Before I went back downstairs, we joined hands and prayed together. Because I understood the significant implications of personality type, because I understood that introverts process experiences differently than extroverts, I was able to be available to love him in ways meaningful to him.

After reading the last few pages, you may have a new perspective on introverts and extroverts, especially if your child's preference is different from yours. Now we move on to consider the different ways people organize the world around them.

What are one or two things you've read in this chapter that you can apply today in the life of one of your kids?

Notes

1. Kay Kuzma, *Building Your Child's Character from the Inside Out* (Elgin, Ill.: David C. Cook Publishing Co., 1988), p. 3.
2. Earle C. Paige, *Looking at Type* (Gainesville, Fla.: Center for Application of Psychological Type, 1983), n.p., adapted.
3. Mark Pearson, *Why Can't I Be Me?* (Grand Rapids, Mich.: Baker Book House, 1992), p. 106.

9

UNIQUE IN ORGANIZING THEIR WORLDS: MORE STRUCTURED OR MORE SPONTANEOUS?

By Gary J. Oliver

Commit to the Lord whatever you do, and your plans will succeed.

—PROVERBS 16:3

It wasn't long after Carl was born that another difference between him and his sister Kelsey became obvious. In fact, of all the ways in which people's personalities can differ, the two presented in this chapter can be the most frustrating. *Judging* and *perception* are known as the lifestyle attitudes. They reflect two different lifestyle orientations and two different ways people relate to the outside world.

"My house doesn't need to be spotless," Kathy began, "but I do like to keep things clean and neat." The look on Paul's face told me that, at least from his point of view, Kathy really did need to have things spotless. Kathy continued to share that since Kelsey had become a teenager, a growing source of irritation and conflict centered around "my daughter's unwillingness or inability to keep her room clean." Kathy continued, "It might not be so bad if she kept her bedroom door closed, but she acts as if the entire house is her personal closet."

When I asked Paul for his perspective, he said that Kelsey's sloppiness wasn't that big a problem for him. But before he could complete his sentence, Kathy jumped in with an emphatic tone of voice and said, "That's just because you are as messy and unorganized as she is!"

After a brief pause, I asked, "What about Carl?"

Paul responded, "When it comes to his preference, Carl and Kathy are exactly alike." He continued, "His room is spotless, his bookshelf is organized and there are never any clothes lying on the floor."

Judgers: Plan Your Work, Work Your Plan

It didn't take long for us to discover Kelsey and Carl's personality preferences on this last MBTI category. Carl, like his mother, Kathy, clearly prefers a judging (J) lifestyle—which doesn't mean that Carl is a judgmental person. Those who prefer a judging (J) lifestyle are decisive, planned and orderly; they relate to the external world in a structured and organized way.

Even as a tot Carl loved to line up his toys in a straight line. He had a place for everything, and he would be upset if things were misplaced and disorderly. While he can be spontaneous, Carl prefers order and structure. He loves to plan ahead and complete projects. He enjoys knowing what the schedule is and following it. He doesn't want to be late for his Sunday School class, and he doesn't like surprises. Too much change throws him off.

As Paul and Kathy discussed Carl's preference for structure and organization, I shared with them a story I heard about a "hard-core" structured person. The story took place in a small midwest town close to the Mississippi that from time to time experienced floods. It had been raining for several days and the river was flooding over its banks. One family had moved their valuables up to the second floor of their home.

The daughter was looking out the window at the rising water flowing down the street in front of their home when she shouted,

"Mom, come here!" Her mother sensed the urgency in her voice and ran over to the window. "Mom, I think there must a whirlpool around our house. Most of the water is running down the street, but there is this brown hat that keeps coming around our house." Her mother didn't understand but decided to stay at the window to see what she was talking about.

Sure enough, in less than a minute her mom saw a brown hat that appeared to be floating around the house. As soon as the mother saw the hat, she turned to her concerned daughter and said, "Oh, don't worry about that, Honey. That's just your dad. Don't you remember? Yesterday he said that he was going to mow the lawn tomorrow, 'Come hell or high water!'"

Those who have a structured preference don't just *like* to plan, they *need* to plan. Their motto is "Plan your work; then work your plan." Not only does Kathy have a Day-Timer, but she also enjoys knowing what the schedule is and abiding by it. One of her favorite parts of the Day-Timer is the six-year planner. She feels more secure when she can look ahead and know what's going on.

As I listened to Kathy talk about her frustrations with Kelsey, I was reminded of another hard-core organizer I had met. Several years ago when I was visiting Hearst Castle in San Simeon, California, I met a couple on vacation. As we talked, they shared that he had recently retired from the army and that they were on a three-month vacation. I said, "That sounds great. You must be having a wonderful time."

"Actually," the wife said, "we're exhausted." She added that they had planned their vacation for years. In fact, her husband had planned all 90 days of the vacation. He had mapped out the trip, determined how many miles they would drive each day and where they would stop. In fact, he had even made reservations for all 90 nights. They were just starting the fourth week of their dream vacation and, "we're so exhausted that he has decided to cancel all of the remaining reservations and just 'take one day at a time,'" she said.

Structured people not only like calendars, but they also like lists. In fact I know some people who make up lists and put things on the list that they have already done just because it feels good to cross them off. When I shared that insight, Paul turned to Kathy and laughed. Kathy broke out in this huge smile and said, "Well, it does feel good to look at one of my lists and see some things already crossed off."

Perceivers: Work at Play, Play at Work

Kelsey clearly prefers a perceiver (P) lifestyle and relates to the outer world in a very casual and laid-back manner. She tends to be more unstructured, adaptable and spontaneous. Once again it's important to understand how these words are used. Those who prefer perception aren't necessarily more perceptive than J's. They are, however, more curious and flexible; they also handle changes well. Perceivers are the free spirits of life.

> A PILE OF PAPERS IS TO THE STRUCTURED PERSON NOTHING MORE THAN A MESS TO BE CLEANED UP. A PILE OF PAPERS IS TO A FREE SPIRIT IS LIKE COMPOST; IF YOU LEAVE IT THERE LONG ENOUGH, SOMETHING GOOD WILL HAPPEN.

Kelsey couldn't care less whether things are in a straight line or scattered all over the floor. She enjoys surprises and responds well to the unexpected. Kelsey is easily distracted. In fact, Kathy made the humorous observation that "Kelsey can get lost between the front door and the car." She starts a lot of projects but often has difficulty completing them because something else catches her attention. She is a lot of fun and brings fun and laughter to those around her. Change is no problem for Kelsey. In fact, change helps her relieve monotony or boredom.

If you aren't sure if your child prefers judging or perception, one simple way to find out is to glance at your son or daughter's bedroom. The room of the structured person is neat and orderly. Books are organized by topics and are a half-inch from the edge of the shelf. The desk is uncluttered and the files are neatly organized in the file cabinet. Clothes are neatly folded and organized by color.

If your child prefers perception, after you walk in the door, you may have to call out your son or daughter's name to see if he or she is there. Why? Because you can't see if he or she is behind the piles of books and papers stacked on the desk. Plus, you may have to step around piles of clothes scattered on the floor.

An important distinction between the structured person and the free spirit is that the structured person files things horizontally and the free spirit files things vertically. A pile of papers is to the structured person nothing more than a mess to be cleaned up. A pile of papers is to a free spirit like a pile of compost; if you leave it there long enough, something good will happen.

Those who are structured, however, need to be careful not to assume that the "piles" of the free spirit are unorganized. They may *appear* to be unorganized. However, if you ask for a certain report, the perceptive will go to the third pile, reach down about a foot-and-a-half from the top, reach in and pull out the report you were looking for. You see, many of them organize things differently than their more obviously structured counterparts.

Another difference in this dimension that frustrates many parents is the way perceivers handle deadlines. This is one of the differences that became evident to Paul and Kathy early in their children's schooling. When Carl gets an assignment, he discusses the project with his teacher, asks Paul or Kathy to take him to the library and jumps in.

When Kelsey gets an assignment, she talks about it with her friends, thinks about some of the possibilities for it and then moves on to something else. A couple of days before the project is due, she may remember that the paper is due soon and suddenly becomes intensely focused on getting it done.

Kathy finally started to understand that Kelsey is "wired" differently than she. Her natural way of doing things—what comes easy for her—is not necessarily the best way and certainly not the only way. Amazingly, Kelsey would frequently get A's on those papers.

The following lists provide a brief summary of some of the differences between those who prefer a judging lifestyle and those who prefer a perceiving lifestyle. If you're like most people, you will find some things that describe you in both lists. However, you will probably be able to identify one of the two as your preferred way of functioning.

Judger	Perceiver
Prefers an organized lifestyle.	Prefers a flexible lifestyle.
Needs definite order and structure.	Likes going with the flow.
Their motto is "Work now; play later."	Their motto is "Play now; work later." or (even better) "Play while you work."
Likes to have life under control.	Prefers to experience life as it happens.
Enjoys making decisions.	Enjoys getting more information.
The product is more important than the process.	The process is more important than the product.
The most important part of a trip is arriving at the destination.	The most important part of the trip is traveling to a destination.

Judger	Perceiver
Likes clear limits and categories.	Likes freedom to explore without limits.
Feels comfortable establishing closure.	Feels comfortable maintaining openness.
Can't relax until the task is completed.	Can easily interrupt a task if something more interesting comes along.
Enjoys deadlines and likes to plan in advance.	Meets deadlines by last-minute rush.
May seem demanding, rigid and uptight to P's.	May seem disorganized, messy and irresponsible to J's.[1]

What are some of the benefits of understanding your child's J/P preference? What are some possible consequences of not understanding your child's preference?

Review each of the lists and imagine what it would be like to have one preference but to live in a home where you were expected to be the total opposite. Imagine what it would be like to be a judging child who was talked to and expected to act like a perceptive child. What would the message be? Would there tend to be more miscommunication and conflict? Would you tend to feel misunderstood and out of place? Would you be more likely to think that something was wrong with you? Would you wonder if God had made a mistake in placing you in this family?

KEYS TO PARENTING THE STRUCTURED CHILD (JUDGER)
Be sensitive to the child's time clock. Time is very important to a J. If you

say you'll be somewhere at a certain time, be there. "One of the greatest sources of frustration in our family has been that Kelsey is always late," Kathy said with more than a hint of irritation.

"Well, she's not always late," Paul retorted. "Besides," Paul continued, "Kathy not only wants to be somewhere on time, but she also likes to be there 15 minutes early. That seems like a waste of time to me, and I'm sure Kelsey feels the same way."

Follow through on your commitments to J's. If judgers ask for something to be done by a certain date, and if their request is reasonable, make sure it is done by that date. Be prompt and follow through on your commitments. Don't make promises that you aren't willing to keep. Most J's would rather have someone say no than to commit with great intentions when they are unable to fulfill the commitment.

Don't mess up their space. J's love organization and structure. Usually, there is a place for everything, and everything goes in its place. They don't just love organization—they need it. When you use their things, put them back where you got them. This shows respect for them and will make it more likely for them to respect you.

Let them know when something is going to be different from usual. Most J's don't like surprises and spur-of-the-moment changes. They can view change as disruptive. In fact, it's much more difficult for most J's to change than for P's to change. When a last minute change occurs, J's are likely to experience frustration.

Don't assume that they are angry. Most J's are so goal-driven that when something moves them off their task or when they are slowed down, they can become even more intensely focused, more frustrated and respond in ways that may *seem* angry. If you accuse J's of being angry, their frustration is likely to increase and lead to anger.

Encourage their flexibility. J's can become too rigid, inflexible and dogmatic, restricting not only their own lives but also the lives of others. They have a tremendous need for closure, which sometimes comes across as a need to control. Paul made the insightful observation that, "When we were first married, I thought Kathy had this tremendous need to control everything. I'm beginning to see that what I perceived as Kathy's need to control was more her need to wrap things up so she could move on to the next item on her list. Her precious list."

I observed that what had frustrated Paul early in their marriage was now a major source of frustration between Kathy and Kelsey. "I thought God had used Paul to make me more flexible than I ever wanted to be," Kathy said. "I think God may be wanting to use Kelsey to teach me that I have a bit further to go."

Encourage their attempts at play. Many J's have a hard time playing. I know, it has been one of my greatest struggles. J's don't play golf; they work at lowering their handicap. They don't play tennis; they work on improving their backhand stroke. When J's structure their days, rarely do they include time for play. Somehow play just doesn't get on their "to do" lists. And if it's not on the calendar, it probably won't happen. You might want to share with your J's the following quote from a delightful little book, *Meditations for Parents Who Do Too Much:*

> Parents who do too much are overbooked, our weekdays jammed full of errands and activities, with no room left for spontaneity or surprise. If something comes up—some "irresistible distraction"—some unexpected fork in the road, we can't take advantage of it, because we fear that if we veer off our route even slightly, we may never find our way back.
>
> Living by the calendar is a necessary evil, especially in these fast-paced times. But we should not be so overscheduled that we can't be lured away when something just happens to turn up. Our kids are as overcommitted as we force them to be, and with no time left to follow a whim or chase a shadow, their lives, too, may feel orchestrated and unspontaneous.[2]

KEYS TO PARENTING THE FREE SPIRIT (PERCEIVER)

Be sensitive to their need for flexibility. P's organize their life much differently than J's. At times the organization may seem nonexistent, but it's there. Practice going with the flow. Remember that there is more than one way of planning, preparing, organizing and doing things.

Honor the fact that P's have their own ways of organizing their important things. Remember, you aren't doing them a favor by ignoring their natural bent and trying to squeeze them into your mold. I had one P tell me, "My wife is an organizer. Her motto is 'I love you and have a wonderful plan for your life.'" He continued, "I know she has the best of intentions, but it bugs the dickens out of me."

Well, it "bugs the dickens" out of a lot of people who experience someone trying to control who they are and how they are to do what someone else does.

Be open to their requests for more information. While J's have a great need for closure, P's have a need for openness. One of the weaknesses of some J's can be wanting to bring closure to a situation or discussion before enough information has been gathered. Many J's believe they are doing the P's a favor by bringing immediate closure.

Kathy said, "One of Paul's many strengths as a dad is that he doesn't jump to conclusions. When the kids are fighting, I'm more likely to walk in, assess what's going on and divvy up the consequences. Sometimes I'm right; sometimes I'm wrong." She added that Paul is much more likely to take the time to ask a few more questions and then decide on the appropriate consequences.

Enjoy and even celebrate their spontaneity. Some of the best opportunities to discuss spiritual things with P's can come during a spontaneous moment: when they come home from school, after dinner or when they're getting ready for bed. Know that some of the most teachable moments you may have with your kids will be during those unprogrammed times.

Understand that some P's have a shorter attention span than J's and may be more easily distracted. What appears to a J to be a distraction or interruption can also be an opportunity for a new insight, a new experience or a new opportunity to grow. It can become a window into your child's life.

Learn to communicate your concerns using shorter sentences. Paul expressed frustration at the way Kathy could, at times, go on and on. "Sometimes I wish she would just get it out and get on with it. I hate lectures."

Of course, Kathy's immediate response was usually a frustrated or insulted, "I'm not lecturing!" Well, what may not seem like a lecture to a J can feel like one to a P.

Remember that when P's, especially NP's, change the subject, it may not be because they're bored or don't care about the topic; it's consistent with how God has made them. They tend to have a shorter attention span, are more easily distracted and don't like to be pinned down. They think better by casting a wider conversation net while many J's feel more secure in what can become a too narrowly focused rut.

How Paul and Kathy Became More Understanding Parents

A normal part of being a family is dealing with each other's differences. Some degree of frustration resulting in conflict is inevitable in any relationship. Clashes between different personality types are to be expected. But when we understand personality type and the different relational languages God has given each of us, we can significantly decrease the unnecessary conflicts and misunderstandings that plague many families. We can speak to our children in their unique languages. As they sense that we have taken the time to understand them, they will be much more likely to take the time to understand us.

With the insights of personality type, you're less likely to spend time trying to squeeze your child into your own mold. You are also less likely to attempt changing things that really shouldn't be changed. However, when something can and should be changed, you are much more likely to be able to communicate that need for change in ways your child will be able to hear and understand. You are more likely to be in a place where God can use you to help your child become the unique person God designed him or her to be.

When Paul and Kathy understood that many of their own differences, as well as those of Kelsey and Carl, were simply the result of the way God had made them, they didn't view each other so negatively. They began the process of learning how to benefit from each other's gifts.

Paul realized that while he was an introvert and his father and grandfather had been introverts, he could benefit from developing some extroversion skills. He discovered that it really wasn't that difficult to talk more to Kelsey, especially about her daily events. He began to understand that what was "small" talk to him was "valuable" talk to his daughter. He learned that by thinking out loud with her, rather than doing it all in his head and announcing his conclusion, she began to better understand what was important to him and what kinds of information he needed for responding to her requests.

Kathy realized that Carl's quietness and withdrawal wasn't necessarily a passive-aggressive way to punish her. It was, in part, how God had made her son. She realized that while she was a full-blown extrovert, she could benefit from developing some introversion skills. Kathy learned to be more comfortable with, even to value, silence and time alone. She learned that while it was OK to think out loud, sometimes it was much better to think before speaking and to weigh the consequences of a statement before verbalizing it.

Kathy discovered that Carl was more likely to hear her and be open to change when she gave him reasons that were logical. Her emotional pleas tended to fall on insensitive ears. Emotionalism was like a foreign language to him. Kathy learned that Kelsey was more receptive to suggestions when she showed more sensitivity. When Kathy's requests were based on the best interest of those involved, and not just her need for control or structure, Kelsey was not only more open but also at times even enthusiastic to them.

In these chapters we've only been able to scratch the surface in introducing the important insights of personality type as identified by the Myers-Briggs Type Indicator. I'm not suggesting that the MBTI insights will transform every family. They won't. However, even with this brief overview, I'm sure you can see how invaluable these insights can be—not only in understanding your child but also in communicating your love and God's truths more meaningfully to that child.

As parents we have the greatest influence on how our children learn, how they understand themselves and others, and how well they grow according to their God-designed bents. The differences in personality type appear to profoundly affect people's learning styles and developmental patterns.

You can become aware of how your own personality preferences and expectations either blend or clash with those of your child. You can learn how to speak your child's language, thus increasing the probability of clear communication. Understanding personality differences between you and your child will help you to nurture, encourage and positively impact your child.

I strongly encourage you to do additional reading on personality type. At the end of chapter 5, I've included helpful resources which are packed with practical illustrations of how to apply these insights in your marriage and family.

Take Action

Before moving on to the next chapter, please take a couple of minutes to complete the following exercise. I've included a brief summary of the MBTI categories. On each of the four lines I'd like you to ascertain your preference and the preferences of your other family members. If you believe that you have a strong preference for introversion, write your name closer to the I. If you think you're an introvert but it's not a strong preference, write your name closer to the middle. Do this with all four of the preferences, and have all other family members repeat the process.

E_____I

Direction of Focus and Interest: Does it flow mainly to the outer world of actions, objects and people or to the inner world of concepts and ideas?

Extroverted types are regarded as primarily focused on the outer world of people, objects and actions, tending to become caught up with whatever is happening around them.

Introverted types have more of an inward focus and tend to detach from the external world in favor of attending to concepts, ideas, thoughts and internal images.

S_____N

Information-Gathering: Do you focus more on the immediate realities of direct and personal experience? Do you focus on the inferred meanings dealing with relationships and possibilities of experiences in the future?

Sensing types focus on perceptions received directly through the sense organs, noticing concrete details and practical aspects of a situation in the here and now.

Intuitive types rely on a more impressionistic approach in order to maximize their spontaneous hunches. They prefer to deal with abstract, inferred meanings and the hidden possibilities in a situation as they look toward the future.

T_____F

Decision Making: In making decisions, are you more likely to rely on logical order and cause and effect, or on priorities based on personal importance, values and relationships?

Thinking types rely on logical structures to clarify and order particular situations; they are skilled at objectively organizing material, weighing the facts and impersonally judging whether something is true or false.

Feeling types are adept at understanding others' feelings and analyzing subjective impressions based on their judgments of personal values.

J_____P

Lifestyle: Is the preference for living systematically, well organized, and attempting to control events or with flexibility and spontaneity, curiously awaiting events and adapting to them?

Judging types are structured, organized and systematic, living in a planned, orderly way, seeking to regulate their environment and control it.

Perceiving types are more flexible, curious and open-minded, going through life in a spontaneous way, and aiming to understand life and adapt to it.[3]

Now, starting with the extroversion/introversion attitudes, go through each one of the four and ask yourself the following simple questions:

1. What is one way God might want to use our differences in this area to strengthen me and our family relationships?
2. What is one thing about the opposite preference that I could incorporate into my own life for greater balance and effectiveness?
3. What is one of my child's strengths that God might want me to incorporate into my own relational tool chest?

Notes

1. Earle C. Paige, *Looking at Type* (Gainesville, Fla.: Center for Application of Psychological Type, 1983), n.p., adapted.
2. Jonathan and Wendy Lazear, *Meditations for Parents Who Do Too Much* (New York: Simon & Schuster, 1993), October 22 selection.
3. M. Carlyn, "An Assessment of the Myers-Briggs Type Indicator," *Journal of Personality Assessment* 42, no. 5 (1977), pp. 461-473.

Section III

TRAINING YOUR CHILD

10

CULTIVATING A SPIRITUAL FOUNDATION: LIFESTYLE DISCIPLESHIP

By Gary J. Oliver

All your sons [and daughters] will be taught by the Lord, and great will be your children's peace.

—ISAIAH 54:13

The sore that had been on my tongue for several months had become so painful that I finally decided to see a specialist. The physician told me not to be concerned about it and prescribed a medication for me to gargle. A month later it was still there, so I returned for a second visit and asked for a biopsy just to make sure it wasn't cancerous. She assured me that I had nothing to worry about and prescribed more gargle.

When after two more months I returned for a third visit and she told me there was nothing to worry about and prescribed an anesthetic, I decided to seek a second opinion. I was going to be driving through Lincoln, Nebraska, to celebrate Easter with my wife's family in Omaha and called a friend of mine, Dr. Ed Stivers, who is an ear, nose and throat specialist to ask if he could to take a look at it. He was most gracious and came in on his afternoon off to see me. After taking my history and looking at the sore, Dr. Stivers suggested that it probably wasn't anything to be too concerned about but he thought it would be wise to biopsy it just to make sure. He said I could call him on Saturday morning for the results.

Confronted with My Legacy

I really wasn't too concerned until I heard his voice on the phone the next day. He told me that the biopsy had come back positive and that he should operate first thing Monday morning. Suddenly, and I do mean suddenly, my whole perspective on life changed. Other people got cancer, not me. It wasn't fair. It just didn't make any sense. I was young, healthy, faithfully serving the Lord and the father of two young boys. This couldn't be happening to me.

Between Saturday and Monday morning I evaluated my life in ways I never had before. Would the surgery be successful? Would I still be able to talk? Would I be understandable? I thought about the best- and worst-case scenarios. I knew God was in control. I knew that I could trust Him. I knew that He would never give me more than I could handle. I also knew that I had cancer.

As I thought about what my life had meant up till then and what was most important to me, I reflected on my relationships with Christ, my wife, Carrie, and my boys. I asked myself what my legacy would be as a father if God decided to take me home. In what ways would my boys' lives be different because I had been their father? Would they know and follow the Lord? Would their values reflect the clear teaching of Scripture? Would they want to live for Jesus?

By God's grace, the surgery went well. The surgeons were able to remove all of the cancerous tissue and the margins were clean. After a few months of recuperation, my speech was almost normal and most people couldn't tell that a portion of my tongue had been removed. However, that isn't the most important thing that emerged from my surgical experience.

Though I'm not glad that I had cancer, I do thank and praise God for the time of reflection I went through. During my time of recovery, God made it clear that one of the most important tasks of my life wasn't how many people I would counsel, how many books I would write, how many people I would speak before or how many boards I would serve on; rather, that my role as a husband and father needed to become a much higher priority.

Developing a Spiritual Root System in Your Child

As Norm and I prayed about writing this book, we realized that our challenge would not be merely to compile a list of creative ideas about how to encourage kids to grow spiritually. Some excellent resources are already available on that subject, and we will share some of those with you at the end of this chapter.

The real challenge would be to help you, the reader, know how to understand the unique combination of gifts, talents and personality preferences of your daughters and sons to help them develop a heart for Jesus. As a parent, I've discovered that it's one thing to hear ideas that have worked with somebody else's children; it's a much greater challenge to know how to cultivate the spiritual root system of your own child.

We've prayerfully written this book to help you cultivate and communicate your own relationship with Christ in such a way that you will better understand your children and be much more likely to raise spiritually healthy and emotionally intelligent kids who love Jesus, look like Jesus, act like Jesus, reflect Jesus and want to spend time with Jesus.

If you've read this far, you understand that there is a battle raging for the heart of your son or daughter. You know that as a parent, you can still make a significant difference in your child's life by cultivating a climate for change. You have gained a new understanding of the unique bent, or design, of your child and have some insights on how to speak the truth of God's promises and love to your child in ways he or she can better understand. In this chapter we turn a corner to look at the power of lifestyle discipleship in helping you help your kids cultivate a heart for Jesus.

In Deuteronomy 6:4-6, Moses instructs parents to follow God's commands themselves and then in verses 7-9 to

> Repeat them again and again to your children. Talk about them when you are at home and when you are away on a journey, when you are lying down and when you are getting up again. Tie them to your hands as a reminder, and wear them on your forehead. Write them on the doorposts of your house and on your gates (*NLT*).

Now here's the $64,000 question: What does it look like in twentieth (and twenty-first) century terms to talk about and repeat truth again and again when we are at home, on a journey, lying down and getting up? Norm and I have spent more than 15 years thinking about, praying about, reading about and talking to numerous successful Christian parents about that very question. The following is what we've learned.

1. DELIGHT YOURSELF IN THE LORD

Recently a good friend shared a story he found on the Internet. Henry Winston had been a diamond merchant in New York City for many years. It seems that several years ago a man came into the store to buy a particular diamond. Winston arranged for his best salesperson, or at least his most knowledgeable one, to show the man the diamond. The salesperson went to the vault and took the diamond out. The salesperson talked to the potential buyer about the clarity and cut of this stone and the potential for appreciation. They talked about scarcity in the world market of this particular kind of diamond. Within a few minutes the man said, "No thanks," and he started to leave the store.

As he was leaving the store, Henry Winston said, "Excuse me, do you mind if I personally show you the diamond myself?"

The man said, "No, I don't mind. I've come a long way. I'd be willing to look at it one more time." Winston took the diamond out. He didn't talk about clarity and cut. He talked about its beauty, its unique color and the joy of ownership. He talked about the pleasure that this diamond brings to people who see it. Within a few minutes the man was writing out a check for the full value of the diamond.

As he was writing out the check, he said, "Mr. Winston, I am puzzled. That same diamond was shown to me only a few minutes ago. I didn't want it. You showed that diamond to me and something changed. Why am I buying the diamond from you?"

Henry Winston said, "The man who showed you the diamond first is my most knowledgeable salesperson. He understands the color, cut and clarity of diamonds. He knows more about diamonds than anyone in the store, myself included. But I would double his salary if I could just give him something I possess. You see he knows diamonds, but I am in the business because I love diamonds."

So what does this have to do with raising kids with a heart for Jesus? Our children are the buyers. Our Lord is the diamond, and we are the salespersons. When they look at our lives, do they merely see someone who knows about God, who believes the right things and who avoids the wrong things, or do they see someone who is in an intimate and growing love relationship with Jesus Christ. Our primary call isn't to be good parents. Our primary call is to model a vibrant and vital love relationship with the living God.

I remember hiking with my boys to the top of the Teton range, sitting by Lake Solitude, looking at the reflection of the majestic Tetons in the crystal-clear water, talking about the One who created this beauty, and singing "Majesty." This was one of those special times when we shared the sweetness of delighting in the Lord. In chapter 2, we shared a statement from Andrew Murray that is well worth repeating:

Not in what we say and teach, but in what we *are* and *do*, lies the power of training. Not as we *think* of an ideal for training our children, but as we *live* do we train them. It is not our wishes or our theory, but our will and our practice that really train. It is by living the Christ-life that we prove that we love it, that we have it; and thus will influence the young mind to love it and to have it, too.[1]

> WHEN WE'RE SOLD ON THE GRACE AND MERCY AND
> LOVE OF OUR LORD JESUS CHRIST, OUR DELIGHT IN HIM
> AND OUR PASSION FOR HIM WILL BE CAUGHT BY THOSE
> WHO ARE WATCHING US THE MOST CLOSELY.

Let me put it as simply as I can. The most important sale you will ever make is not to your employer, to your customer, to your spouse or, believe it or not, even to your kids—it's being sold yourself! When we're sold on the grace and mercy and love of our Lord Jesus Christ, our delight in Him and our passion for Him will be caught by those who are watching us the most closely. But if you don't really believe, if you aren't deeply committed, if they don't see that intensity of love and commitment in you, if the values of Christ aren't seen in the daily decisions you make, if you don't delight in the Lord, the passion will never transfer. Some of the information might transfer, but the passion for Jesus won't.

2. DEFINE TRUE SPIRITUALITY

When I was a little boy growing up in an evangelical church, I was impressed with the heroes of the Bible. I remember hearing messages on the importance of being a mature Christian. At that time I equated maturity with getting old. As I grew older, I began to equate maturity with other things. A mature Christian was solid, stable, well versed in Scripture, good at prayer, able to give a quick and correct theological perspective, and abstained from all the things good Christians should abstain from. That was my view then.

In Ephesians 3:19 Paul tells the Christians in Ephesus that he prays that they will come to know the love of Christ which surpasses knowledge. If you read this passage quickly, it sounds as if Paul is asking them to do the impossible. How can they know something that "surpasses" their ability to know? The answer is simple. What Paul is really telling them is that he wants them to move past mere head knowledge of the truth and experience a deep heart knowledge. In Paul's mind, heart knowledge always surpasses head knowledge.

A heart for God isn't measured by how much we know and what we abstain from. It involves a yearning to spend time alone with Him in prayer and to eagerly turn to His Word to learn more about Him. It involves a desire to put His Word into practice and see His faithfulness in action. God doesn't give us knowledge to show others how intelligent or quick and clever we are. He doesn't give us knowledge to prove how right we are and how wrong everyone else is. God gives us knowledge to transform our hearts, to renew our minds and to change our behavior, so others can see what a wonderful God He is.

True spirituality is characterized by many things, not the least of which is a mom or dad who hungers and thirsts after righteousness. Our world has trained us to hunger and thirst after pleasure, stimulation, novelty, satisfaction, possessions, blessings and success. Our culture pressures us to model materialism rather than maturity. We live in an addictive generation that is controlled by desires for possessions and other things that will help us look successful. God did not create us to hunger and thirst after experiences, blessings and success.

When we truly hunger and thirst after righteousness, we don't merely avoid things that we know are bad and harmful. We also avoid things that tend to dull or take the edge off our spiritual discernment. In my own life I've discovered that there are some things in the world that in themselves are quite harmless and perfectly legitimate. Yet when I find myself spending much of my time with them, my desire and passion for the things of God decrease. These are some of the things that I must avoid and encourage my kids to avoid. John Piper says it best:

> The greatest enemy of hunger for God is not poison, but apple pie. It is not the banquet of the wicked that dulls our appetite for heaven, but our endless nibbling at the table of the world. It is not the X-rated video, but the prime-time dribble of triviality we drink in every night. For all the ill that Satan can do, when God describes what keeps us from the banquet table of His love, it is a piece of land, a yoke of oxen, and a wife (Luke 14:18-20). The greatest adversary of love to God is not His enemies, but His gifts. The most deadly appetites are not for the poison of evil, but for the simple pleasures of earth. When these replace an appetite for God Himself, the idolatry is scarcely recognizable and almost incurable.[2]

Dorothy Sayers often said that the only business of the Christian, in the end, is to be crucified.[3] In his classic book, *The Cost of Discipleship*, Dietrich Bonhoeffer wrote:

> The Cross is laid on every Christian. The first Christ-suffering which every man must experience is the call to abandon the attachments of this world....As we embark upon discipleship, we surrender ourselves to Christ in union with His death—we give our lives to death....When Christ calls a man, He bids him come and die....In fact every command of Jesus is a call to die, with all our affections and lusts."[4]

The Bible tells us that we have been transformed into the image of Christ and that God has designed us to be like Him. Because He really lives His life in us, we are able to walk even as He walked (see 1 John 2:6), do as He has done (see John 13:15), love as He has loved (see John 13:34; 15:12; Eph. 5:2), forgive as He forgave (see Col. 3:13) and have the mind of Christ Jesus (see Phil. 2:5). Therefore, we are able to follow the example He has left us (see 1 Pet. 2:21) and lay down our lives for the brethren as He did (see 1 John 3:16).

Because He became like us, we can become like Him. As we are willing to be identified with Him, we can become like Him. If we are identified with Him and becoming like Him, our kids will be much more likely to follow.

In Luke 9:23 Christ taught, "If anyone would come after me, he must deny himself and take up his cross daily and follow me." What do these words of Jesus look like in the context of parenting? If we want to be His disciples, if we want to be like Him, we must daily choose to take up His cross and follow Him. Christ didn't magically hang on the cross. He was nailed to the cross.

The Cross is a daily decision we make. It's not always fun. It's not always easy. As a parent, it's often easier for me to be cross than it is to model the Cross. As parents, we have many opportunities each day to choose the Cross. You can give a compliment when you feel like criticizing. You can listen to your daughter when you have other things on your mind. You can refuse to make a certain hand gesture when that reckless driver cuts you off. You can let your kids experiment with doing it their way rather than insisting it be done your way. You can love your kids enough to allow them the freedom to make their own mistakes. You can continue listening when you don't like what you're hearing. You can show them what it means to bear all things, believe all things, hope all things and endure all things (see 1 Cor. 13:7).

3. DEMONSTRATE THE DISCIPLINES

Let's face it: When you cut to the chase, molding and shaping the spiritual character of your child is the most significant work any parent can do. But how can we help our children develop godly character in a society that doesn't know the meaning of integrity? Disciplining our children so they will behave well and not embarrass us isn't enough. We agree with Kay Kuzma:

> True character development must begin on the inside with correct motives, unselfish desires, and pure thoughts that come as a result of having a close relationship with God. When kids are spiritually healthy, we don't have to worry about them catching society's 'colds'![5]

Some call this shaping process discipleship or spiritual formation. Spiritual formation goes beyond spiritual information. Spiritual formation is the process by which the character and attributes of Christ are formed in us. A key component of spiritual formation is the development of core spiritual disciplines.

We agree with Richard Foster that superficiality is the curse of our age. The doctrine of instant satisfaction is a primary spiritual problem. The desperate need today is not for a greater number of intelligent people, or gifted people, but for deep people. God has given us the disciplines of the spiritual life so that through them God can transform us. In his classic book, *Celebration of Discipline*, Foster categorizes and discusses some of the core disciplines: The Inward Disciplines (Meditation, Prayer, Fasting, Study); The Outward Disciplines (Simplicity, Solitude, Submission, Service); and The Corporate Disciplines (Confession, Worship, Guidance, Celebration). Foster writes:

> Picture a narrow ledge with a sheer drop-off on either side. The chasm to the right is the way of moral bankruptcy through human strivings for righteousness....The chasm to the left is the way of moral bankruptcy through the absence of human strivings....On the ledge there is a path, the disciplines of the spiritual life. This path leads to the inner

transformation and healing for which we seek. We must never veer off to the right or the left, but stay on the path....As we travel on this path, the blessing of God will come upon us and will reconstruct us into the image of His Son Jesus Christ. We must always remember that the path does not produce the change; it only puts us in the place where the change can occur. This is the way of disciplined grace.[6]

Remember, merely doing the disciplines doesn't create disciples. Merely performing the spiritual kinds of behaviors doesn't automatically produce a passion for our Lord. I've met people who had the spiritual disciplines down pat but whose lives didn't reflect the power and passion and reality of Jesus. However, I've never met a godly man or woman who didn't regularly practice the spiritual disciplines.

At times, there is a fine line between doing spiritual things and being a spiritual person, between discussing the truths of Christ and demonstrating the person of Christ. As Christian parents, our goal is to rear boys and girls who can do both.

I discovered that training in spiritual formation and the spiritual disciplines doesn't have to wait until our kids are adults. There are specific ways we can parent our kids and things we can model for them right now that will lay a strong foundation for a closer walk with the Lord. Here are a few simple examples.

Every weekday morning Carrie and I get up to read and pray before the boys are awake. We don't ask the boys to get up with us, but sometimes if one of them wakes up early, he will sit in on our prayer time together. Later in the morning, about 10 minutes before I take the two older boys to the car pool, we sit down and read the Psalms and/or the chapter of Proverbs for the day. Sometimes we will discuss it then or on the way to school, and sometimes we end up not having time for a discussion.

Almost every evening I go into each one of the boys' rooms after they have gone to bed to spend a few minutes with them. This has become another Oliver tradition. We chat about the day and the plans for tomorrow, I may give each of them a little back rub and then we'll pray and kiss each other good night. Sometimes the chat lasts five minutes; other times it may last a half hour. The length of time isn't as important as building the discipline or habit of ending each day talking to each other, talking to the Lord and expressing our affection for each other.

For several years I have fasted on a regular basis. So far the longest has been for three days. A couple of the guys in my covenant group have completed 40-day fasts. I haven't asked my kids to fast, but they have asked quite a few questions about fasting. In October 1997 when Promise Keepers held the Stand in the Gap rally in Washington, D. C., I let the boys know that I was going to fast one day a week and asked them if they would pray for me during that time.

Each of the boys, entirely on his own, said he'd like to join me. We talked about what fasting is, what it isn't and why people fast. We discussed various types of fasts. I read a couple of quotes from Richard Foster's book to them. We decided to do a fast where you only drink liquids. However, that seemed a bit much for my eight-year-old son, so after some creative thinking, he decided to abstain from sugar one day a week.

When we arrived in Washington, D.C., a couple days before the rally, we took the boys to the PK prayer center. Promise Keeper leaders had divided the city into sections and were signing up individuals and families to go to one of the sections of the city for a prayer-walk. None of us had ever done this before but we were game, so we signed up. On the next day we took the subway to a part of the city I didn't even know existed. For two hours, we walked through the neighborhoods praying for the people, the marriages, and the families and the churches represented there.

As you can see, there is nothing complex or exotic in how we try to model the disciplines. The key is that as parents we don't demand them, we demonstrate them.

Our kids won't remember the talks, the lectures or the logic. They will remember our times together. They will remember what they saw. They will remember that Mom and Dad were people of the Word, of prayer, of fasting, of fellowship, of solitude, of simplicity, of meditation, of celebration and of worship.

4. DEVELOP A SENSITIVE CONSCIENCE

Eli was a man chosen of God. In many ways, he was successful as a priest. He had led Israel for 40 years. He was powerful, influential, honored. He was respected, a hard worker, faithful in many things. But Eli discovered that success in one area does not guarantee success in another. Because he failed in his role as a parent, because he wasn't able to help his sons develop a sensitive conscience, Eli eventually lost his influence in his role as a priest. His failure to lead his sons brought reproach upon both God and the Tabernacle.

Here's what we read in 1 Samuel about Eli's sons:

- "Eli's sons were wicked men; they had no regard for the Lord" (2:12).
- "This sin of the young men was very great in the Lord's sight" (v. 17).
- "His sons, however, did not listen to their father's rebuke....And the boy Samuel continued to grow in stature and in favor with the Lord and with men" (vv. 25,26).
- "And the Lord said to Samuel: 'See, I am about to do something in Israel that will make the ears of everyone who hears of it tingle. At that time I will carry out against Eli everything I spoke against his family—from beginning to end. For I told him that I would judge his family forever because of the sin he knew about; his sons made themselves contemptible, and he failed to restrain them'" (3:11-13).
- Eli's grandson was named Ichabod, which means "No glory" (see 4:21).

Our children are growing up in a post-modern society influenced by situation ethics. Our kids are told that there are no absolutes. Right and wrong are negotiable. There is no such thing as ultimate truth. Our generation is similar to that of Jeremiah when he wrote, "They dress the wound of my people as though it were not serious. 'Peace, peace,' they say, when there is no peace. Are they ashamed of their loathsome conduct? No, they have no shame at all; they do not even know how to blush" (Jer. 8:11,12).

Eli's sons didn't develop a sensitive conscience and they didn't know how to blush. They became desensitized to their own sin and ignored the teaching of God and the warnings of their father. The Bible teaches that "the heart is deceitful...and desperately wicked" (Jer. 17:9, *KJV*). Our child's root problem isn't a lack of good nutrition, more information or better socialization. It's not low self-esteem and inadequate opportunities. It's that he or she, like us, is a sinner. The Bible makes it clear that it is not primarily a head problem; it is a heart problem. Tedd Tripp writes:

> The central focus of childrearing is to bring children to a sober assessment of themselves as sinners. They must understand the mercy of God that offered Christ as a sacrifice for sinners. How is that accomplished? You must address the heart as the fountain of behavior and the conscience as the God-given judge of right and wrong. The cross of Christ must be the central focus of your childrearing.[7]

The Bible has a lot to say about dealing with sin:

> If we claim to be without sin, we deceive ourselves and the truth is not in us. If we confess our sins, he is faithful and just and will forgive us our sins and purify us from all unrighteousness (1 John 1:8,9).

No temptation has seized you except what is common to man. And God is faithful; he will not let you be tempted beyond what you can bear. But when you are tempted, he will also provide a way out so that you can stand up under it (1 Cor. 10:13).

In the same way, count yourselves dead to sin but alive to God in Christ Jesus. Therefore do not let sin reign in your mortal body so that you obey its evil desires. Do not offer the parts of your body to sin, as instruments of wickedness, but rather offer yourselves to God, as those who have been brought from death to life; and offer the parts of your body to him as instruments of righteousness (Rom. 6:11-13).

Brothers, if someone is caught in a sin, you who are spiritual should restore him gently. But watch yourself, or you also may be tempted. Carry each other's burdens, and in this way you will fulfill the law of Christ (Gal. 6:1,2).

God's purpose in guidance is not to get us to perform the right actions; His purpose is to help us become the right kind of people. The first word of Christ's message was "repent." Real-life Christianity begins with a sense of sin. Unfortunately, repentance isn't a popular concept in today's world. To repent means that I must acknowledge my weakness, my blind spots, my selfishness, my pride, my narcissism. The Bible, as well as the experience of every parent, teaches us that children are not born morally neutral. Our children need direction, correction and instruction.

What does that look like from a concerned parent's perspective? Our kids will never develop a sensitive conscience unless they see one in action. Their hearts will not be broken by their sinfulness unless they see our hearts broken by our sinfulness. Fortunate is the child whose parents are desperately sorry for their own sins. Fortunate is the child whose parents can acknowledge their own unworthiness, for it is those parents who will indeed be comforted. Fortunate is the child whose parents will confess their sins, for according to Psalm 51:17, the broken and contrite heart God will never despise. Fortunate is the child whose parents model Psalm 15:2-5:

> Anyone who leads a blameless life and is truly sincere. Anyone who refuses to slander others, does not listen to gossip, never harms his neighbor, speaks out against sin, criticizes those committing it, commends the faithful followers of the Lord, keeps a promise even if it ruins him...such a man shall stand firm forever (*TLB*).

Here is one way you can make this practical. I know of a parent who sat the entire family down in front of the TV and gave each of them a tablet and pencil. He told them they were going to watch a couple of shows as a family and asked them to list anything they saw on those programs that the Bible might consider a sin. They then watched the regular evening news program and two of the most popular situation comedies.

After the shows were over, they began to share their lists. The entire family was surprised at how long each person's list was. As they read what they had written down, this wise father asked why each particular behavior was a sin, what the Bible says about it, what specific passage spoke to that sin, what might be the consequences of doing it and what some options would be for the Christian. This was a simple exercise that made a lasting impression on this family and cultivated a more sensitive conscience.

5. DELIVER HEALTHY ROLE MODELS
Nathan was more than just a little nervous. He didn't know exactly where we were going. He didn't know exactly what he was going to be asked to do. He didn't know exactly who was going to be there.

But at the same time he was excited. He had looked forward to this day for several months. He knew that when he turned 13, he would be invited to get together with the other men in my covenant group and a few other close friends for his "rites of passage" ceremony.

He knew he would spend at least an hour answering a variety of questions including some about his faith, his salvation experience, his love for the Lord, his view of what it means to be a man, his perspective on moral purity and his plan to keep himself pure, and the role of prayer and Bible study in his life.

We walked into the hotel room in downtown Denver, and there were the men—the president of a major seminary, some well-known leaders of some Christian ministries, and his grandfather. Several months earlier, each of these busy men had blocked out this afternoon on their calendars and prayerfully prepared for this time. They had come prepared to ask Nathan questions, to share the "one thing" they wished they had known at his age and to give him a simple gift as a symbol of a character trait God had laid on their hearts to share with him.

It was a simple time. There was a lot of laughter and a few tears. These men opened their hearts to my oldest son and welcomed him at the gateway to his life as a man of God. If there was one theme to those several hours, it was to remind Nathan of the importance of being a man of prayer and a man of the Word, of being a Promise Keeper.

Since that time, my son Matthew has also turned 13 and experienced a similar ceremony. This kind of ceremony isn't just for boys. It can be done with daughters as well. Both boys point to that time as one of the most significant events in their lives. Throughout the book we've talked about the importance of models for our kids. But they need more than just Mom and Dad. There will come a time, perhaps during the adolescent years, when our kids won't want to talk to Mom and Dad. They may think we won't understand. Perhaps they'll be right.

If we have other friends that they are close to, that they have spent time with and whom they respect, they will be more likely to turn to them. Last night, one of the couples in our group came over. Before they left, we spent close to an hour sharing what God had been doing in our lives. One of our sons decided to stay in the living room with us to listen. That night when I was tucking him into bed he said, "Dad, I always like it when Dale comes over. He makes me think."

I don't know if my 16-year-old son will ever feel that he can't talk to me. Odds are good that he will. If and when that time comes, whether he chooses to or not, he will have spent time with several other Christian families and couples that he knows he can call and talk with.

6. DISCUSS YOUR OWN SPIRITUAL JOURNEY, MISTAKES AND ALL

In the first beatitude, Christ taught that God blesses those who are poor in spirit, or "those who realize their need for him" (Matt. 5:3, NLT). Our generation struggles with confusion between self-confidence, self-assurance, self-expression and self-esteem. This preoccupation with self has led to a cultural narcissism that not only ignores but also looks down upon the greatest virtue of all: humility.

According to D. Martyn Lloyd-Jones, to be poor in spirit doesn't mean that we are insecure weaklings who have no confidence or courage and are unable to make a decision. What it does mean is that we have "a complete absence of pride...a consciousness that we are nothing in the presence of God."[8]

When Paul went to Corinth, he didn't go with a cocky self-confidence based on his extensive vita and a laundry list of his top 10 accomplishments. He went "in weakness and fear, and with much trembling" (1 Cor. 2:3). Paul was aware of his strengths, but he was also aware of his total dependence on his Lord Jesus Christ.

Fortunate are the children whose parents realize their own helplessness, their limitations, their weaknesses and their blind spots and who boldly take those tendencies and lay them at the foot of the Cross. Fortunate are the children whose parents share their weaknesses and spiritual struggles with them, who ask their children to join in praying for them and who share God's answers to those prayers with their children. Fortunate are the children whose parents model the words of that great hymn "When I Survey the Wondrous Cross" by Isaac Watts:

When I survey the wondrous Cross
On which the Prince of Glory died,
My richest gain I count but loss,
And pour contempt on all my pride.

As we learn what it means to pour contempt on all of our pride, our kids will see in us the true basis of spiritual power. As our children see that we really do believe that Christ's death for us and our sins upon the Cross is alone what saves us, as they see us function as if our sins really are forgiven, as we demonstrate that we are children of God, heirs and joint-heirs with Christ, as they see us confess our sins and then manifest the joy and power of being forgiven, they will be exposed to an irresistible dose of truth.

On a regular basis, Carrie and I share with our boys what God is doing in our lives, what we are learning, how we are growing and some of the things the Holy Spirit is convicting us of. When appropriate, we share where we're struggling, how we've been disappointed, how we're hurting and how we've failed. We let them know that we believe in the power of prayer by asking them to pray for us. Then we share the answer with them when it comes.

Any parent can do this. It doesn't take any advanced degrees or any special courses. As we model transparency and teachability, we build a climate of acceptance, affirmation and safety. We communicate that it is OK to make mistakes. They learn that failure isn't fatal or final. They discover new ways to apply biblical truth. They see that spiritual maturity, the process of becoming "conformed to the image of His Son" (Rom. 8:29, *NASB*), is a process that takes time and proceeds in a series of small steps.

If you want to leave a legacy, you must live a legacy. By helping our children visualize truth, we get beneath the surface of their lives into their heart zones, we take truth out of the realm of dull, boring and empty abstractions. Show them what the daily Christian life looks like—don't just tell them. Draw them a map. Be a living illustration. Make them see. Help them feel. Make them understand. Cause them to care. Let your kids see you doubt, hear you ask hard questions and grapple with moral issues. Healthy parents encourage questions because they know that questions provide opportunities for answers.

7. DEEPEN YOUR PRAYER LIFE

For those living in Colorado, it seemed too good to be true. Once again, the Denver Broncos were playing in the Super Bowl. There was a mixture of excitement and fear. Why fear? Well, the Broncos had been there four times before and had lost every time. Some of the losses were spectacular.

The Packers were an easy favorite to win and to deliver Denver its fifth Super Bowl defeat. However, this was a different Denver team and perhaps John Elway's last chance at the elusive Super Bowl ring. It was a hard-fought game. By the end of the fourth quarter, it appeared that a Denver victory might be possible. But these were the powerful Packers, and they weren't about to quit.

Green Bay had the ball and was close to the goal line. It was the fourth down and the end of the fourth quarter. Brett Favre tried to complete a pass, but John Mobley batted it away at the last second. Denver got possession of the ball with only 28 seconds left on the clock. A Denver victory was sure. The outcome was certain. All John Elway had to do was hold on to the ball and get down on his knees. That's exactly what he did and the Denver Broncos went on to upset the outstanding Green Bay Packers and, against all odds, become the Super Bowl champions. John Elway got his ring. There was joy in the Mile High City.

Several weeks after the game, I was talking with my good friend John White. He had taken his family to that game and as we talked, he described what it was like to watch the final seconds. Then he shared with me an insight the Lord had given him. He reminded me that parenting is much like the final seconds of that game. We have so little time to win the battle for our children's hearts. Elway won the game by falling down on his knees and holding on to the ball. That's the same way we will win the game of parenting. The most important thing we can do is to hold on to God's promises and get down on our knees.

The purpose of prayer isn't that we get ahold of the answer but that we get ahold of God. I am amazed by the number of boys and girls who grow up in Christian homes who have little appreciation for the significance of prayer. We believe that this dimension of parenting is so important that we have devoted all of the next chapter to it.

Christ said, "Wherever your treasure is, there your heart and thoughts will also be" (Matt. 6:21, *NLT*). If I were to ask your kids what is your mom and dad's treasure, what is most important to them, what would they tell me? Are they aware of your family being any different than the average secular family? If so, what are some of the differences?

In the process of writing this book, God has helped me to see that at times there are aspects of my family that aren't that much different from secular families. Oh, we are clearly Christian and our values permeate most of what we do. But at times we're too active, busy, driven by sports, school and church activities. I'm sad to say that there have been times when the following observation by Tedd Tripp has applied to me:

We pander to their desires and wishes. We teach them to find their soul's delight in going places and doing things. We attempt to satisfy their lust for excitement. We fill their young lives with distractions from God. We give them material things and take delight in their delight in possessions. Then we hope that somewhere down the line, they will see that a life worth living is found only in knowing and serving God.[9]

I've worked with many families who had no problem being gone three or four nights a week for baseball practice but somehow couldn't find the time for regular family Bible reading and prayer. What are we teaching our kids when church, youth group, times of Bible study and prayer come in a distant second to some athletic activity?

Our children can learn to love the Lord. They can learn the importance of living for Him. They can begin to develop spiritual disciplines. They can be used of God to impact the world around them. As we close this chapter, let me encourage you with a true story:

> Doris Howard trained her daughter to love the Lord. By the time she was a sophomore in high school, she was leading a Bible study in a classroom every Friday morning before school.
>
> Two years later she had inspired 13 kids from other campuses to do the same. Two years after that, those 13 kids had grown to become 3,000 on-fire teenagers committed to telling every junior-high and high-school student in Wichita about their faith in Jesus Christ. Those 3,000 young people personally invited 30,000 area students to a youth rally. Of the 30,000 who were invited, 10,000 showed up, and 6,000 made a written commitment to follow Christ.[10]

Your children may not start a movement that leads to 30,000 kids attending a youth rally. But with your help, your model and your prayers, that seemingly ordinary son or daughter can "become conformed to the image of His Son" and be used of God to make a significant difference for the Kingdom.

Notes

1. Andrew Murray, *How to Raise Your Children for Christ* (Minneapolis, Minn.: Bethany House Publishers, 1975), p. 12.
2. John Piper, *A Hunger for God* (Wheaton, Ill.: Crossway Books, 1997), p. 14.
3. David Coomes, *Dorothy L. Sayers: A Careless Rage for Life* (Oxford: A Lion Book, 1992), p. 182.
4. Dietrich Bonhoeffer, *The Cost of Discipleship* (New York: Macmillan Publishing Company, Inc., 1961), p. 99.
5. Kay Kuzma, *Building Your Child's Character from the Inside Out* (Elgin, Ill.: David C. Cook Publishing Co., 1988), pp. 10-11.
6. Richard Foster, *Celebration of Discipline: The Path to Spiritual Growth* (New York: Harper & Row, 1978), p. 7.
7. Tedd Tripp, *Shepherding a Child's Heart* (Wapwallopen, Pa.: Shepherd Press, 1995), p. 145.
8. D. Martyn Lloyd-Jones, *Studies in the Sermon on the Mount, Volume One*, (Grand Rapids: Wm. B. Eerdmans Publishing Company, 1967), p. 50.
9. Tripp, *Shepherding a Child's Heart*, p. 66.
10. Joe White, *Faith Training* (Colorado Springs: Focus on the Family, n.d.), p. 5.

Reading Resources:
Spiritual Formation for Kids

Dobson, Shirley and Pat Verbal. *My Family's Prayer Calendar, 1998*. Ventura, Calif.: Gospel Light, 1998.

Kuzma, Kay. *Building Your Child's Character From the Inside Out*. Elgin, Ill.: David C. Cook Publishing, 1988.

Ledbetter, J. Otis and Kurt Bruner. *The Heritage: How to Be Intentional about the Legacy You Leave*. Colorado Springs, Colo.: ChariotVictor Publishing, 1996.

Murray, Andrew. *How to Raise Your Children for Christ*. Minneapolis, Minn.: Bethany House Publishers, 1975.

Tripp, Tedd, *Shepherding a Child's Heart*. Wapwallopen, Pa.: Shepherd Press, 1995.

Weidmann, Jim and Kurt Bruner. *Family Night Tool Chest, Book 1*. Colorado Springs, Colo.: ChariotVictor Publishing, 1997.

White, Joe. *Faith Training: Raising Kids Who Love the Lord*. Colorado Springs, Colo.: Focus on the Family Publishing, 1994.

Worthington, Everett L. and Kirby. *Helping Parents Make Disciples*. Grand Rapids: Baker Books, 1995.

Reading Resources:
Spiritual Formation for Adults

Blackaby, Henry and Richard. *Experiencing God*. Nashville, Tenn.: Broadman and Holman, 1997.

Bonhoeffer, Dietrich. *The Cost of Discipleship*. New York: Macmillan Publishing Company, Inc., 1961.

Bright, Bill. *The Transforming Power of Fasting and Prayer*. Orlando, Fla.: New Life Publications, 1997.

Curtis, Brent and John Eldredge. *Sacred Romance*. Nashville, Tenn.: Thomas Nelson, 1997.

Foster, Richard. *Celebration of Discipline: The Path to Spiritual Growth*. New York: Harper & Row, 1978.

Manning, Brennen. *Abba's Child*. Colorado Springs: NavPress, 1994.

Martyn Lloyd-Jones, D. *Studies in the Sermon on the Mount, Volume One*. Grand Rapids: Wm. B. Eedrmans Publishing Company, 1967.

Murray, Andrew. *How to Raise Your Children for Christ*. Minneapolis, Minn.: Bethany House Publishers, 1975.

Piper, John. *A Hunger for God*. Wheaton, Ill.: Crossway Books, 1997.

Rumford, Douglas J. *Soul Shaping: Taking Care of Your Spiritual Life*. Wheaton, Ill.: Tyndale, 1996.

11

PRAYER: THE PARENTS' NOT-SO-SECRET WEAPON

By H. Norman Wright

"I prayed for this child, and the Lord has granted me what I asked of him. So now I give him to the Lord. For his whole life he will be given over to the Lord." And he worshiped the Lord there.

— 1 SAMUEL 1:27,28

How are you praying for your child? What *is* the best way for parents to pray for their children, especially when desiring them to become more like Jesus? Is there a set way, a formula, principle or guidelines to follow? Just how important is praying for your children?

This chapter is a compilation of the thoughts of several praying parents and what they have done through the years. Even before you consider how and what to pray for, remember that the first step is doing what Hannah did in the passage quoted at the beginning of the chapter. She gave her child back to God. She relinquished her child.

"Loan of a Life"

Years ago, a Christian publishing house developed a ministry to help prospective parents. It was called "The Cradle Roll Program."

This program provided written materials to assist parents who were preparing for the birth of their child. The title of the material was called "Loan of a Life," which reflected the fact that children don't really belong to us. They are *not our possession*. We have been entrusted with their care and, in the natural progression of life, they will be relinquished at a given point in time to form their own families. Actually, you will relinquish them in many different ways all through their lives as they progress toward maturity. Understanding ahead of time what this process entails makes it much easier to handle.

> To understand what relinquishment is we must first understand what God is like and what the essence of His relationship to us is. As He is to us, so must we (so far as possible) be to our children.
>
> God's attitude as a parent combines loving care and instruction with a refusal to force our obedience. He longs to bless us, yet He will not cram blessings down our throats. Our sins and rebellions cause Him grief, and in His grief He will do much to draw us back to Himself. Yet, if we persist in our wrongdoing He will let us find, by the pain of bitter experience, that it would have been better to obey Him.
>
> To relinquish your children does not mean to abandon them, however, but to give them back to God, and in so doing to take your own hands off them. It means neither to neglect your responsibilities toward them, nor to relinquish the authority you need to fulfill those responsibilities. It means to release those controls that arise from needless fears, or from selfish ambitions.[1]
>
> To relinquish our children is to set them free. The earlier we relinquish them the better. If we unthinkingly view them as objects designed for our pleasure, we may destroy their capacity for freedom. We may also cripple ourselves. Having made

our children necessary to our happiness, we can so depend on them that we grow incapable of managing without them.[2]

Seeking the Presence of God

One of the best descriptions of a parent praying comes from Stormie Omartian in her book *The Power of a Praying Parent.*

Prayer is much more than just giving a list of desires to God, as if He were the great Sugar Daddy/Santa Claus in the sky. Prayer is acknowledging and experiencing the presence of God and inviting His presence into our lives and circumstances. It's seeking the *presence* of God and releasing the *power* of God which gives us the means to overcome any problem.

The Bible says, "Whatever you bind on earth will be bound in heaven, and whatever you loose on earth will be loosed in heaven" (Matthew 18:18). God gives us authority on earth. When we take that authority, God releases power to us from heaven. Because it's *God's* power and *not* ours, we become the vessel through which His power flows. When we pray, we bring that power to bear upon everything we are praying about, and we allow the power of God to work through our powerlessness. When we pray, we are humbling ourselves before God and saying, "I need Your presence and Your power, Lord. I can't do this without You." When we don't pray, it's like saying we have no need of anything outside of ourselves.

Praying in the name of Jesus is a major key to God's power. Jesus said, "Most assuredly, I say to you, whatever you ask the Father in My name He will give you" (John 16:23). Praying in the name of Jesus gives us authority over the enemy and proves we have faith in God to do what His Word promises. God knows our thoughts and our needs, but He responds to our prayers. That's because He always gives us a choice about everything, including whether we will trust Him and obey by praying in Jesus' name.

Praying not only affects *us*, it also reaches out and touches those for whom we pray. When we pray for our children, we are asking God to make His presence a part of their lives and work powerfully in their behalf. That doesn't mean there will always be an *immediate* response. Sometimes it can take days, weeks, months, or even years. But our prayers are never lost or meaningless. If we are praying, something is happening, whether we see it or not. The Bible says, "The effective, fervent prayer of a righteous man avails much" (James 5:16). All that needs to happen in our lives and the lives of our children cannot happen without the presence and power of God. Prayer invites and ignites both.[3]

Now does this mean you receive everything you pray for? No. Of the 650 prayers in the Bible (not including the book of Psalms), 450 of them have recorded answers. All prayers are answered, but they are answered according to the wisdom of God. Jesus did say prayers would be answered: "Everyone who asks receives" (Matt. 7:8). Answers could be yes, no, direct, indirect, immediate or deferred. Our prayers are responded to by a loving God.

How to Pray Effectively

Which of you, if his son asks for bread, will give him a stone? Or if he asks for a fish, will give him a snake? If you, then, though you are evil, know how to give good gifts to your children, how much more will your Father in heaven give good gifts to those who ask him! (Matt. 7:9-11).

Remember when you pray there isn't one set way of praying. We can pray anywhere, anytime (2 Tim. 1:3).
We can share our deepest, most troubling feelings and

know God will not be shocked or deaf to our requests (Ps. 102:17; Lam. 2:19).

We can pray haltingly, simply, confusedly (Ps. 69:33; Rom. 8:26).

We can pray alone or with other believers (Dan. 6:10; Acts 2:42-47).

We can pray ecstatically, carried along by God's Spirit or factually, driven by our commitments when all feelings fail us (Ps. 102:23-28; Eph. 5:18,19).

We can pray silently, wordlessly (Ps. 5:1; Matt. 6:6).

We can pray over and over for the same thing (Luke 18:1-8).

There are guidelines to follow when we pray:

Pray reverently. Keep in mind God's holiness and greatness. Pray with genuine respect and humility (Eccles. 5:1,2; Matt. 6-9).

Pray sincerely. The words don't matter as much as a parent's heart. We are to bring a deeply felt desire to see God act for our children and a willingness to do our part to make God's solutions possible (Ps. 51:17; Matt. 6:7,8; Heb. 10:22).

Pray in faith. Simply and completely trust in God's commitment to your children's best interests and in His power to act on your behalf (Jer. 32:17; Heb. 11:6).

Pray with purity. Don't let prayers be hindered by any known sin in your heart or life: we could have unfinished business with God, our neighbor or a family member. We may need to take action before we pray (Prov. 15:8; Mark 12:38-40; Jas 4:8; 1 John 3:21,22).

Pray according to God's will. Submit your personal desires to God's greater glory and purposes. It is important to test our wishes for our children against the Word of God (Matt. 6:10; 1 John 5:14).

Pray in Jesus' name. We have access to the Father only through Jesus' name and by His merits. His name is the power above all powers on earth (John 15:16; Eph. 2:18).

Pray thankfully. It helps to recall God's past goodness

and His faithful character and then surround every new request with thanksgiving and praise (Ps. 22:3; Phil. 4:6).

Pray boldly and persistently. Jesus taught that a loving Father is waiting to give us His best, and it's better than we could ever imagine. Make your requests known, and continue to expect answers (Luke 18:1-8; Acts 12:5; Heb. 4:16).[4]

> AS PARENTS, WE NEED TO PRAY CONSTANTLY FOR OUR CHILDREN. WHAT CAN WE PRAY FOR? WELL, EVERYTHING.

If you want an example of a parent who prayed for his children, look at Job. In the first chapter you discover that after Job's children feasted, Job would have them purified. "Early in the morning he would sacrifice a burnt offering for each of them, thinking, 'Perhaps my children have sinned and cursed God in their hearts'" (v. 5). He was concerned and faithful in bringing them before the Lord.

John Bunyan made a noteworthy comment about prayer many years ago. He said,

> You can do more than pray
> after you have prayed
> But you cannot do more than pray
> until you have prayed.

One of the guiding passages of Scripture for the way we are to pray is from 1 Thessalonians:

Pray without ceasing (5:17, *NKJV*).

What Paul is talking about here are frequent, brief prayers expressed while we are walking, waiting for a phone call, driving (with eyes open!) or any time. God is not concerned about the setting, only that we pray.

Praying Constantly and for Everything

As parents, we need to pray constantly for our children. What can we pray for? Well, everything, but if you want specifics, here are a few: Pray for your children's spiritual growth. Pray for their character development and any character defects. Pray also for their views and attitudes about themselves, their ability to say no to temptation and their daily difficulties. Pray for the kinds of friends they will have, protection when they date and wisdom when they select their future partner. Above all, praise God for each of your children, who they are and who they will become.

Sometimes parents become discouraged when they pray. Their children still have problems and they think God isn't answering their requests. Consider how the parents in the following paragraphs responded to similar concerns.

We parents must allow our concept of prayer to be shaped by scriptural reality, for then we will understand that our prayers are not tools with which to manage God. Rather, the opposite is the case, because God uses our prayers to manage us, to bend our will to him and brand our soul with his character. When parents truly pray for their offspring, their prayers bind both their soul and the souls of their children into a mystery that ultimately deepens the life of each.[5]

Often the silence of God is a mute sign of a greater answer. Oswald Chambers explained:

Some prayers are followed by silence because they are wrong, others because they are bigger than one can understand. It will be a wonderful moment for some of us when we stand before God and find that the prayers we clamored for in early days and imagined were never answered, have been answered in the most amazing way, and that God's silence has been the sign of the answer.[6]

Sometimes parents have asked, "What exactly should we be praying for when we pray for our children?" Here are some items to consider by the authors of *How to Pray for Your Children*:

1. That Jesus Christ be formed in our children (see Galatians 4:19).
2. That our children—the seed of the righteous—will be delivered from the evil one (see Proverbs 11:21, *KJV*; Matthew 6:13).
3. That our children will be taught by the Lord and their peace will be great (see Isaiah 54:13).
4. That they will learn to discern good from evil and have a good conscience toward God (see Hebrews 5:14; 1 Peter 3:21).
5. That God's laws will be in their mind and on their hearts (see Hebrews 8:10).
6. That they will choose companions who are wise—not fools, nor sexually immoral, not drunkards, nor idolaters, nor slanderers, nor swindlers (see Proverbs 13:20; 1 Corinthians 5:11).
7. That they will remain sexually pure and keep themselves only for their spouses, asking God for his grace to keep such a commitment (see Ephesians 5:3, 31-33).
8. That they will honor their parents (see Ephesians 6:1-3).[7]

Praying the Bible

One of the newer approaches to praying for children in the past few years is to "pray the Bible" for our children. This is simply using passages of Scripture to formulate prayers or actually saying the verses back to God and making them your own petitions. This is definitely a biblical pattern, as we see it again and again in the Scriptures.

> Jesus and His disciples sang the psalms together as part of morning and evening prayers. And when Jesus was experiencing His greatest agony on the cross, Jesus cried out the words of a psalm: "My God, my God, why have you forsaken me?" (Psalm 22:1).
>
> Many other Bible passages are recorded prayers. Some of the best known are the prayers of Moses after the escape through the Red Sea (Exodus 15); Hannah's song at the temple (1 Samuel 2); Jeremiah's lament over Jerusalem (Lamentations); Jonah's plea for grace (Jonah 2); the song of Mary after the angel's visit (Luke 1:46-55); "The Lord's Prayer" (Matthew 6:9-13); Jesus' prayer for His disciples (John 17:6-19); and Paul's prayers for a young church (Ephesians 3:14-21).[8]

WHEN WE PRAY THE SCRIPTURES FOR OUR CHILDREN, WE GROW IN OUR OWN PERSONAL RELATIONSHIP WITH THE LORD. IT IS READING THE LOVE LETTERS GOD HAS WRITTEN TO US.

There is tremendous value in praying the Scriptures. It is a way to help us resist becoming stuck in a rut. Perhaps you are different, but there are times when I experience a prayer blockage. Words, ideas and phrases seem to have taken a vacation from my mind. It is difficult not only to get started but also to keep it flowing. Scripture gives us structure as well as direction.

It is a way to remember God's character, promises, past faithfulness and goodness, which we tend to forget. It is also a memory activator. It helps to bring balance into our own thought life. Jeremiah said, "Yet this I call to mind and therefore I have hope: Because of the Lord's great love we are not consumed, for his compassions never fail" (Lam. 3:21,22).

When we pray the Scriptures, we can pray more directly in God's will. Scripture can be used to evaluate our motives and reveal the direction for our prayers.

It also helps us pray with a greater sense of confidence and expectancy. When we focus on God's promises, we have a greater assurance of what He will do. We also learn to trust Him for accomplishing what He will do in His own way and time.

When we pray the Scriptures for our children, we grow in our own personal relationship with the Lord. It is reading the love letters God has written to us. Reading these by praying them for our children instills His words within us even more.

Finally, praying in this manner opens us more so the Holy Spirit can minister to us.[9]

Quin Sherrer and Ruthanne Garlock provide some helpful suggestions in this regard.

One especially effective tactic involves personalizing verses of Scripture as you pray, such as replacing the pronouns with the names of the children or people for whom you're interceding. For example, Psalm 23:3 could be personalized in this way: "Thank you, Lord, that you guide my son Keith in the paths of righteousness for your name's sake." The verse takes on added potency as both an expression of praise to the Lord and a declaration of truth to the enemy.

We pray differently for children during various phases of their lives. For instance, the following prayer for a child who is either a student or an employee combines several verses:

Lord, may my child like Daniel show "...aptitude for every kind of learning, [be] well informed, quick to understand and qualified to serve in the king's palace"

(Daniel 1:4). May he/she "speak with wisdom and tact," and may he/she be "found to have a keen mind and knowledge and understanding and also the ability... to solve difficult problems" (Daniel 2:14; 5:12). Lord, endow my child with "wisdom and very great insight, and a breadth of understanding as measureless as the sand on the seashore" (1 Kings 4:29).

Another way to personalize these same Scripture verses would be to speak them aloud about your child: "My child will be found to have a keen mind and knowledge and understanding and ability to solve difficult problems. He/she does have wisdom and insight and breadth of understanding as measureless as the sand on the seashore." By hearing the Word of God—even from our own lips—we stand firm on his truth as applied in our very own family. And in doing this we have strengthened our own faith.[10]

Kent Hughes, a Bible teacher, and his wife, Barbara, share the concept of taking prayers from the Scripture and modifying them for your own family. Consider this Scripture passage:

I pray that out of his glorious riches he may strengthen you with power through his Spirit in your inner being, so that Christ may dwell in your hearts through faith. And I pray that you, being rooted and established in love, may have power, together with all the saints, to grasp how wide and long and high and deep is the love of Christ (Eph. 3:16-18).

Now look at this family's adaptation of the same passage. This is an activity you may want to do for your own family.

Ephesians 3:16-18 for the family: Father, we pray that out of your glorious riches you will strengthen our children with power through your Spirit in their inner beings, so that

Christ may dwell in their hearts through faith. And we pray that our children, being rooted and established in love, may have power, together with all the saints, to grasp how wide and high and deep is the love of Christ, and to know this love that surpasses knowledge—that they may be filled to the measure of all the fullness of God.[11]

Submitting Ourselves in Prayer

When you pray for your children, do you also pray for yourself? Sometimes the changes we pray for in our children don't materialize because we're not seeking some needed changes in our own lives.

What change needs to be made in your life? What do you need to pray about? Sometimes the insight of other parents can help us develop sensitivity to changes we need to make. Consider this prayer from *The Power of a Praying Parent*:

> Lord,
>
> I submit myself to You. I realize that parenting a child in the way You would have me to is beyond my human abilities. I know I need You to help me. I want to partner with You and partake of Your gifts of wisdom, discernment, revelation, and guidance. I also need Your strength and patience, along with a generous portion of Your love flowing through me. Teach me how to love the way You love. Where I need to be healed, delivered, changed, matured, or made whole, I invite You to do that in me. Help me to walk in righteousness and integrity before You. Teach me Your ways, enable me to obey Your commandments and do only what is pleasing in Your sight. May the beauty of Your Spirit be so evident in me that I will be a godly role model. Give me the communication, teaching, and nurturing skills that I must have. Make me the

parent You want me to be and teach me how to pray and truly intercede for the life of this child. Lord, You said in Your Word, "Whatever things you ask in prayer, believing, you will receive" (Matt. 21:22). In Jesus' name I ask that You will increase my faith to believe for all the things You've put on my heart to pray for concerning this child.[12]

Perhaps one of the best ways to pray for ourselves is in the following anonymously written prayer:

Dear God,
I am powerless
and my life is unmanageable
without Your love and guidance.
I come to You today
because I believe that
You can restore and renew me
to meet my needs tomorrow
and to help me meets the needs of my children.
Since I cannot manage my life or affairs,
I have decided to give them to You.
I put my life, my will,
my thoughts,
my desires and ambitions in Your hands.
I give You each of my children.
I know that You will work them out
in accordance with Your plan.
Such as I am,
take and use me in Your service.
Guide and direct my ways
and show me what to do for You.
I cannot control or change my children,
other family members or friends,
so I release them into Your care

for Your loving hands to do with as You will.
Just keep me loving and free from judging them.
If they need changing, God,
You'll have to do it; I can't.
Just make me willing and ready
to be of service to You,
to have my shortcomings removed,
and to do my best.
I am seeking to know You better,
to love You more.
I am seeking the knowledge of Your will for me
and the power to carry it out.

Praying for Our Children in Good Times and Bad

All too often we limit our praying for our children to the times when we have concerns for them or they are in trouble.

One of the most frequent questions parents ask is, "How should I pray for my children when they're in trouble?" But the other side of the coin is, "What's the best way to pray for my children when they're doing well and living for the Lord?"

In Colossians 1:2, Paul called the Colossians "faithful brothers in Christ." They were living for the Lord, but Paul saw they still had a need for prayer. If your children are committed to the Lord, keep in mind that Satan, the great deceiver, is not too happy about this. Godly children are still going to face temptations. They can get discouraged and will face greater peer pressure and ridicule than others. That is because they are nonconformists living in a society that has totally different values.

For this reason, since the day we heard about you, we have not stopped praying for you and asking God to fill you with the knowledge of his will through all spiritual wisdom and understanding (Col. 1:9).

In Jesus's great prayer in which He committed His followers to God's keeping, He prays:

"I have revealed you to those whom you gave me out of the world. They were yours; you gave them to me and they have obeyed your word....For I gave them the words you gave me and they accepted them....I pray for them. I am not praying for the world, but for those you have given me, for they are yours....protect them by the power of your name—the name you gave me—so that they may be one as we are one" (John 17:6,8,9,11).

If Jesus prayed this way for His spiritual children, then we as parents should pray even more for our believing children that they will be protected by the power of Jesus' name. We can pray, "Dear Lord, I bring my children to You. They have heard the Word of God which I have taught them, and they have believed. Now keep them, protect them by the power of Your name, Lord Jesus Christ. Don't let the Evil One steal away the teaching they have received, but rather let it grow in them. Make them mighty men and women of God to Your honor and glory."[13]

Praying for Character Development in Our Children

David and Heather Kapp provide specific examples of how to pray for the character development of children.

Dear Lord,
I spend all day trying to shape my children's characters, but only work from the outside. I'm afraid I may not be get-

ting through. Lord, You hardly look at the outside because You know that the inside is what matters (1 Sam. 16:7). How can I teach my children integrity?

I worry sometimes that my kids will grow up having mastered all the right words and actions but not be changed through and through by You. Then they'll fold when the pressure mounts.

Lord, use Your Spirit and Your Word to penetrate their innermost natures (Heb. 4:12). Make them whole and healed all through so that the beauty people see on the outside is true of their hearts as well. Only You can accomplish this, Lord.

Save my children and me from deceiving ourselves—and along the way keep making us whole all through by Your work of grace (Ps. 119:29).

Amen

Lord Jesus,

It is my joy and honor to pray for my children. Each one is a miracle in the making, growing from year to year into a creation that only You can see completely (Ps. 139:16). I absolutely believe in this miracle going on right under my nose!

Yes, O God of miracles, I know it's happening—in spite of ill, cranky, foolish, wandering, and obstinate kids (and their parents). I know it's happening in spite of my inability to see the miracle or on some days even to care much about it. Yes, You are up to something grand here! Lord, today I ask that You would grow in my children the courage to want, reach for, and cherish Your best. We do not want to be like those who give up on our destiny and are lost (Heb. 10:39, PH). You changed cowardly, small-spirited fishermen into world ambassadors, leaders, and heroes of faith. Change us too, Lord! you are able to do immeasurably more than all we ask or imagine, because Your immense power is at work in us (Eph. 3:20).

Fearfulness and timidity are *never* what You give! Your gifts to us through Your Spirit are

—power to overcome all obstacles

—love that changes us and those we love

—self-discipline to stay the course (2 Tim. 1:7).[14]

You can pray for immediate specific concerns as well as specific future issues as well.

One of the concerns of every parent is not only who their son or daughter dates, but also whom they will marry. Many parents become anxious about this—especially when their child's choice of a partner appears to lack wisdom. Some parents begin praying for their son or daughter's future partner when their child is just an infant. This is a wise decision and can bear fruit later on when the time arrives for them to choose a mate. You may want to be praying about this now. You may find that the following prayer serves as a good initial step for you.

Prayer for the Future Spouse of a Daughter or Son

Dear Father God,
please send your Holy Spirit
in search of a good spouse
for my daughter (son).

I pray that this chosen one
may be full of love for you, God,
and one who accepts your Son, Jesus,
as his (her) Savior.

May the spouse of my adult child
be strong, good, loving and prudent.

Please give my child
the patience to wait
for the spouse you have chosen.

If she (he) has impatiently
gotten close in hurtful or sinful ways
to another man or woman,
please heal and cleanse her (him)
of the wounds and stain
of those relationships.

Please give (name of adult child)
the gifts and virtues he (she) needs
to be a good spouse
for the one you have chosen.[15]

Keeping a Personal Prayer Journal

Quin Sherrer and Ruthanne Garlock suggest a unique approach to praying for children—keeping a personal prayer journal. I would recommend that you read their book *How to Pray for Your Children*. This is what Quin said:

For nearly 25 years now I've kept personal prayer journals, which I fill with requests, words of praise, reports of answered prayers and specific lessons I'm learning through prayer or Bible reading.

In the first section of my notebook, I glue a picture of LeRoy and myself and write out our prayer Scriptures. The next three sections contain pictures and prayer requests for our three children and their families. The last section is reserved for others outside our family. Here I place names (and a few pictures) of young people I pray for in the mission field, my children's friends, relatives and some government officials.

In the section for an individual family member, I write Scripture prayers as well as practical prayers I'm praying for that child daily. I often record the date beside specific requests. Later I add the day and the way God answered. This has taught me much about God's perfect timing.

During one period I was praying for a daughter away from home who needed a new apartment with lots of storage space. I brought that before the Lord and daily thanked Him that He would provide her with lots of closet space. When He did, I wrote, "Thank You, Lord," and scratched that petition.

Here are some entries from my prayer journal over the years.

Heal Her Broken Heart

Lord, our daughter's heart is broken. Please comfort her. It was her first touch of love, and now he's dumped her for another girl. Her pride is wounded. She feels rejected, worth nothing. Oh, Lord may she realize how much You love her and we love her. Heal her hurts. Bring other Christian friends into her life who can help fill the void left after losing her special friend. Help her get her priorities in order and realize her real purpose in life should be to love and please You. Thank You for Your everlasting arms around our daughter—Your daughter.

Help Her Accept Herself

Lord, our daughter is almost two heads taller than the other girls in her class. She feels like a giant. Show her You made her just like she is for a purpose. You know what You have in store for her, not only in her physical makeup but with the abilities You have given her. She's struggling hard right now to find her true identity. Please help her see she is special and unique, just as each of Your children is.

Help Me Be an Encourager

Lord, he's not doing as well in school as I'd like. Help me accept his pace. Though I'd like better grades, keep me from pushing him beyond his capacity. Show me how to encourage him, right where he is.

Accomplish Your Will

Today accomplish Your will in my children's lives, Father. Have mercy on them according to Your lovingkindness.

Son's Specific Talent

For my son, who is a graphic artist, I wrote: "May Keith be filled with the Spirit of God, with skill, ability and knowledge in all kinds of crafts—to make artistic designs and to engage in all kinds of artistic craftsmanship" (see Exodus 35:31-33).

Wisdom and Discernment

Lord, give my children wisdom about what they are to look at and listen to. Help them avoid those things that would defile their minds (1 Peter 1:13-16).

Lord, let my children hate this rock music that is so attractive to them now when they are in their teens. May they have a desire to hear music restful for their souls.

Answer:

Some ten years later when I was Christmas shopping with my oldest, she was so repelled by the loud rock music, she said to the store manager, "Will you please turn your music down or off if you want me to stay and shop here."

Inside I was praising God for answered prayer. Soft, soothing music is her choice nowadays.

Sample Prayer Journal Page

Child's Name _____

Thank You, Lord, that You know

the plans You have for _____   PASTE

to prosper and not harm him/her,   PHOTO OF

but to give him/her hope and a future.   CHILD

I pray that my child will not stand in the   HERE

way of sinners or sit in the seat of mockers.

May my child's delight be in the law of the Lord

as he meditates on it day and night

(see Jeremiah 29:11; Psalm 1:1,2).

Dear Father, may_____, like Your Son Jesus, grow in wisdom and stature, and in favor with You and the people his/her life touches. Give him/her a listening ear to parental instructions. Help him/her to pay attention that he/she may gain understanding (see Luke 2:52; Proverbs 4:1).

May the Spirit of the Lord rest upon my child, _____—the Spirit of wisdom, understanding, counsel, might, knowledge and the reverential and obedient fear of the Lord (see Isaiah 11:2, *Amp.*). I pray the eyes of his/her heart may be enlightened in order that he/she may know You better. I pray that Christ may dwell in his/her heart through faith and that_____ will be rooted and established in love (see Ephesians 1:17; 3:17).[16]

How will you begin praying for your child today?

Notes

1. Reprinted from *Parents in Pain* by John White. © 1979, by InterVarsity Christian Fellowship of the USA, p. 165. Used by permission of InterVarsity Press, P.O. Box 1400, Downers Grove, IL 60515.

2. Reprinted from *Parents in Pain* by John White. © 1979 by InterVarsity Christian Fellowship of the USA, p. 164. Used by permission of InterVarsity Press, P.O. Box 1400, Downers Grove, IL 60515.

3. Stormie Omartian, *The Power of a Praying Parent* (Eugene, Oreg.: Harvest House, 1995), pp. 18,19.

4. David and Heather Kapp, *Praying the Bible for Your Children* (Colorado Springs: Waterbrook Press, 1998), p. 10, adapted.

5. *Common Sense Parenting* by Kent and Barbara Hughes © 1995, p. 91. Used by permission of Tyndale House Publishers, Inc. Wheaton, IL. All rights reserved.

6. This material is taken from *Daily Thoughts for Disciples* by Oswald Chambers, p. 75. Copyright © 1994 by the Oswald Chambers Publications Assoc. Ltd. Originally published by Zondervan Publishers ©1976. Used by permission of Discovery House Publishers, Box 3566, Grand Rapids, MI 49501. All rights reserved.

7. Quin Sherrer and Ruthanne Garlock, *How to Pray for Your Children* (Ventura, Calif.: Regal Books, 1998), pp. 33,34.

8. Kapp, *Praying the Bible for Your Children*, p. 15, adapted.

9. Ibid., pp. 15-18, adapted.

10. Servant Publications, *The Spiritual Warrior's Prayer Guide*, Quin Sherrer and Ruthanne Garlock, © 1992, p. 156. Used by permission.

11. *Common Sense Parenting* by Kent and Barbara Hughes, ©1995, p. 85. Used by permission of Tyndale House Publishers, Inc. Wheaton, IL. All rights reserved.

12. Omartian, *The Power of a Praying Parent*, pp. 13,14.

13. Reprinted from *How to Pray for Your Children* by Quin Sherrer, p. 76. ©1986 Quin Sherrer. Used by permission of Aglow Publications, a ministry of Aglow International.

14. Kapp, *Praying the Bible for Your Children*, pp. 161 and 166.

15. As found in Ronda De La Sola Chervin. *A Mother's Treasury of Prayers* (Ann Arbor, Mich.: Servant Publications, 1994), p. 181. Adapted from *The Spiritual Warrior's Prayer Guide* by Quin Sherrer and Ruthanne Garlock.

16. Sherrer and Garlock, *How to Pray for Your Children*, selections from chapter 2.

12

THE HEALTHY FAMILY

By H. Norman Wright

By wisdom a house is built, and through understanding
it is established; through knowledge its rooms are filled
with rare and beautiful treasures.

—PROVERBS 24:3,4

I have always enjoyed raising animals. As a child, I had baby chickens, ducks and cats. As an adult, I have ventured into the world of puppies. Many think it is simple and easy to raise these animals; it isn't. It takes the right conditions and atmosphere. If you have ever incubated eggs, you know what I mean. You just don't let the eggs sit there. Not only do they have to have a constant temperature from the lamp, but they also need to be turned from time to time. When puppies are born, they need to be handled with care. Not only do you keep other dogs away, but if you touch another dog other than the puppies' mother, you also need to wash your hands before touching the puppies. Why? Their immune system is not working yet. They are too susceptible.

The Atmosphere to Help Your Child Become More Like Jesus

The atmosphere of our family has much to do with our children becoming more like Jesus. There are things to avoid and elements that must be there. Let's consider what happens in a family and what needs to be done.

Have you ever helped your kids build some complicated design, perhaps a model airplane or a Tinker Toy forklift? I don't know about you, but I need a detailed plan in front of me for what piece goes where. Surely family life is one of the most intricate designs of all, consisting of many complicated relationships thoroughly intertwined with the world around us. Of course, not every healthy family will look as though it were pressed out of the same mold. True to God's infinite creativity, diversity abounds.

Is there a model we can work toward in building our families? I have discovered several in plowing through various books and studies on the subject. Lots of folks claim to be experts these days. Who can we trust with our most precious project?

If you told a medical doctor, "I am healthy," he would use certain basic criteria to determine the accuracy of your diagnosis. Let's say you went to a family therapist and asked, "Is my family healthy?" What criteria would the therapist use in his or her analysis? Let's examine some basic building blocks.

Building Blocks for a Healthy Marriage

THE MARRIAGE RELATIONSHIP

Of the myriad factors involved in family life, the most important is the marital relationship. It is the foundation stone on which all the other pieces of family structure will be built. We need to distinguish between the marital unit of husband and wife and the parental unit. Each element will have its own roles and responsibilities. Two people may be both partners and parents, yet keep the roles separate.[1]

A family always faces an uphill battle if the marriage is sick. A warm, caring, supportive relationship contains the best ingredients for nurturing children. Given all the books available today about marriage, no lack of information is available about this subject.

HOW DOES THE FAMILY DEAL WITH POWER?

When you think of power, what comes to mind? For our purposes, I would define "power" as each individual's capacity to influence another person; or the ability to make our own thoughts and feelings the main force in making decisions.

Power within a family can be sorted out in various ways. It could be equally shared by all members. On the other extreme, one particular person might totally dominate the rest. Within a dominated family, opportunities for developing close or intimate relationships are greatly diminished. A strongly dominant spouse or parent usually cannot handle intimacy. In a healthy family, power is shared by the spouses, while they gradually give their children more and more opportunities to learn how to use power in a healthy way. They teach their children to become independent.

FAMILY CLOSENESS

A third characteristic we look for in a healthy family is both the amount and kind of family closeness. Being close as a family is important, but it must also be balanced with the freedom of each individual to express his or her own individuality and have access to some private space for retreat when necessary. It means you recognize and accept needs that come from personality differences as well.

Either emotional starvation or smothering within the family can be extremely detrimental. Personal boundaries are often violated in either situation. The absence of warmth and affection can create enormous insecurity and love hunger. The other extreme of holding on too tightly and controlling others leaves too little opportunity for individuality and intimacy.

Both intimacy and autonomy need to be encouraged within the family. If not, all the members, especially the children, end up stunted in their capacity to form healthy relationships with adults later on. How well do family members bond together? How well are individual boundaries established and respected? All these issues add crucial building blocks to the healthy family.

Just as families are all different, so each individual develops his or her own unique personality. The following message needs to be heard very clearly: It is okay for you to be who you are and for me to be who I am.

THE PATTERN OF COMMUNICATION
The fourth area to evaluate is the pattern of communication that occurs within the family. Is each person encouraged to talk, to share feelings, likes and dislikes? Does everyone enjoy total freedom in expressing feelings or are some emotions on an unspoken forbidden list?

In some families, anger is all right and affection is not. In others, just the opposite may be true. Some families forbid the expression of all feelings. Some families carry a prevailing mood that seems to permeate the atmosphere—ranging from warm to polite to angry to depressed to hopeless.[2]

We all grow and function best when we live in an atmosphere of acceptance. Do the members of the family listen to each other? I mean *total listening* using both eyes and ears. Too many family conversations are nothing more than dialogues of the deaf. We are called by the Scriptures to be listeners "be...[a ready listener]" (Jas. 1:19, *Amp.*). "He who answers a matter before he hears the facts—it is folly and shame to him" (Prov. 18:13, *Amp.*).

The parents must set the example. By adapting their own style of communication, they help everyone else learn the principles of speaking the other's language. We all need to be especially sensitive to gender and personality differences that can create various ways of responding.

Are family members allowed to speak for themselves? Perhaps you have been with a family in which individuals interrupt one another constantly, speak for one another and complete sentences for other family members. Such a nasty habit can often develop without our even realizing it.

Within the framework of communication patterns, individual

adeptness in problem solving and conflict resolution especially reflects the growth and progress of the family unit. Learning to negotiate is a skill couples need to learn and then teach their children.

> FAMILIES WHO CONTINUE TO GROW IN HEALTHY WAYS FOCUS ON WHAT WORKS RATHER THAN ON WHAT DOESN'T.

In a healthy family, you assume that conflict will occur; it is an opportunity for growth. Did you ever wonder what conflicts took place in Jesus' family? Between Jesus and His parents or His brothers? I wonder how they were resolved.

Conflict is an opportunity for the Holy Spirit to guide us and heal us.

Families who continue to grow in healthy ways focus on what works rather than on what doesn't. They look for the times when problems are resolved and discover what greased the wheels so they can do it again. They resolve to learn from their experiences rather than getting bogged down in an unproductive fixation on what went wrong.

Adapting and Growing

Several years ago, the Chicago Cubs won the divisional championship. As often happens, one of their leading hitters suffered a batting slump during the season. The manager noticed this player was spending extra time in the clubhouse evaluating films of his performance. In trying to discover what he was doing wrong, he was scrutinizing tapes taken during his slump. Unfortunately, watching those films only reinforced his bad habits!

The manager complimented him on wanting to do something about the problem. Then he suggested to the batter that he begin watching films of when he was doing his best at the plate, really striking the ball with power. The ballplayer took his manager's wise advice. When he focused on what worked before, it began to work again.

Life is full of challenges for all of us. One of the most difficult is dealing with an upheaval in our lives because of some loss or tragic event. How well families handle crisis situations as well as the more frequent changes can also be a barometer of health.

Common transitions—such as a child leaving for school or getting married or returning home again—offer countless opportunities for the entire family to adapt and grow. How well individuals handle their own response to these times of change and how they respond to one another are both reflections of family health.[3]

Many families are thrown into total disarray by a sudden crisis or unforeseen change. They perceive the disruption as a threatening enemy, something to be feared. Other families may recognize the difficulties presented by the crisis but set their sights on learning from the particular problems and people involved.

The courage of one family could be a model for us all. The mother underwent surgery, requiring a hospital stay of 27 days. Her husband and three children—ages 7, 11 and 14—had to carry on without her. They cooked, cleaned and discovered how to complete tasks that were totally foreign to them. Mom's return home required another period of readjustment for everyone until she could resume her former responsibilities. Fortunately, the entire family met together on several occasions to share how they felt, what they were learning and how the family was changing because of the mother's absence.

Such crises can either strengthen or weaken relationships. Problems are the opportunities of life that allow both the individual and the family to grow. The apostle Peter described this challenge when he said:

Beloved, do not be amazed and bewildered at the fiery ordeal which is taking place to test your quality, as though something strange (unusual and alien to you and your position) were befalling you.

But insofar as you are sharing Christ's sufferings, rejoice, so that when His glory [full of radiance and splendor] is revealed, you may also rejoice with triumph [exultantly] (1 Pet. 4:12,13, *Amp.*).

Being Loving Parents

Finally, the mother and father in a healthy family fulfill God's call to be loving parents. Being totally responsible for growing children is a tall order. Let's consider some of the necessary ingredients in healthy parenting.

Have you ever wondered as a parent, *What in the world am I doing spiritually for my child?* Many parents have asked that, especially after a particularly stressful, unproductive, disastrous and exhausting day.

One parent said, "There are days when I question whether I've accomplished anything. It seems like I follow one child for a while and then another, either trying to head off a pending disaster or trying to salvage the remnants of the most recent one. Is this what parenting is all about? Is this what I'm supposed to be accomplishing with my life? How can I draw them closer to Jesus? I feel like a janitor."

Another parent reflected, "Parenting is a lot different than I ever expected. Some days I think I'm more of a chauffeur and other days the enforcer of homework. Then there are the times when I'm a censor for TV programs and the chef of a fast-food diner! I wanted my life to count for something as a parent, but I wonder at times what it is. Have I lost sight of something? Am I putting my time and energy into the right areas or is there something else I should be focusing on? Where is teaching them to be more like Jesus in all of this?"

Sometimes the task of parenting seems to be survival more than anything else. It is easy to become immersed in the tasks and activities of running the home, of putting out brushfires instead of focusing on our calling as Christian parents.

In the past, there were times when God called His people back to their primary purpose. Given today's hectic schedules, it may be helpful to refocus on our calling as parents. Consider these thoughts and read them aloud each day for a month. You won't lose sight of them if you do that.

> The primary goal of child rearing is to produce godly character in children so that God will be glorified. This perspective transforms the task of child rearing. Our goal is no longer merely to resolve family conflicts and find a little peace. Now we are participating in God's great program of the ages. We are shaping lives for eternity. We are helping to form each child's character so that he or she reflects God's glory.[4]

The Many Roles of Parents

Yes, it is tough being a parent. It is just plain hard work; and you have to be flexible in the multitude of roles you need to play as a parent. The more you can flex to the various roles, the greater influence you will have in the life of your child. As you consider these roles, consider which of them were helpful to you as you were growing up.

TEACHER/COACH
You will function at times as *teacher/coach*. Do you know what this means? You will be assisting your child to develop some new skill, as well as improve an old one. It is a role in which you will need to give hands-on help at times and then let your child learn some things on his or her own. You are not functioning as a high-powered, intense, yelling football or basketball coach, but think of yourself as a

birthing coach. You are there to help bring about something that usually happens naturally.

In doing this, discover what it is your child wants to learn, and when you interact with him, concentrate on what he knows and wants to know. *First, ask your child to show you what he already knows.* Then you can ask what the child wants or needs to know and then show him. Give your child an opportunity to learn by trial and error. Welcome your child's questions.

LEADER/GUIDE

You will also function as *leader/guide*. This is where you help your child explore areas she can't on her own. Knowing she has your support, she is able to accomplish this.

On several occasions, I have hired a bass guide to help me develop my proficiency at bass fishing, as well as to learn about a new lake. If I had not been with a guide, it would have taken me 10 times as long to learn what I learned. You will need to structure the learning experience in such a way that your child feels comfortable with the amount of risk involved. Be sure to use praise and positive reinforcement as your child moves ahead in any new endeavor. Ask what she has learned and what it means to her.

MENTOR/SAGE

One of your roles is to respond as a *mentor/sage*. Think of yourself as an actor in a play, but you don't have the leading role; you are a supporting actor. You respond as a mentor/sage when you look for ways to help your child discover what he already knows. We all have our own perception of what we think a mentor is or does. This role, however, is one in which you clarify questions rather than give answers. You help shed light on issues. This is difficult.

Most of us try to rescue our children when we either see them struggling or they don't seem to be getting it. Sometimes we express ourselves by exhibiting a sense of frustration and irritation. This dampens the learning desire on the part of your child. The rule here is restrain—restrain—restrain! Let your child discover his capabilities. If your child is a preteen or a teenager, this role is very important because this is a time when children this age test their prebelieved values and come face-to-face with conflicting value systems to a heightened degree.

Remember you may hear statements you don't want to hear. Your tendency may be to immediately correct and override to make them believe what you want them to believe. Don't! It won't work. Your role is to help your child search by asking questions. Help her search out the truth.

FRIEND/COMPANION

The *friend/companion* is a role that slowly evolves as your child grows older. When your child becomes a teenager, you will find this is developing. This is where you do something you mutually enjoy. It can develop in childhood to some degree. I started my daughter, Sheryl, fishing when she was five. We have had many enjoyable outings together and she catches as many fish as I do. In fact, on one trip to Canada she not only caught the largest northern pike of the trip (22 pounds) but also the largest caught in that lake all year. Was she ever excited and was I ever proud of her!

It is important to take time for these opportunities. This is where your playful side has a chance to emerge. Remember that your child may want you to stay in this role longer than you want to or think is best. You will need to work this out.

COUNSELOR/CONFIDANT

At times you will assume a very influential role, which is as a *counselor/confidant.* You become a person who is very trusted because you are a listener, as well as a keeper of secrets. In this role you don't give advice. You may reflect back what you hear your child say or what you sense she is saying. You don't give trite statements when she shares her hurts. You allow and encourage the child to grieve when needed.

PROTECTOR/ADVOCATE

An additional role you will play is *protector/advocate*. It is probably a natural role to play. You are a support system for your child, especially when she is having a difficult time. Being an advocate means you believe in your child and her intentions. You give her the benefit of the doubt while letting her experience the consequences of her actions. When your child makes a mistake or misjudgment, you don't shield her, but help her to learn from it and believe the next time will be different. You do shield your child from hanging on to guilt and from others who won't give her another chance. You focus on intentions rather than just actions. If she misbehaves, you talk with her about what she will do differently the next time.

PROVIDER/SUPPORTER

Finally, you will also be a *provider/supporter*. Parents are the primary providers for all the basic needs of their child, such as food, clothing, shelter and health care. You would be amazed at the number of families who can afford all this but funnel the funds elsewhere for various reasons.

A parent is always a provider in some way, but support means that over a period of years you are assisting your child not to need you. You respond in this way when your child needs a boost in confidence. You believe in her capabilities, and when she enters adolescence, you have helped her prepare for and enter into adulthood.[5]

Being Role Models for Our Children

BE THERE

Other factors are involved as well. Healthy parenting means being there when a child needs you. Coming home to an empty house day after day can have a very negative effect upon a child. He or she may feel abandoned or get into serious difficulty because of the lack of supervision. Even in the midst of work demands, parents can spend adequate time with their children.

PROVIDE PROTECTION

Parents need to provide protection from the normal hazards of life, as well as information and experiences the child is not yet equipped to handle. Media exposure—including television, movies and recordings—needs to be screened, limited and supervised. Children should neither be pushed into anything that is beyond their capabilities nor prematurely exposed to certain activities and experiences. A child is not the fulfillment of a parent's unfulfilled experiences.

CONSIDER CHILD'S UNIQUENESS

Healthy parents are able to determine the child's developmental level so the child doesn't expect too much or too little. They understand and accept age-appropriate behavior, and are able to identify and correct that which is inappropriate. Effective parenting takes into account every child's age and stage of development when assigning privileges and responsibilities. Both the mother and father respect the uniqueness of each child and adapt their responses according to each specific child and situation.

Proverbs 22:6 exhorts parents to "train up a child in the way he should go [and in keeping with his individual gift or bent], and when he is old he will not depart from it" (*Amp.*). Scripture is not advocating favoritism here, but respect for the individuality of the child. Wise parents encourage the child to develop his or her special areas of giftedness.

EXHIBIT AFFECTION

Both physical and verbal affection are necessary expressions of love and acceptance. Regardless of their background and experience, healthy parents take care to provide a role model of healthy marital interaction, as well as giving to the children without exploitation. Children especially enjoy seeing their parents give one another some visible sign of affection such as a loving kiss or a warm hug. How to make up after the inevitable arguments of married life also provides invaluable lessons for life.

ESTABLISH GUIDELINES

Healthy parents establish rules and guidelines for their children, while also teaching them how to discern and establish them when the parents are not around. These rules also need to take into consideration the ability and individuality of each child. The parents remain parents and the children remain children. They understand and respect their positions.

INDEPENDENCE, RATHER THAN DEPENDENCE, IS FOSTERED IN A HEALTHY FAMILY. THROUGHOUT THE PARENTING ROLE IS WOVEN A THREAD OF GRADUAL RELINQUISHMENT OF AUTHORITY AND DECISION MAKING.

FOSTER INDEPENDENCE

Independence, rather than dependence, is fostered in a healthy family. Throughout the parenting role is woven a thread of gradual relinquishment of authority and decision making. The child is enabled to gracefully move from dependence to independence. This means we accept and encourage the fact that our child is going to grow and change. The child needs us to model this for him or her.

Changing and Growing

BUILD TWO-WAY ACCOUNTABILITY

When we parents change and grow, we show our teenagers that it is all right for them to change and grow. In fact, one of the best ways we can restructure our relationships with a teenager is to begin building two-way accountability. What's that? Let's look at its opposite to help define it.

The world structures relationships by setting up a series of one-way accountability systems that comprise a line of authority. At the bottom is the guy who is accountable to his boss, who is in turn accountable to *his* boss and so on, all the way up the ladder to the top. The president or manager may be accountable to a board, and in some companies a profit-sharing program makes the president indirectly accountable to lower-level employees.

One-way accountability is the system most families are familiar with. Kids are accountable to adults, especially parents, *but* not vice-versa.

In two-way accountability, a dad would be willing to go to his teenage son and say, "Son, I'm working on not being anxious and committing everything to God in prayer. I'd like to report my progress to you each evening, and I'd like you to ask me how I'm doing. I'd like you to suggest ways I can learn quicker. And when you notice me getting anxious about something, I'd like you to remind me to commit it to the Lord right away. Okay?"

When the parent initiates two-way accountability, he or she sets the stage for several things to happen: (1) Teenagers will have a model for change that will make change and growth easier to accomplish; (2) teenagers will have a model for voluntary accountability, which, if they develop it, will increase their self-discipline and responsibility greatly; (3) parent-teen communication can become more adult-to-adult rather than a adult-to-child. This may be new, but think about the possibilities.[6]

PROVIDE SPIRITUAL GROWTH

The spiritual dimension of life is lived out in word and deed. Wise parents give direction to each child for his or her spiritual growth. Such spiritual guidance must be integrated into all seven days of the week, rather than remain a mere token expression when Sunday arrives. Personal devotions are most effectively taught—or more aptly "caught"—by what children observe happening in the everyday lives of their parents. The wisest parents endeavor to lead each child to a saving knowledge of Jesus Christ.

WORK AS A TEAM

Healthy parenting requires working as a team whether parents are together or divorced. They publicly support each other and work out their individual differences behind the scenes. Mothers and fathers need to avoid triangulation with the children; this is where each parent pairs off with a particular child against the spouse regarding some issue. Healthy parents don't use the children to communicate to the estranged spouse or get back at him or her.[7]

John White summed it up well when he said,

> What do children need? And how well can parents meet their needs? Children need acceptance. They need praise and appreciation. They need to learn they can trust their parents not to deceive them or to break promises. They need consistency and fairness. They need to feel that their fears, their desires, their feelings, their inexplicable impulses, their frustrations, and their inabilities are understood by their parents. They need to know exactly where the limits are, what is permitted and what is prohibited. They need to know that home is a safe place, a place of refuge, a place where they have no need to be afraid. They need warm approval when they do well, and firm correction when they do wrong. They need to learn a sense of proportion. They need to know that their parents are stronger than they are, able to weather the storms and dangers of the outer world and also able to stand up to their (children's) rages and unreasonable demands. They need to feel their parents like them and can take time to listen. They need perceptive responses to their growing need for independence.[8]

What about your experience with parenting? Does this sound anything like the family you grew up with? Or like your present-day family? Could you initiate any changes that could make these elements of healthy parenting more of a reality? How will this help your child become more like Jesus?

Notes

1. Original survey from Dr. Patricia Love, *The Emotional Incest Syndrome* (New York: Bantam Books, 1990), p. 103, adapted.

2. Jerry Lewis, *How's Your Family?* (New York: Bruner Mazell, 1979), p. 63, adapted.

3. Ibid., pp. 47-49, adapted.

4. Taken from *Parenting with Love and Limits* by Bruce Narramore. ©1979 by The Zondervan Corporation, pp. 25, 26. Used by permission of Zondervan Publishing House.

5. David Domico, *The Influential Parent* (Wheaton, Ill.: Shaw Publishers, 1997), pp. 96-114, adapted.

6. H. Norman Wright, *Quiet Times for Parents* (Eugene, Oreg.: Harvest House, 1995), July 13 devotion.

7. Love, *The Emotional Incest Syndrome*, pp. 102-107, adapted.

8. Reprinted from John White, *Parents in Pain*. ©1979 by InterVarsity Christian Fellowship of the USA, p. 181. Used by permission of InterVarsity Press, Downers Grove, IL 60515.

WHAT YOU GIVE IS WHAT THEY GET (HERITAGE/LEGACY)

By H. Norman Wright

Your statutes are my heritage for ever;
they are the joy of my heart.

—PSALM 119:111

Whether a child wants one or not, he or she receives something from you that you received from your parents—it's called a heritage. If I asked you to define what it is, what would you say? Unfortunately, many are unclear what it really is! Consider this definition from the authors of a book titled *The Heritage*:

> A heritage is the spiritual, emotional, and social legacy that
> is passed from parent to child...good or bad.[1]

Heritage Influences Legacy

Do you know what a legacy is? It means something resulting from, and left behind by, an action, event or person.

Each heritage has three distinct yet interrelated parts, and the three together are stronger than just one or even two together. A heritage ties a child to his past, gives stability in his present life and gives hope for what is to come in the future.

Sometimes parents overemphasize one part more than the others. One part of the heritage is given gourmet attention while the others exist on starvation rations. However, the three are interrelated and influence the others.

THE SPIRITUAL

Perhaps the spiritual is the most neglected. (Although I have seen this overemphasized to the extent that a child ended up being socially inept and his spiritual development didn't draw anyone to Jesus.)

THE EMOTIONAL

The emotional legacy highly influences the spiritual and social. An emotional legacy is a lasting sense of emotional security that has been nurtured in a safe and loving environment.[2] Unfortunately, many children grew up in homes where emotions were not modeled or discussed. The few emotions that were expressed were kept out of sight from the children. No names were given to them and no healthy opportunities were provided for understanding them. Thus, some children wound up as emotionally handicapped adults.

Others grew up in homes where emotional expression was punished and emotional repression was reinforced. Children reared in this setting either consciously or unconsciously told themselves it wasn't safe to feel. For their own survival, their minds were trained to ignore emotions or filter them out or, when one accidentally crept up to the surface, stuff it back down. Children need an environment in which they are free to learn how to experience or express their God-given emotions. This is where the spiritual and emotional heritage come together. Looking at the life of Jesus and how He expressed emotions will help your child become more like

Him. Jesus experienced grief, compassion, sympathy, love, depression, anger, amazement, sadness and sorrow.

How important is the emotional component? In many race cars you will find what is called a stabilizer bar, or the stabilizer system. It keeps the car from going out of control while going around corners at terrific speeds. It prevents it from crashing. It keeps the car from swaying in those dangerous curves.

> The emotional element of the heritage cord is like an auto stabilizer bar; the emotions are to act as a stabilizer to the spiritual and social components. Many a relationship has been lost because of unstable emotions, which produced irrational thinking and actions. Spiritual lives crash and burn each day, while trying to navigate harsh circumstances thrown at them. Why? Because as children growing up their emotions at some point were impaired. Now as adults, without the emotional health to give stability, the other two elements are pushed to the breaking point. As a result, either their relationships or spiritual lives (often both) are abandoned.[3]

IF A CHILD LEARNS HOW TO RELATE WELL, IT ENHANCES
ANY PROFESSION HE OR SHE CHOOSES.

THE SOCIAL

The social heritage comes from learning the skills of interacting with others. It involves learning to care, share, respect, be courteous and be involved in the life of others. Giving a child a social legacy involves helping him or her develop the insight and relational skills for developing healthy stable relationships. Basically, a child needs to be taught about people. This is where the teachings of Scripture come in, for there we find our guidelines. If a child learns how to relate well, it enhances any profession he or she chooses. He or she needs to learn about healthy boundaries, respect, empathy, responsibility for others and especially how to communicate effectively.[4]

Leaving a Legacy by Our Actions

Often we have good intentions to create a positive legacy. Sometimes we allow distractions to drag us off course with our family. Recently, I watched a comedy movie on television called *Battling for Baby*. The battle between two ex-friends who become the grandparents of the same baby was humorous, but at the same time contained a thought-provoking message.

The maternal grandmother—a concert pianist who was terribly uncomfortable with children—was holding her granddaughter at the baby's first birthday party. The mother of the baby looked at her and said, "Mother, it's interesting you're here for her first birthday party. You weren't there at mine. Where were you?"

The grandmother looked surprised. After a moment's reflection she answered, "Well, I guess I was in Vienna." Later on when she was alone in the kitchen, she asked herself, "I wonder what was so important in Vienna that I missed her first birthday?" All of us can ask that same question: "I wonder what was so important that I missed..."

The Word of God is very clear about our calling in a non-Christian society. "And do not be conformed to this world, but be transformed by the renewing of your mind, that you may prove what the will of God is, that which is good and acceptable and perfect" (Rom. 12:2, *NASB*). Sometimes we can be close in our efforts, and yet so far off.

A young man's experience in college best illustrates this fact. He described a father and son who walked onto his job site one morning looking for work. They appeared to have the tools of the trade, as well as the callused hands of those who worked in the building trade. The foreman hired them and put them to work building a foundation for the walls of a split-level ranch home. They went about their bricklaying and completed their task on time.

The next day, however, when the other workers tried to install the metal frames for the windows and doors, nothing seemed to fit. The frames matched the specs on the blueprints, but they just wouldn't go into the openings. The foreman finally came over and stretched his own tape measure across the openings and discovered the problem. Here are the words of the college student:

> I felt frustrated and sad as the foreman asked to see the bricklayer's ruler. He unfolded it and laid it on the floor. Then the foreman stretched out his own tape measure beside it and locked it open.
>
> Amazing.
>
> The difference wasn't much per inch—less than one-eighth—but stretched over the distance, it added up to an expensive blunder. None of the bricklayers knew it could happen. I didn't either. But it did—and it does. When quizzed about the ruler, the unfortunate man said he bought it from "bargain barrel" at a hardware store.
>
> He had bought a lie which made his speed as a brick-layer an illusion. In the end, the vital components of the home would not fit in their rightful place.
>
> He was sincere...but wrong. He was skilled...but disgraced.
>
> His work was a monument to a man who put his faith in an unreliable standard.[5]

So what legacy are you leaving? Each of us is creating our own legacy right at this very moment. I have been doing this for many years. As Tim Kimmel puts it in his book *Legacy of Love*, "Your words, your schedule, your choices, your obedience, the way you savor your victories and the way you swallow your defeats all help to define your life. It is this definition that your children rely on most as they seek to chart their own future."[6]

> WHAT YOU DO, WHAT YOU SAY AND WHO YOU ARE WILL
> LIVE ON. WHAT WILL YOUR LEGACY BE?

What are others receiving from you? What are you giving to help your children become more like Jesus? We don't have any option when it comes to leaving a legacy. We all leave one wherever our feet have touched as we walk through life. However, we do have an option about the kind of legacy we leave. What you do, what you say and who you are will live on. What will your legacy be?

Building a Positive Lasting Legacy

I am enthralled with a story Tim Kimmel tells about his travels around the Bahamas by sailboat. While Tim and his wife were snorkeling the reefs and exploring the various isolated islands, they headed into the harbor of Man-O-War Bay for supplies and repairs. While exploring the island, they stumbled upon a graveyard—a beautiful spot featuring tropical plants and flowers and a white beach in the background. The open graves that had apparently been dug months before puzzled them, though. They had never seen anything like that before.[7]

Returning to the harbor, Tim and his wife met one of the pastors on the island and asked him about the open graves. He explained that because the island rested on a coral platform, digging a grave required several days. Having limited facilities and refrigeration, a body could not be preserved that length of time. Because people were usually buried within a few hours after dying, the government required that two graves be kept ready for the next death.

Tim asked how they could assemble people in time for the funeral. The pastor's answer was interesting and unusual. In the case of a sudden death, they did the best they could to get people together. In the case of a lingering or terminal illness, the funeral was held in advance!

When people were dying, their family and friends would carry them into the church or come to their house for the funeral service. Can you imagine hearing your own funeral service? In most cases, it worked out well and gave the dying an opportunity to hear what others had to say about them. In some cases, though, the people recovered. I wonder if hearing the eulogy in advance—whether good or bad—may have encouraged them to keep on living.

Would you want to hear your eulogy in advance? Do you wonder, like I do, what would be said? What would you want your friends and family to say about you? What would you change now so that your children would be able to say even more positive remarks about you and the influence you had upon their lives? What would they say about your helping them become more like Jesus?

A sobering thought, isn't it? We need to consider this as we move forward to help our children become more like Jesus.

Developing Character Qualities in Our Children

What do you want right now for your child? What are the character qualities you are seeking to develop?

WISDOM

Consider this passage: "And the Child continued to grow and become strong, increasing in wisdom" (Luke 2:40, *NASB*).

As Jesus grew as a child, He wasn't stunted in any way. He moved ahead toward maturity, responsibility and strength. He grew physically, emotionally, intellectually and spiritually. The

Scriptures say *He increased in wisdom*. Perhaps that's the foundation for a child becoming more like Jesus, to grow in wisdom. Proverbs says, "Rightly favored is the person who finds wisdom" (3:13, paraphrased).

Focusing on helping our children discover wisdom will help us as parents concentrate more on what kind of adults they will be rather than on what they will do. We want our children to become men and women of character rather than to be at the top of their classes, CEOs or noted athletes. Building character is more likely to result in children learning to use their capabilities to the best of their abilities as well as reflecting the presence of Jesus in their lives.

INTEGRITY

A person of character is a person of integrity. We need men and women of integrity today, but it is a costly virtue. What will it cost your children? Just a few things such as time, effort, money, and, perhaps, even popularity and respect from the people around them. Integrity is not popular; it makes some people uncomfortable.

The word "integrity" means to be "sound, complete, without blemish, crack, or defect." In the construction business, the concept of integrity refers to building codes that ensure the building will be safe. To have integrity, the building has to be properly designed, comply with all the building codes and function safely in accordance with its purpose. Webster's dictionary has a simple word for it—"honesty."

How will integrity make your child's life better? Let God's Word answer that for you. "The integrity of the upright guides them, but the unfaithful are destroyed by their duplicity" (Prov. 11:3).

Integrity gives you a solid footing. "The man of integrity walks securely, but he who takes crooked paths will be found out" (Prov. 10:9).

Integrity gives you something that lasts. "The days of the blameless are known to the Lord, and their inheritance will endure forever" (Ps. 37:18).

Integrity gives a poor man riches. "Better a poor man whose walk is blameless than a fool whose lips are perverse" (Prov. 19:1).

Integrity pleases God. "I know, my God, that you test the heart and are pleased with integrity" (1 Chron. 29:17).

Integrity makes you more like Jesus. "'Teacher,' they said, 'we know you are a man of integrity and that you teach the way of God in accordance with the truth. You aren't swayed by men, because you pay no attention to who they are.'" (Matt. 22:16).[8]

NONCONFORMISM

Building character into the life of your child means assisting him or her to become a nonconformist just as Jesus was. To be a person of character today means going across the grain of what our society does and believes. Your son or daughter may not wind up where you wish they would be economically, socially, vocationally or even where they live. Are you ready for that? Are you willing to see that happen? Becoming more like Jesus is not an easy step; it is a radical step. It won't be popular with the majority; your child may not appear "well-adjusted" to this world, but that's all right. Dr. Robert Hicks said the following:

My own assessment about Jesus is that—by contemporary standards—He was not very "well-adjusted" at all. In any culture, to be "well-adjusted" is not necessarily the *sine qua non* of mental health. After all, to be well-adjusted to a sick society is in my estimation real sickness! In this light, Jesus was not well-adjusted. He took on His teachers, He disagreed with the authoritative rabbinic opinion, and He created the most disruptive political-economic disturbance one could create in His time by throwing out the money-changers from the Temple compound. In terms of economic impact, that act is comparable to walking into the stock exchange on Wall Street and pulling the plugs on all the computer financial networks, thereby plunging the entire world into economic chaos! It's no wonder the authorities finally came to the conclusion that this "mentally deranged" person had to go (Mark 11:15-18).[9]

These words are something to think about.

Developing Wisdom Rather Than Being a Fool

Wisdom—what is this? The Word of God gives us what we need to know. The book of Proverbs opens with these words:

> The proverbs of Solomon the son of David, king of Israel:
> To know wisdom and instruction,
> To discern the sayings of understanding,
> To receive instruction in wise behavior,
> Righteousness, justice and equity;
> To give prudence to the naive,
> To the youth knowledge and discretion,
> To understand a proverb and a figure,
> The words of the wise and their riddles (1:1-4,6, *NASB*).

What Proverbs is saying is that a person is wise when all his or her life has been shaped by the insights of wisdom.[10]

Wisdom here implies learning from those older and wiser than we are; and when learning occurs, it is incorporated into a person's life by disciplining such areas as emotions, tongue, passions as well as appetites. A wise person is just the opposite of what Proverbs refers to as a fool. Do you know what a fool is really like?

Three Hebrew words are translated "fool." One of them is used almost 50 times in the book of Proverbs. It means a person who is dull and obstinate, and it is a choice he has made. He is not really willing to search patiently for wisdom. He just feels it should be handed to him. He shares his opinions with you quite freely, but they are not worth much. "A wise man thinks ahead; a fool doesn't, and even brags about it!" (13:16, *TLB*). What he says falls flat or comes back to haunt him.

The problem is the fool doesn't learn from his mistakes! "In the mouth of a fool a proverb becomes as useless as a paralyzed leg. A rebel will misapply an illustration so that its point will no more be felt than a thorn in the hand of a drunkard. A rebuke to a man of common sense is more effective than a hundred lashes on the back of a rebel" (26:7,9; 17:10, *TLB*). He likes the way he is. He wants to stay as he is, and he returns again and again to his folly. "As a dog returns to his vomit, so a fool repeats his folly" (26:11, *TLB*).

It is best to avoid this kind of a person. Don't spend time with him. "Be with wise men and become wise. Be with evil men and become evil" (13:20, *TLB*). To be blunt, he is a menace. He is like a loose cannon. If you want to waste your time, spend it with a fool. "If you are looking for advice, stay away from fools" (14:7, *TLB*).

The second Hebrew word is used 19 times in the book of Proverbs. It suggests stupidity and stubbornness. This word is darker or more serious than the first. How do you identify a fool? It is easy. As this verse suggests, as soon as he opens his mouth, he gives himself away. "Even a fool is thought to be wise when he is silent. It pays him to keep his mouth shut" (17:28, *TLB*). He quarrels. Boy, does he quarrel. He doesn't use any restraint or self-discipline. He just goes for it, regardless. "It is an honor for a man to stay out of a fight. Only fools insist on quarreling" (20:3, *TLB*)

The last Hebrew word occurs just three times in the book of Proverbs. It is similar to the others, except for adding the quality of being a bore. The fool is a person whose mind is closed to God as well as to reason. That doesn't leave him with much, does it?

Keep one characteristic in mind about the fool. He hates learning, clear and simple. It is not for him. "'You simpletons!' she cries. 'How long will you go on being fools? How long will you scoff at wisdom and fight the facts?'" (1:22, *TLB*). Give him a warning sign and it doesn't register. He won't learn from what you say or do for him. "Wisdom is a fountain of life to those possessing it, but a fool's burden is his folly"

(16:22, *TLB*). He knows it all. He is right. Don't confuse him with the facts! "A fool thinks he needs no advice, but a wise man listens to others" (12:15, *TLB*). He just won't respond.

"Wisdom is the main pursuit of sensible men, but a fool's goals are at the ends of the earth!" (17:24, *TLB*). For any family to get along they have to have good healthy communication. That involves controlling two things: the tongue and the temper. James talks about the problem graphically:

> But no human being can tame the tongue. It is always ready to pour out its deadly poison. Sometimes it praises our heavenly Father, and sometimes it breaks out into curses against men who are made like God. And so blessing and cursing come pouring out of the same mouth (Jas. 3:8-10, *TLB*).

The fool knows no limits. He violates boundaries. Self-control is a dirty word to him. "A rebel shouts in anger; a wise man holds his temper in and cools it" (Prov. 29:11, *TLB*). What he says weighs heavily on those around him. "A rebel's frustrations are heavier than sand and rocks" (27:3, *TLB*).

This person is an out-and-out troublemaker. He loves to quarrel. "It is an honor for a man to stay out of a fight. Only fools insist on quarreling" (20:3, *TLB*). He expresses everything without regard to the effect it may have on others.

Some people know when to speak and when to shut up but not the fool. It never crosses his mind to be quiet and gain from it.

The fool is a classic gossip. He loves to talk about others, whether the information is true or not. He has an opinion for everything; he is a self-proclaimed expert. "The wise man is glad to be instructed, but a self-sufficient fool falls flat on his face. To hate is to be a liar; to slander is to be a fool" (10:8,18, *TLB*).

What he says will bring him down. It will ruin him. "His mouth is his undoing! His words endanger him" (18:7, *TLB*).[11]

Have you ever taught these principles and guidelines from

Proverbs to your children? It could make a difference. Wisdom, however, goes further than just learning.

> WISDOM...IS THE ABILITY TO DISTINGUISH BETWEEN RIGHT
> AND WRONG, LYING AND TRUTHFULNESS, WHAT IS BEST
> RATHER THAN EXPEDIENT.

The wise person in Proverbs is also wise in his relations with others, actively involved in upholding the standards of righteousness, justice, and equity. These are interpersonal, relational values that assume the importance and commitment of doing what is right, just, and fair to those God brings across our paths. Apparently, moral skillfulness is not just a private affair of individual character alone, but also delves into the dirty mess of social responsibility.[12]

Wisdom also means being discerning about what you hear in life from politicians, leaders, television ads, marketing ploys and newspaper reports. It is the ability to distinguish between right and wrong, lying and truthfulness, what is best rather than expedient.

Too many today reflect the opposite pattern. "The naive believes everything, but the prudent man considers his steps" (Prv 14:15, NASB).

The Hebrew word for *simple* or *naive* presents the idea of "openmindedness" or inexperience that leaves a person open to being conned. One writer describes the naive as "a person of undecided views and thus susceptible to either good or bad influences."

Simple people are way too trusting. They are gullible and believe just about anything. They lack a discerning spirit. The Bible says they like the way they are. Proverbs asks the question, "How long, O simple ones [open to evil], will you love being simple?" (1:22, AMP). Perhaps the reason is they rarely consider the consequences of what they do. They enjoy being openminded. They also lack good moral sense. They're lousy judges of character, and they often develop friendships with others like themselves. They can't seem to recognize evil. "A prudent man sees the evil and hides himself, but the simple pass on and are punished (with suffering)" (Prv 22:3, AMP).[13]

Having wisdom doesn't mean being an isolationist. To live righteously from the perspective of the wisdom literature is not to be a monk, isolated in a cave somewhere. It is to be where the action is, in the mess and stench of life, engaging and enhancing the lives of others because that is what godly living in a fallen world means.

Fearing the Lord Provides Wisdom

Where does wisdom begin or how does a person become wise? It begins with one simple step—fear of the Lord. Look at some of the following passages from Proverbs:

Do not be wise in your own eyes; fear the Lord and shun evil (3:7).

The fear of the Lord adds length to life, but the years of the wicked are cut short (10:27).

A wise man fears the Lord and shuns evil, but a fool is hot-headed and reckless (14:16).

He who fears the Lord has a secure fortress, and for his children it will be a refuge (14:26).

The fear of the Lord is a fountain of life, turning a man from the snares of death (14:27).

Better a little with the fear of the Lord than great wealth with turmoil (15:16).

The fear of the Lord teaches a man wisdom, and humility comes before honor (15:33)

Through love and faithfulness sin is atoned for; through the fear of the Lord a man avoids evil (16:6).

The fear of the Lord leads to life: Then one rests content, untouched by trouble (19:23).

Humility and the fear of the Lord bring wealth and honor and life (22:4).

Blessed is the man who always fears the Lord, but he who hardens his heart falls into trouble (28:14).

Charm is deceptive, and beauty is fleeting; but a woman who fears the Lord is to be praised (31:30).

The fear of the Lord is not the kind of fear most of us think of when the word is mentioned:

Initial fear is not what the Old Testament means by the "fear of the Lord." In fact, when Moses tells the people what God has revealed to him, he explicitly says "do not fear." Moses wanted them to know that they need not fear as if they faced something unknown or unpredictable (the root cause of fear in pagan religions), but to live in sober awareness of who God is.

The Hebrew fear of the Lord was to be unique. In pagan religions people live in constant fear of the spirits which they must seek to appease...Israel's fear of God was rather an awesome realization that the holy God had turned to them and had chosen them to be his people...So fear was not primarily an emotion, but a way of life based on a sober estimate of God's presence and care. Such an attitude includes emotion, but so far from being a disintegrative force, this fear leads to life and satisfaction.[14]

Fear is a healthy recognition of who God is and His presence in our lives. It also necessitates a response on our part to who He is and what He has done for us. It is a submission to who God is and who is really in charge of our lives. His commands and His presence in our lives is for our benefit. "So the Lord commanded us to observe all these statutes, to fear the Lord our God, for our good always and for our survival, as it is today" (Deut. 6:24, *NASB*). Wise people recognize who is in charge of their lives.

You can't force children, however, to live "in the fear of the Lord." They must choose to do so on their own. This is clearly shown in Proverbs.

My son, *if* you will receive my sayings,
And treasure my commandments within you,
Make your ear attentive to wisdom,
Incline your heart to understanding;
For *if* you cry for discernment,
Lift your voice for understanding;
If you seek her as silver,
And search for her as for hidden treasures;
Then you will discern the fear of the Lord,
And discover the knowledge of God.
For the Lord gives wisdom (2:1-6, *NASB,* italics added).

A wise person never stops looking for more truth and wisdom. "A wise man will hear and increase in learning, and a man of understanding will acquire wise counsel" (1:5, *NASB*). "Wise men store up knowledge" (10:14, *NASB*). "The mind of the prudent acquires knowledge, and the ear of the wise seeks knowledge" (18:15, *NASB*). When people stop studying and learning, they stagnate.

Men don't like to hear criticism about themselves. They especially don't like books or seminars that put responsibility at their feet and say they need to change. Perhaps the reason they hear so much about this is their inborn tendency to be defensive, coupled with the fact that many men never (and I mean, never) read a book about marriage or parenting. They base many of their responses on what they saw in their family of origin. Unfortunately, that's not enough. Frequently the wife continues to read and grow. Soon she outdistances him by what she knows, but too often her husband turns a deaf ear to what she says. This is unfortunate. *If God has called a man to lead, it also means reading, learning and growing.* Don't expect your children to do so unless they have a role model to follow.

This leads into another characteristic of people of wisdom. They know they can be wrong and admit it, and they're open to correction.

They way of a fool is right in his own eyes, but a wise man is he who listens to counsel (12:15, *NASB*).

Reprove a wise man, and he will love you, give instruction to a wise man, and he will be still wiser (9:8,9, *NASB*).

It is a badge of honor to accept valid criticism (25:12, *TLB*).

A man who refuses to admit his mistakes can never be successful. But if he confesses and forsakes them, he gets another chance (28:13, *TLB*).

When children see a parent following the advice given in these passages, they have a healthy model and your children will be more open to following God's Word in this difficult area of choosing wisdom instead of foolishness.

Notes

1. J. Otis Ledbetter and Kurt Bruner, *The Heritage* (Colorado Springs: Chariot Victor, 1966), p. 27.
2. Ibid., pp. 60-64, adapted.
3. Ibid., pp. 64,65.
4. Ibid., pp. 61-88, adapted.
5. Tim Kimmel, *Legacy of Love* (Portland, Oreg.: Multnomah Press, 1989), pp. 219,220.
6. Ibid., p. 215.
7. Ibid., pp. 199-201, adapted.
8. John Trent and Rick Hicks, *Seeking Solid Ground* (Colorado Springs: Focus on the Family, 1995), pp. 58-60, adapted.
9. Robert Hicks, *In Search of Wisdom* (Colorado Springs: NavPress, 1995), p. 25.
10. William Dyrness, *Themes in Old Testament Theology* (Downers Grove, Ill.: InterVarsity Press, 1979), p. 197, adapted.
11. Hicks, *In Search of Wisdom*, pp. 194-200, adapted.
12. Ibid., p. 18.
13. Ibid., p. 19.
13. Ibid.
14. Dyrness, *Themes in Old Testament Theology*, p. 162.

WHAT ARE THE QUALITIES OF A BALANCED CHILD?

By H. Norman Wright

It is not only the old who are wise, not only the aged who understand what is right.

—JOB 32:9

What are the qualities of a growing, strong, wise child? What should you look for as your child develops? Your goal is rearing children to the best of your knowledge and capabilities, so they become independent, responsible, mature and reflect the qualities of their Savior. Our calling as parents is to help our children develop in all areas of their lives. Could you identify the qualities of a mature, responsible young adult? Consider the following.

A Growing Child's Mature Qualities

FRUSTRATION TOLERANCE

A growing child will have good *frustration tolerance* and be able to maintain emotional control during frustrating situations and upsets. Parents will avoid rescuing him from frustrating experiences, so he can develop strategies and capabilities to cope with life.

TASK PERSISTENCE

A growing child will develop good *task persistence*. She learns to hang in there when working on a goal. She doesn't rely upon simplistic reasons for stopping to do something such as "it was boring" or "it's too hard" or "it wasn't any fun." Parents of these persistent children have learned to be consistent in keeping their children at a task and refrain from taking over and completing the job themselves. They avoid being rescuers.

PROBLEM-SOLVING SKILLS

A growing child will have good *problem-solving skills*. He has developed this because his parents have resisted removing problems from his life. They are aware of the problems confronting a child, but observe rather than interfere, teach rather than bail out. This kind of child has learned to develop alternatives and then to select one that is workable. Underdeveloped children usually have one option, and often it is aggression.

Research indicates that children who do better in school get along better with others. What kind of home environments do good problem solvers come from? It is more likely they come from a family environment that is more similar to an authoritative style of parenting rather than permissive. This is a home in which there is a healthy pattern of control, the rules are well defined and reinforcement is consistent—*consequences are explored and explained.* Democratic decision making is also a part of the process. The child is encouraged to be independent from an early age according to his or her ability.

The following Driving Agreement is an example of how this was carried out with an adolescent. In this family the daughter would be driving in a few months, so the parents developed and agreed upon a driving contract. It was helpful to them to develop the standards prior to a significant transition in the young daughter's life.

This agreement also cleared the air, so that each person knew what was expected from each family member. This covenant contained restrictions and freedoms and was reviewed every six months to see how it was working and to determine which areas should be revised. The daughter was given time to consider what she thought should be contained in the agreement and then submitted her suggestions to her parents. The parents offered what they felt should be contained in the agreement and then they discussed, negotiated and created their own standard or agreement. When it was finalized, both parents and daughter signed and dated the form, indicating their willingness and commitment to follow the covenant.

Here is the sample covenant that was worked out with the 15-and-a-half-year-old girl and her parents. This is not being shared as one that every parent should follow, but just as an example:

Driving Agreement

1. Before using either car, I will ask either my mom or dad if I can use the car and explain the purpose.
2. If I want to go somewhere for myself, my homework and piano practicing must have been completed thoroughly.
3. During the first six months of driving with my own driver's license, the radio will not be used while driving.
4. During the school year I will be allowed to drive to church on Wednesday nights but cannot take anyone home without prior permission.
5. I will not allow anyone else to use the car under any circumstances.
6. I will be allowed up to thirty-five miles a week and after that must pay for any additional mileage.
7. I will not carry more than five passengers at any time in the Plymouth nor more than three in the Audi.
8. Upon receiving my driver's permit I will be allowed to drive to church and run local errands when either Mom

> or Dad is along. I will assist in driving for extended periods
> of time on our long vacations under all types of driving
> conditions.
> 9. I will not give rides to hitchhikers under any conditions
>   nor will I accept any ride if I should have any difficulty
>   with the car.
> 10. I will either wash the car myself or have it done once
>   every three weeks.
> 11. I will pay half the increase of the insurance costs and in
>   case of an accident I will assume half the deductible cost.

Perhaps this contract could serve as a model for your own situation. It could be changed and adapted for your use. The teenager should have the first opportunity to share her ideas, then the parents, then negotiate.

More than half the items on this list were suggested by the daughter. The word "thoroughly" was added to rule number two by her parents. The dad added rule number three, which was her least favorite one, but one the daughter said she could live with. The reason for the rule was too many times a radio is distracting and often played too loudly.

Driving is a serious privilege and responsibility. When the child is just learning to be on her own, she needs to give her full attention to what she is doing to perfect her skills. Police officers and insurance agents have agreed with this concept. Rule eight indicates a latitude and freedom for her driving experience. This family traveled a great deal in the summer and her parents wanted her to have the experience of driving under varied highway, traffic and weather conditions, so she would be better equipped when on her own.

Even before this covenant was agreed upon, this daughter had earned half the increase of the insurance rate by helping paint the family home.

Some have asked about the consequences should these rules be broken. The father in this case said that nothing had been agreed upon specifically, for two reasons. They as parents were willing to invest trust in their daughter to the extent that they would expect her to live up to the agreement. If, however, there was a violation, the consequences would be discussed with her and she would be asked three questions: Why do you think you did what you did? What will you do the next time? What do you think should be the consequences for this violation of the covenant? She would be asked to provide two or three suggestions. Moreover, she would have sufficient time to think over these ideas and one of them would be selected.

As a parent you can assist your child in learning to be a *problem solver.*

MAKES PLANS

To me, *plan making* is essential. Of course, it will come easier with some personality types than others. Some will resist and react, but it is still possible for them to access the undeveloped part of their personalities. (More on this will be presented later.)

You could ask your child the following questions (adapted according to age):

What is your plan?

Is there anything else you can think of? Let's explore.

What is the first step you need to take?

What if this doesn't work? What then?

What will happen next?

What are the pros and cons of each plan you have thought of?

What are the possible outcomes?[1]

TAKES RISKS

A growing child is willing to step out to *take risks,* to learn the skills needed for new situations. This involves a willingness to risk failure and to be overwhelmed by it. Sometimes your child will succeed and sometimes not. She needs to be valued by you just as much in each situation. A child who doesn't feel capable will live a life of hesitating reluctance. Your belief in her and gentle encouragement may make the difference. Sometimes you may need to loan her your faith and hope because her own is lacking.

HANDLES ADJUSTMENTS AND PROBLEMS

A growing child does not avoid *handling the adjustments and problems* of life. What the child does avoid is the cop-out excuses such as blaming others, denial, escape, faking illness, forgetting, rationalization, etc.

BECOMES MORE INDEPENDENT

A growing child is continually becoming more independent because the parents have been allowing the child to experience life. As soon as the child is capable, the parents allow the child to do what was formerly done for him. Several years ago I was impressed with a wealthy couple who could have afforded servants and maids. When each of their sons reached their twelfth birthday, the boy became responsible for washing and ironing his own clothes. Both are very capable adults today.

Parenting Patterns

The following chart gives three possible parenting styles. The three numbers (0, 12 and 18) indicate the ages of the child as he grows into adolescence.

PERMISSIVE PATTERN

In the first example, we see that during the first 12 years the parents have used the permissive pattern of child raising. When the child becomes an adolescent, however, the parents notice the various changes and problems that occur at this age. The parents become alarmed and concerned. For the first time in the life of their child, they begin to impose restrictions and attempt to regain control. They are met with resistance and conflict, however, because the adolescent has not been accustomed to this new pattern. It is foreign to him.

RESTRICTIVE PATTERN
In the second example, the pattern is reversed. The parents have been restrictive (in a good sense) during the first 12 years, using proper techniques and methods. When the child becomes an adolescent, the parents allow more permissiveness and independence because the child is able to accept this and can function by himself.

Some parents follow the second chart too closely by being totally restrictive during the first 12 years and then suddenly allowing the child a great deal of freedom.

BLENDING OF PATTERNS
The third example indicates that this is a gradual, blending process including restrictiveness as well as teaching the child how to be responsible. Gradually the child is allowed more and more freedom and independence as he indicates that he is capable of behaving or functioning on his own. The parent, in a real sense, has learned how to "let go and let grow." But it is a step-by-step process.

	Three Parenting Styles	
0	12	18
Permissiveness (Independence)	Restriction	
0	12	18
Restriction (Independence)	Permissiveness	

0	12	18

Restriction   Independence

Dependence on Peers

Dr. Elizabeth Ellis suggests that adolescents who have been overly dependent upon their parents often transfer their dependency onto a peer. Ellis explains:

> Unable to manage a period of independence that would normally occur between childhood and the young adult years, these teenagers become emotionally "married" to someone at fourteen. By "married" I mean that they have at least daily contact, sometimes several times a day; they forsake all others in terms of dating or even close friendships; they are extremely jealous and possessive of each other; their mood rises and falls in accordance with how peaceful or stormy the relationship is with the other teen at that moment in time; and they become convinced that they cannot survive without each other. Parents often see these relationships as unhealthy but are powerless to intervene. The strength of the dependency upon the boyfriend or girlfriend is in direct measure a reflection of the strength or the dependency upon the parent.
>
> While attaching oneself to a boy or girl so intensely and so early may grant the teenager a measure of separation from her parent, this approach certainly has its hazards. By becoming "married" at such a young age, the adolescent misses out on mastering some of the developmental tasks of adolescence that need to be dealt with as well.[2]

Parents do have a calling to help their children become increasingly independent. That, however, often feels like a double-edged sword. The child may experience freedom and equality, but the parents may suffer separation and loss. Such growth can bring mutually supportive relationships and at the same time bring along in its wake a lifetime of conflict.

A Declaration of Independence

PREPARATION

I found a practical book a few years ago titled *Leading a Child to Independence*. The authors compared the growing independence of a youngster to America's Declaration of Independence. Independence is something that happens "in the course of human events." Because it is inevitable, we would be better off preparing for it and fostering it. As much as possible, parents need to be in charge of the process rather than be buffeted willy-nilly by the stormy winds of blustering rebellion.

> SOME FAMILIES WIND UP SUFFERING CASUALTIES IN THEIR OWN SMALLER VERSIONS OF THE REVOLUTIONARY WAR IN THE CHILDREN'S QUEST FOR INDEPENDENCE!

When parents do not let go, the entire family suffers consequences. One author said, "It leaves emotionally crippled parents living their lives through emotionally crippled children who then feebly try to perform as adults while avoiding the responsibilities of determining the destiny of their country, offspring, and society. The results are a loss of independence for all—past, present and future."[3]

DISSOLVING BONDS

Another phrase in the Declaration of Independence states that it becomes necessary "for one people to dissolve the political bonds which have connected them with one another." Sometimes a child decides that it is time to leave home. Sometimes the parent reaches that conclusion first. Each party holds the power to make the decision. When it is implemented properly, the bonds can dissolve in a way that is congenial and healthy.

SEPARATION

The Declaration goes on to say that independence is a *separate and equal* station or position in life. For a while, our country was politically and economically dependent upon England. We needed the security and protection of an established power, but America gradually grew to desire a life of its own. England naturally wanted to protect this budding colony. Because it was unwilling or unable to let go, the bloody and costly American Revolution had to be waged to sever the bonds. Unfortunately, some families wind up suffering casualties in their own smaller versions of the Revolutionary War in the children's quest for independence![4]

Examples of Moving Children Toward Independence

Here is the story of how one set of parents, Paul and Jeannie McKean, helped their children move toward independence:

> As the children got older, we began studying Scripture together....Then we started to talk about their quiet times and the things we were learning in our walks with the Lord. From our journals we shared what the Lord was teaching us. If we had a hard week, we felt free to talk about it and soak up the affirmation of our family. We took our concerns to the Lord in a spirit of oneness.
>
> We also helped Tanya and Todd develop goals for their own lives. In 1983, we became familiar with Master Planning Associates, which helped us consider questions

such as "What are you dreaming of accomplishing five to twenty years from now?" Or "What needs do you feel deeply burdened by and uniquely qualified to meet?" We helped our children assess the milestones they had already passed and the ideas they would like to see become reality. We talked about colleges and careers and our purpose in life. Together we were able to dream dreams, some of which have already come true.

As the children became more independent, Paul and I let them organize some of the family days. Each of the four of us planned one Sunday each month. Todd's favorite activity was cross-country skiing; Tanya enjoyed relaxing at Dana Point Harbor.

One of the most practical things we did during our family times was talk about events to come. Each week we got out the calendar, looked at the commitments, and then planned the rest of the week. When the children were little, they were most interested in free time for play; but little by little their activities began to match ours. Looking at the calendar together has helped us take an active interest in one another's lives and avoid the miscommunications which plague busy families. Therefore we were better able to pray for each other and to understand the pressures and opportunities we shared.[5]

When asked about her parents' approach in helping them grow toward independence, Tanya replied: "My parents have made a lot of decisions for me and yet have made me make a lot of decisions. They have given me freedom when I've shown I can handle it responsibly—and even when I haven't been responsible, just to let me know I'm an individual who has worth and importance. I know now that I am quite intelligent and I can make decisions. Later on I will become responsible in certain areas that I might not be doing well in right now."

Todd also expressed his appreciation:

As I look back, I know my parents have really cared about our lives and what we've been interested in. They haven't said "Kids, we're going to do this because your father and I want to do this," or anything like that.

They consulted us about activities we wanted. We spend at least an hour or two doing something with our parents each weekend—different kinds of activities that kids usually do. My dad and I got a little airplane that we put fuel into, and we held it by a string as it flew around in the air. We also got interested in train sets and spent some of our activity time on them. That was really fun! I know most of my friends' parents never took time for special activities with them; so I feel that really shows my parents' interest in my life.[6]

Bart Campolo in a letter to his father, Tony, reflected on how his parents helped him grow. He talked about freedom:

That's what real freedom is, I think: the understanding that in a world filled with choices and decisions, under tremendous pressure from other people and our own desires, amid the paralyzing fear of mistakes or failure, loving God and loving His people are the only things that really matter, and doing those things is a decision that we genuinely have the ability to make in every situation.

You and Mom didn't let me do whatever I wanted to, Dad, but you gave me my freedom nonetheless. I think I finally appreciate it.

Love,
Bart[7]

What can parents do to help their children grow, mature and become independent?

Parenting Approaches

ARCHITECT-PARENTS

Fact: We can guide our children. *Fallacy:* We can control and shape their lives the way we want them to turn out. I have seen parents so obsessed with having their children become what they wanted that they are still pursuing this exercise in futility when that child is in his or her thirties! These parents remind me of an architect.

Have you ever seen an architect at work? He goes to the drawing board and, in very intricate detail, designs the end product, whether it be a new home or a shopping mall. There are still parents who believe they are totally responsible for what the child becomes. Architect parents mentally design all aspects of their child's life, including the end product. They have a very clear and definite picture of what they want their child to become. They carefully dictate and control their child's activities, choices and relationships. They screen what he is exposed to and make sure he plays and socializes with the "right" children. The words "ought" and "should" are frequently heard in this family.

We all have the tendency to mold our children to match the design we have for their lives. If their unique tendencies threaten us, we try to make these differences disappear. Basically, we are comfortable with others who are like us. Thus we unwittingly attempt to fashion our children into a revised edition of ourselves. We want them to be created in our image, but that puts us in conflict with God who wants them to be created in His image.

It is very easy to abuse parental authority by compelling children to deny their individuality and conform to behaviors which violate their identity. As parents, one of our great challenges and delights is to honor our child's uniqueness and accept what cannot be changed in him. We are called to guide them, not remake them.[8]

A modified architectural approach can be used as long as the plans are very flexible and custom designed to fit the child.

EXPLORER-PARENTS

Because 1992 marked the 500-year anniversary of his arrival in America, Christopher Columbus filled the news. When we think of explorers, his name often comes to mind, along with the pioneers of the seventeenth and eighteenth centuries in this country. Such people are risk takers.

Those who become parents take on the role of an explorer as well, whether they want to or not. To properly teach, guide, encourage or nurture their children, parents must patiently observe and study each child to discover his or her unique personality traits and learn each one's characteristics. The better parents know those, the better equipped they will be to prepare the child for life.

The same process of exploration happens when two people marry. The amount of new information to discover and process can be literally overwhelming at times. The spouses who put in the necessary time and energy to explore their partner's uniqueness have a much better time adapting and adjusting and, consequently, enjoying marital fulfillment.

What is the role of explorers? They search and ask. They are inquisitive, but they learn in a way that doesn't violate the boundaries of others. Explorer-parents are in a good position to implement and encourage the maturity and independence of their children.

FARMER-PARENTS

Once many explorers or pioneers found what they were looking for, they gave up their search to become farmers. Parents can learn to make this role change as well. Farmers consider each plant variety unique: they don't force potatoes to be tomatoes, in other words.

Farmer-parents will recognize the uniqueness of each child and nurture that person to full maturity and fruitfulness. Likewise, a spouse will not attempt to make the partner conform to a former romantic interest or an ideal created in his or her imagination.

Many of my relatives own large farms in Minnesota, Iowa and South Dakota. They have all discovered the importance of timing, planting the right varieties, needing the proper soil and the essential ingredients to put into the soil. They also realize they cannot do it all themselves. Many farmers know that success at growing good crops is the result of a partnership.

> The idea of partnership in farming is a strong one. We realize that not much will happen if the farmer doesn't throw himself wholeheartedly into bringing crops to fruition. That's his responsibility, and all his efforts lead to a productive harvest. But, it is equally true that nothing happens at all if God doesn't do His part. The farmer works with an absolute dependence on God to provide sun and rain. Even the farmer who doesn't believe in God knows, too well, the limitation of his powers.

ALL THREE OF THESE MODELS—THE ARCHITECT, THE EXPLORER AND THE FARMER—PROVIDE AN ATMOSPHERE THAT FOSTERS GROWTH.

The active farmer wants pears to be pears, spinach to be spinach, avocados to be avocados and peas to be peas. He rejoices in the identity of what is planted and does everything to nurture each crop according to its own nature. While farmers are highly active in the nurturing of their crops, they must also learn to yield to circumstances over which they have no control. In the full knowledge of God's splendid grace, they sometimes face the inexplicable.[9]

In partnership with God, farmer-parents are able to empower their children to mature and release them to independence. They rely in large measure upon encouragement, and those who are encouraged usually develop confidence.[10]

All three of these models—the architect, the explorer and the farmer—provide an atmosphere that fosters growth. As parents diligently explore their children to discover their unique qualities and gifts, they are better able to cultivate and nurture their individualities without forcing them to become something they are not. Spouses would benefit from following this approach with their partners as well.

Creating Life Experiences for Children

A growing child has a healthy sense of identity and accepts who he or she is in a healthy way. Often this is developed by creating a reservoir of life experiences. I am thankful for the way my parents made sure I had many experiences in life, such as earning multiple merit badges in Boy Scouts and learning how to help them repair and do upkeep on their three rental houses.

My parents helped me learn a variety of things. I learned how to care for animals such as dogs, cats, chickens and rabbits. They had me take piano and clarinet lessons (which led to a band scholarship at USC, which paid half the tuition!). My parents trusted me to learn and properly use a BB gun, a 22 rifle, shotguns, and took me on many trips. No, I didn't come from a wealthy home, but a hardworking frugal home where there was a belief that "you can learn to do it." We played and laughed a lot as well.

HANDLING EMOTIONS

A growing child is capable of handling the gamut of emotions we all experience. The older we become the more complex our emotions become. A child needs to learn to put a name to every emotion experienced, needs to discover their cause, what they mean, the destructive and constructive uses and how to properly express them.

A growing child is able to handle the stresses and especially the accumulation of stressful events.

CONCERN FOR OTHERS

A growing child has a concern for other members of his family and friends rather than just being concerned with his own needs. The parents expose their children to the needs and hurts of others in their community. They may take on a family to help at Christmas or all year long for that matter. Tony Campolo suggests the following:

> A family that puts happiness first cannot help but produce essentially selfish children. Happiness is a selfish goal. There must be a better way.
>
> As far as I am concerned, that better way is to redefine the family as a missionary team. What that means is that parents who want their kids to become bona fide Christian disciples have to communicate by example and experience that following Jesus involves more than a person's salvation.
>
> Practically, I think, that means that every member of a Christian family needs to understand that the primary purpose of that family is not to achieve economic prosperity or even happiness, but to love and serve God and meet the needs of other people.
>
> Every family needs a "reason to be" outside of itself and its own well-being. Kids need to see in their parents' lives that life is a gift from God which He means for us to pass along. When a family begins to understand itself as a missionary team, it becomes a creative entity, with members always on the lookout for a lonely person in need of a home-cooked dinner with friends, or a neglected kid who would love to come along on an outing, or an old person who needs help cleaning up the house. Kids develop a sense of compassion that offers their parents opportunities to help them discover how to express genuine

love and understanding to people in need. Spiritual gifts and personal strengths assert themselves and can be encouraged and confirmed. Mutual love becomes mutual respect.[11]

REALISTIC GOALS
Growing children have realistic goals. They are able to look to the future and continue after a goal. They may experience setbacks, but they find alternative ways to pursue what they want to obtain. They want to move forward.[12]

Developing Effective Parenting Styles

For children to become mature and become more like Jesus in all ways, what kind of parenting style will help to accomplish this?

In another chapter, we talked about the characteristics of a healthy family. Perhaps what is said here may repeat what was expressed, but will also expand what is needed in the family.

Studies of children who are successful and competent at life skills (and who have a faith that works) tend to have parents (or a parent) who have some of the following characteristics.

EXUDE WARMTH
The parents of competent children create a home characterized by warmth. How do you define warmth? Expressions of love, affection and affirmations of a child's worth. It means sitting down with a child and helping her understand her value in not only her parents' eyes, but also in God's eyes.

One parent spent time sharing with her child the following thoughts for months until the child realized the significance of what these words meant for her life. This parent thought sharing this thought and the following can help all people realize they have value:

Our understanding of who God is and how He wants to

bless our lives is enriched when we realize that He is committed to performing good in our lives. It says in God's Word: "Surely goodness and love will follow me all the days of my life, and I will dwell in the house of the Lord forever" (Psalm 23:6); "I will make an everlasting covenant with them: I will never stop doing good to them...I will rejoice in doing them good and will assuredly plant them in this land with all my heart and soul" (Jeremiah 32:40-41).

A few years ago, I heard a choir sing an anthem based on Zephaniah 3:17. I had never heard the song before. The words were printed in our church bulletin, and I have read them many times since because they encourage me, inspire me and remind me of what I mean to God.

And the Father will dance over you in joy!
He will take delight in whom He loves.
Is that a choir I hear singing the praises of God?
No, the Lord God Himself is exulting over you in song!
And He will joy over you in song!
My soul will make its boast in God,
For He has answered all my cries.
His faithfulness to me is as sure as the dawn of a new day.
Awake my soul and sing!
Let my spirit rejoice in God!
Sing, O daughter of Zion, with all of your heart!
Cast away fear for you have been restored!
Put on the garment of praise as on a festival day.
Join with the Father in glorious, jubilant song.
God rejoices over you in song![13]

God is patient and available. He has chosen to spend time and attention on you (2 Peter 3:9).

God is kind and gracious on your behalf. He has chosen to bring help and intervention into your life (Psalm 103:8).

God will work all things for your good. God desires to give you His support and encouragement. You can trust Him (Romans 8:28).

God values you as His child. He is constantly affirming and building you up. You have value because He created you and because you are in Christ (John 1:12).

God has included you in His family. You now belong to Him (Ephesians 1:4-5).

God desires intimate fellowship with you. You are valuable and priceless in His eyes (Revelation 3:20).

God loves you just as you are. You don't have to try to earn His love (Ephesians 2:8-9).

God accepts you regardless of your performance. He sees who you are more than what you do (Psalm 103:8-10).

God forgives you for your sins and failures and does not hold them against you. You can be trusted to do right and to come to Him when you've done wrong, knowing that He has chosen to forgive you (1 John 1:9).

God is just, holy, and fair. He will treat you fairly and, when He disciplines you, it will be done in love and for your own good (Hebrews 12:5-8).

God is reliable and is with you always. He will stick by you and support you (Lamentations 3:22-23).[14]

MAKE RULES CLEAR

Competent children come from a home in which there is firm control over major issues. The child can explain what the rules are, understands them, and knows their purpose as well as consequences for infractions. The parents provide reinforcement along with discussion of what infractions happened as well as what they expect from their child the next time. Listen to what Jack and Judith Balswick say about this parenting style:

> While some parenting styles encourage growth and are empowering, others hinder or block growth either by fostering dependency or by expecting self-reliance prematurely.
>
> Early attempts to understand parenting styles made a distinction between *permissive* versus *restrictive* parenting. Proponents of the permissive style, while not rejecting the need for discipline, stressed that a child's greatest need is for warmth and security. Those holding to the restrictive style, while not rejecting parental affection, emphasized that a child's greatest need is for discipline, responsibility, and self-control.
>
> In hundreds of studies done on parenting styles over the last thirty years, two factors—parental control and parental support—have emerged as the most important elements in good parenting. The term *parental control* means that you, as a parent, actively provide guidelines, set limits, direct and redirect your child's behavior in some desired direction. The term *parental support* refers to the affirmation, encouragement, and general support that you give to assure your children that they are accepted and cared for.
>
> Some parents are great at teaching right behavior but not so good at following through in their own lives. In effect they tell their children, "Do as I say, not as I do." Children will understandably feel resentful when parents fail to live by the standards they preach. Children recognize

the incongruence and may be disrespectful or rebellious when parents make demands.

On the other hand, parents who model right behavior but never provide explanations and good reasons for the values and beliefs they hold are also lacking appropriate skills. It is important that parents guide, equip, and empower their children by taking time to give the *whys* of the behavior they expect from them. It's balance we're looking for, perhaps best described as a disciplining role.[15]

Sometimes the way our children respond can be an insight into what we have taught. We never know how what we do will affect them.

A pastor one Sunday told the story of backing his car out of the garage and hearing a snap. He stopped and discovered his favorite fishing pole had been left behind the car. It now was in two pieces.

He walked into the house and asked, "Who was using my fishing pole?"

"I was, Dad," his five-year-old son said.

"Look at it now," he said, holding up the two pieces. "What happened?"

"I was playing with it and set it against the garage door. I forgot to put it away."

The father realized it must have fallen down behind the car. He wasn't pleased, but neither was he going to cry over spilled milk—or broken poles.

"Well, thank you for telling me," he said quietly and went back to the car.

As the pastor told his congregation: "I didn't think much more of it, but two days later, my wife told me that when she and our son were at Sears, he said, 'Mom, I've got to buy Dad a new fishing pole. I broke his other one.

Here's my money.' And he handed her his savings of two dollars.

"'That's nice of you to offer,' she said. 'But you don't have to do that.'"

"'I want to, Mom,' he said. 'I found out something. I found out that Dad loves me more than he loves his fishing pole.'"[16]

What kind of parent are you?

CREATE CONSISTENCY

The parents of competent children have a healthy level of emotional detachment and little to no enmeshment. A big factor is the aspect of consistency on the part of the parents. The child can both expect and rely upon each parent to be the same in terms of enforcing rules and doing what the child was expected to do. This pattern gives a sense of stability to the child.

DEMONSTRATE DEMOCRATIC DECISION MAKING

I don't know how you feel about the process of decision making, but a consistent finding in study after study of successful parenting is that democratic decision making is very effective. Children are invited to share their opinions and are encouraged to look at issues in different ways. The result is an ability to think for themselves.

Parents who hold back and contain their inclination to help, assist their children in becoming independent. Children are given household responsibilities appropriate to their ages.

TEACH SOCIAL SKILLS

The parents of competent children place a strong emphasis on teaching the children appropriate social skills. They are quite insistent that the children abide by and incorporate guidelines at an early age. Respect, politeness and control of anger are musts in the child's life. Sibling interaction includes *no* verbal or physical abuse of one another.

ENCOURAGE NONCONFORMITY

One final element was mentioned by Dr. Elizabeth Ellis:

Lastly, many of these homes where we find healthy parents and healthy kids are homes where *nonconformity* is encouraged. It seems that the parents' emphasis on independence, self-sufficiency, and democratic decision making in the home also contributes in some way to helping these children march to the rhythm of their own drum. They are a bit rebellious away from home and often challenge authority figures. While teachers may be uncomfortable with this at times, children from these homes seem more imaginative and more capable of formulating original ideas. They are not as strongly swayed by peer pressure, but instead are guided by *inner values and principles.*[17]

Notes

1. Elizabeth M. Ellis, Ph.D., *Raising a Responsible Child* (Secaucus, N.J.: Citadel Press, 1996), pp. 78-80, adapted.
2. Ibid., p. 22.
3. Paul and Jeannie McKean, *Leading a Child to Independence* (San Bernardino, Calif.: Here's Life Publishers, 1986), p. 21.
4. Ibid., pp. 21-32, adapted.
5. Ibid., pp. 134,135.
6. Ibid., pp. 144,145.
7. Tony and Bart Campolo, *The Things We Wish We Had Said* (Dallas, Tex.: Word Publishing, 1989), p. 63.
8. Tim Kimmel, *Legacy of Love* (Portland, Oreg.: Multnomah, 1989), pp. 55,56.
9. Ralph Mattson and Thom Black, *Discovering Your Child's Design* (Colorado Springs: David C. Cook Publishing Co., 1989), p. 196.
10. H. Norman Wright, *The Power of a Parent's Words* (Ventura, Calif.: Regal Books, 1991), pp. 51-54, adapted.
11. Campolo, *The Things We Wish We Had Said*, pp. 179-182.
12. Ellis, *Raising a Responsible Child*, pp. 13-35, adapted.
13. "And the Father Will Dance." Lyrics adapted from Zephaniah 3:14,17 and

Psalm 54:2,4, arranged by Mark Hayes.

14. William and Kristi Gaultiere, *Mistaken Identity* (Grand Rapids: Fleming H. Revell, 1989), pp. 183-186, adapted.

15. Jack and Judith Balswick, *The Dual-Earner Marriage* (Grand Rapids: Fleming H. Revell, 1995), pp. 173-174, 179-180.

16. Marshall Shelly, "Helping those who don't want help," *Christianity Today* (1986), pp. 65,66, adapted.

17. Ellis, *Raising a Responsible Child*, p. 77.

PARENTING THE ANGRY CHILD

By Gary J. Oliver

A crushed spirit who can bear?
—PROVERBS 18:14

"How many times have I told you not to interrupt when I'm on the phone?"

"Christopher, I'm sick and tired of your leaving a mess all over the house. This may be hard for you to believe, but I'm not your personal maid."

"If the kids don't stop fighting, I'm going to commit myself."

"You are in real trouble now. Just wait till your Dad gets home."

"If I've told you once, I've told you a hundred times...don't take things out of this drawer without asking."

"I've had enough. If this happens again, you're going to be in serious trouble. I'm not kidding. I really mean it this time."

Have you ever heard parents make statements like these? Have you ever heard yourself make such statements? If you've been a parent for very long, you've experienced the kind of frustration and discouragement reflected in these comments. While it is true that children can be our greatest source of joy, they can also be our greatest source of frustration—especially when dealing with the emotion of anger.

Anger, a Horrifying Encounter with Our Worst Selves

Spiritual maturity can be measured in many ways. One of them is by the degree we are able to bring our emotions under the lordship of Christ and express them in constructive ways. One of the most significant challenges of parenting is to help our children understand the important role of emotions and help them develop healthy ways to express those emotions. Of all the God-given emotions, anger is the most challenging.

Anger can be one of the major bumps in the road to modeling a Christ-centered life for our children. Many Christian parents feel discouraged or defeated by the ways in which they deal with conflict and anger. The fact is that most parents see situations involving conflict and anger as something to be avoided. However, we've discovered that these kinds of situations present us with a unique opportunity to model for our kids the difference that Jesus Christ can make in a person's life and in a family.

Parents struggle more with their own anger than any other emotion. They also report a more difficult time knowing how to deal with their children's anger. Nancy Samalin has done a great job of expressing what I have heard hundreds of parents express and, quite frankly, what I have experienced as a parent:

For many families, home is a battleground, filled with constant bickering, shouting matches, and exhausting power struggles. Often, parents' complaints appear so frivolous they hardly seem worth the effort of doing battle over. Parents are amazed that they can go from relative calm to utter frustration in a few seconds. An uneaten egg or spilled juice at breakfast can turn a calm morning into a free-for-all. In spite of parents' best intentions, bedtime becomes wartime, meals end with children in tears and food barely touched, and car rides deteriorate into stress-filled shouting matches....Whatever its source, we often experience parental anger as a horrifying encounter with our worst selves. I never even knew I had a temper until I had children. It was very frightening that these children I loved so much, for whom I had sacrificed so much, could arouse such intense feelings of rage in me, their mother, whose primary responsibility was to nurture and protect them."[1]

"I've had it. I give up. I quit!" Steve said with a quiet desperation. "I've tried everything I can think of to help Trever with his anger, but nothing seems to work. The more I try to help him with his anger, the more he resists. I hate to admit it but the more he resists, the more frustrated I get. When my frustration reaches a certain point, I lose it. And then I feel guilty because I'm modeling the very thing I don't want him to do."

Steve is a sensitive and gracious man who loves the Lord, his wife and his children. He really wants to be a good dad. But all his life he has struggled with the emotion of anger. And he's not the only one. Both his father and his grandfather had problems dealing with their anger.

When Steve and Twila's first child was born, one of Steve's prayers was that he would be able to help his children learn how to deal with their anger. He didn't want to model for his kids what he had seen as a child. That's what has made his struggle with Trever especially frustrating and discouraging.

Most of the time, Trever is a positive little guy who is a joy to be around. But when he doesn't get his way or his little brother takes one of his toys, the good times are over. I don't know about you, but most parents I've talked with can easily relate to Steve's experience.

Of all the emotions God has given us, anger is usually the most difficult for parents to deal with, both in ourselves and in our children. Why? What's so unique about anger? To understand, we must begin by realizing that anger isn't the real problem. The real problem is that most of us don't understand what anger is and why God has given it to us. How can it be used constructively to achieve positive goals?

Anger: A Gift or a Time Bomb?

Why, of all the various emotions, has anger had such a bad reputation? Why do so many people have a totally negative view of it? Is all anger bad? Is being angry always a sin? Is it possible for the energy of this "enemy" emotion to be constructively redirected? Can anger be used to mobilize us rather than neutralize us? In what ways can this unwelcome and potentially destructive emotion be considered a gift rather than a time bomb?

Is your initial response to the word "anger" positive or negative? Whenever I ask that question at least 90 percent report that their initial response is negative. Most Christians view anger from an almost exclusively negative perspective. If we are going to be able to help our children understand and deal with this God-given emotion, we need to understand a few things about it.

1. ANGER IS A GOD-GIVEN EMOTION.

One of the most basic aspects of being a person is that we were created in God's image. This means every individual is an image-bearer. Even though God's image in man and woman has been damaged and distorted by sin, we are still image-bearers. Part of what it means to be made in God's image is that we, like God, have a variety of emotions and are able to experience the emotions of others.

One of these emotions is anger. From Genesis 4:5 through Revelation 19:15, the Bible has a lot to say about anger. In fact, in the Old Testament alone, anger is mentioned approximately 455 times with 375 of those passages referring to God's anger. The only emotion the Bible talks about more than anger is love.

What exactly is anger? Anger looks like different things to different people. People use many different words to describe the emotion of anger such as "rage," "fury," "wrath," "resentment" and "hostility." Webster defines anger as "emotional excitement induced by intense displeasure." Many experience anger as a strong feeling of irritation or displeasure.

2. ANGER IS A SECONDARY EMOTION.

Whenever you or your child experience the emotion of anger, it is always in response to another emotion or combination of emotions. Though many factors can contribute to our anger, we've found three primary causes: hurt, frustration and fear.

Hurt is often caused by something that has already happened—something in the past. When we are hurt, we feel vulnerable and open to more hurt. This is especially true of kids who are very sensitive. David and Daniel are eight-year-old twins. David is an especially sensitive little boy. His brother Daniel is also sensitive, but David has learned how to let things roll off of him.

One day David came home from school and stormed into the house steaming mad. "Perry was making fun of us on the bus. I hate him. If he does it again tomorrow, I'm going to hit him right in the face."

When their mom, Karen, asked Daniel his view of what had happened, he replied, "Perry makes fun of everyone. It's no big deal. If you just ignore him, he goes away." Both kids encountered the exact same situation with two different ways of responding. One made a negative interpretation and assumed the worst; the other made a positive interpretation and assumed the best.

David personalized what Perry had said and experienced hurt. The automatic defense mechanism most people use to protect against hurt is anger. When we get angry at someone, it tends to erect a wall between us; then we can hide behind that wall. The unhealthy expression of anger produces distance between individuals, and many people feel safer with that distance.

If we sit on our hurt, it can become bitterness and resentment that can flare up into aggression, rage and violence. That's what happened with Joseph and his brothers. Jacob's favoritism with Joseph (see Gen. 37) caused his brothers to be jealous. Have you ever experienced what it's like to know you are not as good as or loved as much as someone else? His brothers sat on their hurt feelings until the hurt grew to the point that they wanted to kill him. In Genesis 37:18, we read that "they plotted against him to put him to death" (*NASB*).

Frustration is an emotion that takes place in the present. We can become frustrated by blocked goals or desires or by unmet expectations. It is especially easy for children to experience frustration. Their young bodies are developing and at times they feel awkward. Their minds are developing and they are confronted with many things they don't understand. They can't stand back and weigh their current experience against a memory bank of previous similar experiences. The present is all there is.

> WHILE HURT DEALS WITH THE PAST AND FRUSTRATION DEALS WITH THE PRESENT, FEAR FOCUSES ON THE FUTURE—EVENTS THAT HAVEN'T YET HAPPENED.

Frequently the things that lead to the greatest frustrations have one main characteristic—they really aren't very important. Yet at the time, they appear to be of major significance. This is especially true with children.

Marsha had been working hard building a tower with her Legos. She was trying to balance a large section of blocks on top of a narrow tower she had erected, but it kept falling off. After the third try, Marsha threw the section across the room, frantically tore apart what she had already made and stormed out of the room saying that she was "never going to play with those stupid Legos again."

We need to examine our own lives and the lives of our children to identify frequent sources of frustration. What kinds of situations cause you to become frustrated? Do any specific individuals cause you more frustration than others? What situations or individuals have frustrated you this past month? When are you most vulnerable to experiencing frustration? How do you usually respond when you are frustrated?

While hurt deals with the past and frustration deals with the present, **fear** focuses on the future—events that haven't yet happened. Tom heard his seven-year-old sister coming up the stairs and thought it would be a great idea to hide behind the door and scare her when she walked into the room. When Lois walked into the room, Tom did a masterful job of jumping out from behind the door with a blood-curdling scream. Her first response was to scream. Her second response was to kick Tom and then run downstairs to "inform" her mom that Tom was being mean to her. Tom hadn't touched Lois, but when he activated her fear, she experienced the secondary emotion of anger, and he experienced a kick.

Many people associate fear with vulnerability and weakness. Some people, especially men and boys, find it less threatening to express anger than fear, so they respond to situations in which they are anxious or afraid by getting angry. When you or one of your children are experiencing the emotion of anger and aren't sure where it is coming from, ask yourself, *Is there something that I am afraid of that could be triggering my anger?*

3. ANGER WEARS MANY DISGUISES AND IT CAN BE HARD TO IDENTIFY.

Sometimes it's hard to tell when our children are experiencing anger. Anger can hide behind many different masks, especially with our kids. Anger can appear as criticism, silence, intimidation, hypochondria, numerous petty complaints, depression, gossip and blame, stubbornness, half-hearted efforts, forgetfulness and laziness. An important step in helping our children understand their anger is to study our children and discover the ways they experience and express anger.

4. ANGER IS ENERGY.

When we experience anger, our minds and our bodies prepare us to act. Anger involves physical and emotional energy. Since anger is energy, we can either spend it or invest it. We *can* help our children learn to harness and channel that anger-energy in healthy, positive and constructive ways. As your children learn creative ways to invest the God-given anger-energy, as they develop more effective anger management skills, as they learn how to approach anger from a biblical perspective, you will have helped them develop one of the most powerful sources of motivation available to humankind.

5. ANGER INVOLVES A PHYSICAL STATE OF READINESS.

When understood, the emotion of anger can provide tremendous energy to right wrongs and change things for the good. When it is misunderstood, anger can lead to negative, destructive actions such as emotional, verbal or even physical abuse and violence.

Unfortunately, many parents have bought into the myth that because anger is a powerful emotion, it can't be controlled and so must at all costs be avoided. They have been taught to deny, suppress, repress or ignore their anger. They have never understood this powerful emotion, so they have never learned to deal with it constructively. People talk about the dangers of anger. But the danger is not with the anger; the danger is in misunderstanding the emotion and not knowing how to make it work for us.

We can't always control when we *experience* anger, but with God's help, we can learn to control how we choose to *express* that anger. It's easy to confuse the emotion of anger with some of the unhealthy and irresponsible ways people choose to express it. For example, many parents and educators confuse anger and aggression, but they're not the same. Anger is an emotion; aggression is an action. Anger is often associated with rage, but there is an important difference: Rage is anger that is out of control.

When our children have been hurt or wronged, their first response is usually to experience anger. The next step is that their fallen human nature wants revenge. Anger can easily distort their perspective, block their ability to understand and thus limit their ability to see things clearly. Potentially, there are great benefits in allowing ourselves to experience and express anger. There are also, potentially, devastating consequences in allowing ourselves to be controlled by our anger.

6. ANGER IS ONE OF THE MOST DIFFICULT EMOTIONS TO ADMIT.

It's not too hard to say I'm worried or sad. It can be a bit awkward to say, "I'm depressed." But for most of us, admitting that we are angry is almost impossible—especially in evangelical circles. It's as if the admission suggests a lack of maturity or spirituality or self-control.

However, because anger is such a difficult emotion to admit, our kids need to hear us identify our anger, admit our anger and model what to do about it. One of Satan's most effective tools for imprisoning Christians is repressed and suppressed anger. I've worked with many good Christian leaders who wouldn't admit their anger. And yet it wasn't much of a secret; everyone around them knew it. Gaining victory over unhealthy expressions of anger is a powerful way for Christian parents to model the practical difference Christ can make in a life.

7. ANGER CAN BE HEALTHY OR UNHEALTHY.

When our anger is healthy, it is usually of moderate intensity and doesn't consume us. We are not overwhelmed by it. It helps us attain our goals. Unhealthy anger, on the other hand, tends to control us. It distorts our perspective, robs us of energy, blurs our focus and creates more turmoil.

In Christian circles, not enough has been written on the positive side of anger. Anger has tremendous potential for good. Anger can be a signal that something is wrong. Anger can alert us to the fact that we are in danger or that our rights are being violated. Anger can provide us with immediate energy to deal with a crisis or take constructive action to right a wrong.

For most parents the emotion of anger is considered negative, a problem, something to be eliminated or solved. What we so often fail to see is that every problem is really an opportunity in disguise—an opportunity to learn, to grow, to mature, to be used of God to make significant changes for the good.

If there is any place where our faith can make a visible difference, it is in the way we allow it to transform how we deal with anger.

Simple Keys for Helping Your Child Cultivate Healthy Anger

I've talked with many parents who wait until they are in the midst of a knock-down, drag-out anger episode with their children before they want to know what they can do when their child is angry. That's not the place to begin. The best time to help your children deal with their anger is before they become angry.

One of the most helpful things a parent can do is to normalize the emotion of anger. Talk about emotions with your children. Share your own emotions with them. Help your sons and daughters to understand what emotions are and where they come from. Make sure they know that emotions aren't good or bad, right or wrong.

Take the time to open the Bible and share what God has to say about this important emotion. Don't just read it to them, have them read it for themselves. You might share passages such as James 1:19,20, "My dear brothers, take note of this: Everyone should be quick to listen, slow to speak and slow to become angry, for man's anger does not bring about the righteous life that God desires," and Ephesians 4:26,27, "'In your anger do not sin': Do not let the sun go down while you are still angry, and do not give the devil a foothold."

It's natural for children to experience joy, surprise, delight, fear, hurt, frustration, disappointment, discouragement, depression and anger. Teach them how to identify and name their emotions. Ask them what they are feeling. Help them develop a vocabulary for their emotional life. This makes it easier for them to understand their own emotional life as well as talk about it with you.

Let your kids know that you are encouraged when they identify their anger. This suggests that they are growing in their understanding of their emotions. It indicates that they are learning how to deal with this powerful emotion in healthy ways.

Carrie and I have worked with each one of our three sons to help them name their emotions. One evening when we had company, our son Matthew came up and asked if he could talk to me. I excused myself from a conversation, lowered myself so that we were eye-to-eye and asked him what was up. He said, "Dad, I'm angry."

My first response was, "Thanks, Matt, I appreciate you letting me know." But as I said it, I realized that what I said might need a bit more clarification, so I added, "Matt, I'm glad that you know when you are angry and that you want to talk about it." His ability to identify and label his emotion made it much easier to help him deal with a difficult situation. Now he could express his anger in a constructive way rather than in a destructive fashion.

Go to the library and pick out books that talk about emotions. We've written a book specifically to help parents and children understand anger. *Hip Hop and His Famous Face* deals with a bunny named Hip Hop who lives in the Wonder Woods. All of the other animals like him, until he lets his anger take control of them. Then they want to stay as far away from him as possible. This story helps kids look through the eyes of Hip Hop to learn constructive ways for dealing with anger. Stories provide children with alternative ways to understand and deal with their own experience. Many children find it easier to learn from other children's (or an animal's) experiences than from an adult's experience.

Make sure that your home is a place where it is safe for your children to experience and express a wide range of emotions. Let them know that in your family, it is OK to be angry. At the same time, let them know that there are acceptable and unacceptable ways of expressing anger. Make sure they know what the unacceptable expressions are and what the consequences will be when they choose to respond in those kinds of ways.

Pray with your children about their emotions. Talk about their emotions with them and then thank God for the gift of emotions. Don't leave out the gift of anger. As you thank God for anger, thank Him for the specific positive things that can come from anger. If you have seen your child respond to anger in a positive way, thank God for what he or she is learning about his or her anger.

Make sure your child's environment isn't a setup for anger. Monitor nutrition and make sure your son or daughter gets plenty of rest. Be aware of your child's schedule and the pressures he or she faces. It's amazing how busy many children's lives can be. The challenges, the expectations and the demands continue to grow. Most of us are more vulnerable to frustration when we are tired. We can eliminate a lot of unnecessary frustration and pain from our families by making periodic environmental adjustments.

Study each of your children. When are they most likely to experience anger? What kinds of situations increase the probability that they will become angry? How do they usually express that anger? What is the most effective way to communicate with them when they are angry?

We've already talked about the importance of what we model for our children. Watch your verbal and nonverbal communication when you discipline them. What is your immediate reaction when your child has an angry outburst? If you are like most parents, you want to shut it down. I've heard countless parents, including myself, respond with statements such as, "You shouldn't be angry." "There's no reason to get mad." "I'm sick and tired of you arguing. If you don't stop it right now, I'm really going to get mad." What do those kinds of statements teach our children about anger?

Talk to your children about your own anger. When you are angry with your children or someone else say, "I'm angry." If you are angry with one of your children and are concerned that the emotion is controlling you rather than you controlling it, tell them that you need to take a time-out to process your anger. On several

> AVOID UNNECESSARY POWER STRUGGLES....
> EVEN IF WE DO WIN THE BATTLE...THEY [CHILDREN] CAN
> RETALIATE BY BECOMING SPIRITLESS, REBELLIOUS,
> DELINQUENT OR NEUROTIC.

occasions I've told one of my kids, "I'm experiencing a lot of anger right now, so I need to take a few minutes to cool down and think about it. I'm concerned that I might express it in ways that wouldn't be helpful. I'll be back in a few minutes and we'll talk about the consequences for what you've done."

Major on majors. Avoid unnecessary power struggles. Children have more time and energy to resist us than we have to force them into doing and responding exactly as we think they should. Even if we do win the battle and get them to do what we've asked, exactly the way we think they should perform, they can retaliate by becoming spiritless, rebellious, delinquent or neurotic.

Helping Your Children Understand and Deal with Their Anger

1. HELP YOUR CHILDREN BE AWARE OF THEIR ANGER.
Justin would not be considered an angry child. He rarely appears to be angry. One of the many myths regarding anger is that if a person doesn't look or appear to be angry on the outside, then he or she doesn't have a problem with anger; he or she is clearly not an angry

person. But while Justin does not appear to be an angry person on the outside, he is like a battlefield on the inside.

If he has had a difficult day at school, Justin is more quiet when he comes home and tends to isolate himself in his room. He is more likely to be negative and critical of everything and everyone. His mom has learned to watch for these symptoms. When she sees them, she knows that this is frequently the way Justin acts when he is angry.

How often are you aware of your children being angry? What situations do they encounter that might make them more vulnerable to anger? How do their bodies respond to anger? What are their physical manifestations of anger? How do they treat others when they are angry? What is unique about the ways in which each of your children experiences and expresses anger?

2. WHEN YOUR CHILDREN ARE AWARE OF BEING ANGRY, HELP THEM PROCESS THEIR ANGER.

When your children are feeling overwhelmed by strong emotions, it is tempting as parents to jump in and want them to get over it. This is especially true with the emotion of anger. Even the best parents are tempted to give their children advice and tell them what to do.

However, when our children are in the midst of powerful emotions, they have a hard time listening to anyone. The last thing our children want is advice or criticism; they want to be understood. They want us to understand what they are feeling. Many parents have found that simply taking the time to sit down and listen to the child is enough to release his or her angry feelings.

Make sure you pick the right time to talk with your children. Take into account their personality types. Most extroverts like to process things externally. They like to talk about things right away. Most introverts prefer to process things internally. They like to think about it before they talk about it. Being insensitive to your child's preferred way of processing anger could only increase frustration and thus increase his or her anger, making it more difficult if not impossible to deal with.

Eventually, you will be able to help your children develop other words for their anger. When one of your children says, "I'm angry," you can respond by asking, "Do you think your anger is from being afraid, hurt or frustrated?"

3. HELP YOUR CHILDREN ADMIT THEIR ANGER AND ACCEPT RESPONSIBILITY FOR IT.

Someone has said that one of the major effects of original sin is seen in our tendency to blame someone else for our problems. When God confronted Eve in the garden and asked her what happened, she blamed the serpent. When God confronted Adam, he first blamed Eve and then blamed God.

We live in a society of victims. Nothing is ever my fault; it's always somebody else's fault. When "everybody else" is responsible, then nobody is responsible. One of the characteristics of a godly person is the ability to take responsibility for his or her actions. If sin was involved, the person should confess it and seek to make it right. This is especially true with the emotion of anger.

We can teach our children that when we are angry, it is easy for us to blame someone else and say, "It's your fault; you made me angry." This is especially true with brothers and sisters. If your child has a brother or sister, that child has a built-in cause for all of his or her problems.

But as our children see us take responsibility for our anger, as they see us be angry and yet not sin, as they see us speak the truth in love, it is more likely that they will follow our example. Over time we can teach our children that though other people can say or do things that cause hurt or frustration, we are responsible for how we choose to respond. If we are angry, the anger is ours, and choosing how to express it is our responsibility.

4. HELP YOUR CHILDREN DECIDE WHO OR WHAT WILL HAVE CONTROL.

This is a very important step for both children and adults.

However, it's a bit more difficult for children. They haven't had the time to develop some of the discipline and control that we adults have. They don't have the understanding of consequences that we do. But this is their opportunity to learn discipline and control.

When our children become aware that they are angry, we can help them learn that they are faced with a choice. They can either allow the emotion of anger to dominate and control them, or they can, with the help of the Holy Spirit, choose to control the anger and invest the anger-energy in healthy ways.

A simple yet powerful response can be, "Honey, I can tell that you are feeling a lot of anger right now. It's OK to experience anger. I'm glad you're able to talk about your anger. It sounds like you've got some good reasons to be angry. Now you need to decide: Are going to let your anger control you, or do you want to control your anger? Do you remember what happened last week when you let your anger get out of control? Do you want that to happen again? Would you like me to pray with you to ask God to help you deal with your anger in a healthy way?"

Obviously, the way you talk to your children depends on how old they are and where they are in the process of their individual emotional development. But however you choose to express it, your children can be helped to understand that as soon as they are aware of their anger, they can and need to make a decision to either control their anger and deal with it constructively or let their anger get out of control and lead to more problems.

5. HELP YOUR CHILDREN IDENTIFY AND DEFINE THE CAUSE OR SOURCE OF THE ANGER.

Children get angry for many of the same reasons adults get angry. Anger is a normal response to all kinds of daily events that can produce fear, hurt and frustration. Be careful not to overreact to your child's anger. Remember that anger is a secondary emotion.

Ask yourself these questions: Where is the anger coming from? What's the real issue? What is his or her anger about? Often a child's anger is communicating a need that he or she may not be aware of. Your son or daughter may be frightened, sad, insecure or confused and it comes out as anger.

Once your child has become aware of his or her anger and has had time to cool down, it's often possible to begin exploring the cause of the anger. When you begin this process, your child may be clueless about what triggered the anger response. But as you talk about fears, hurts, insults, rejection and disappointments, the door of awareness and recognition will often open. Take time to explore what happened on that day or on the previous several days. Listen. Ask questions. Let your child ramble. As you take the time to understand, you will help your daughter or son understand themselves. At the same time, you will communicate your love, support and encouragement.

6. HELP YOUR CHILDREN CHOOSE THEIR RESPONSES AND DEVELOP THEIR OWN SOLUTIONS.

Anger can be dealt with in many ways. Some are constructive; some are destructive. Some of the destructive ways to deal with anger are to stuff, deny, suppress or repress it. One of the most destructive ways of dealing with anger is to ventilate it or dump it on someone else. Ventilating anger tends to increase rather than decrease it. That's why it is important for us to help our kids move from a "what's the problem?" mode to a "what can I do about it?" mode.

One way of initiating the sixth step might be to say, "Julie, now that you know your anger came from being frustrated with your brother, you can decide what you're going to do about your frustration. What would you like to do?"

As much as possible, allow children to develop their own solutions to their problems. You may have to prime the pump a bit more with younger children, but as they get older, they will develop their own wide range of responses to choose from. If Julie didn't have any ideas, you could say, "I can think of four different ways you can handle your frustration. If you want to hear them, I'd be happy to share them with you. Think about it and let me know."

7. HELP YOUR CHILDREN REVIEW THEIR RESPONSE TO THE ANGER.

This is a step that many parents leave out. For years I was one of those parents. After a couple of days have passed, ask your child what he or she learned about dealing with anger from what happened. What went well? What would he or she like to have done differently? What did he or she learn? What would he or she like to do next time?

This conversation doesn't need to take more than a few minutes. It should involve what the child learned and not what you as a parent think the child should have learned. This brief conversation can easily turn into a lecture; if that happens, you've undermined the process and robbed your son or daughter of a great learning experience.

Remember that learning how to understand and deal with emotions is a lifelong process. I know I'm still working at understanding and dealing with my own emotions, and so are you. It takes time, trial and error, but the product is worth the process. Encourage each little step your child takes. Congratulate your child whenever possible. Praise him or her for even making an effort in a healthy direction.

During those times, remember that Romans 8:28 is true. God can cause all things to work together for good—your disappointments, your discouragements, even your mistakes. In fact, the act of being open and honest about your own emotions can provide a powerful learning experience for your children. It lets them know that you are human. It shows them in practical ways that what you are telling them really works. When you show them that you can learn from your mistakes, they see that they can learn from theirs.

Before going on to the next chapter, take a couple of minutes to complete this quiz on each of your children. Then pick one specific thing you've read in this chapter that you can apply in the lives of your children during the coming week.

How Angry Is Your Child?

Child's Name: _____

The following inventory covers the more common signs of anger in children. All children occasionally manifest these signs, but if several of them are persistent or if your child evidences many of them, you may have a problem.

Rate each statement according to the following scale and enter the rating in the the appropriate space:

0 = My child never or rarely does this.
1 = My child occasionally does this (no more than once a month).
2 = My child often (once a week or so) does this.
3 = My child does this frequently (daily or several times a week).

Rating

_____1. My child blames others for his or her troubles.

_____2. My child throws or breaks things whenever he or she feels frustrated or irritated.

_____3. Whenever my child gets angry, calming him or her down takes a lot of placating.

_____4. My child does not like change of any sort and becomes angry when change is forced on him or her.

_____5. My child changes the rules of games when playing with other children.

_____6. My child says spiteful or hateful things whenever he or she is thwarted.

_____7. My child is negative, deliberately slow and resists doing what he or she is told to do to the point that discipline becomes a standoff.

_____8. My child seeks out arguments or reasons to become upset, even when everything is at peace.

_____9. My child ostracizes, scorns, and complains about others.

_____10. My child loses control when she or he is angry and shows it with facial expressions or body language.

_____11. My child uses foul language whenever he or she gets angry.

_____12. When my child is learning something new, he or she easily becomes frustrated and wants to do something else.

_____13. My child is stubborn and refuses to do what he or she is told to do unless you use the right tone of voice or approach.

_____14. My child's friends don't like to play with him or her because he or she is such a bad sport.

_____15. My child gets into fights with other children and has great difficulty controlling his or her temper when teased.

_____ Total Score

Test Interpretation

0-5 Your child is remarkably free of anger and is not prone to frustration. If anything, he or she may be a little too passive—but don't try to change this!

6-10 Your child is showing a normal degree of anger and irritation, but a higher score (nearer 10) is more appropriate for younger children (under 6) and a lower score (nearer 6) is more appropriate for older children.

11-15 Your child is beginning to show an above-normal degree of anger response. Again, a higher score is more appropriate for younger children. Some attention to your child's response may be needed.

16-20 Clearly your child has a problem with anger and should receive your attention.

Over 20 Your child has a serious problem with anger, especially if he or she is already of school age. Take immediate steps to help your child cope with his or her anger, and seek professional help, if necessary.[2]

Notes

1. Nancy Samalin, *Love and Anger: The Parental Dilemma* (New York: Viking Penguin, 1991), p. 5.
2. Archibald D. Hart, *Stress and Your Child* (Dallas, Tex.: Word Publishing, 1992), pp. 110,111.

16

NURTURING THE OPPOSITIONAL CHILD

By H. Norman Wright

*Fathers, don't aggravate your children. If you do,
they will become discouraged and quit trying.*

—COLOSSIANS 3:21, (*NLT*)

Years ago we moved into new offices. Just before we moved in, the owners of the building recarpeted the complex. For some reason, however, the initial carpet order was 20 yards short, so new carpet was laid in all the rooms except one until the second order arrived two weeks later.

When the final 20 yards were laid, I noticed something unusual. The carpet was the same brand, the same design and the same color, but it was just a shade off from matching the original order. When I asked the installer about it, he said that the dye lots of the two orders were different.

"Even though the company attempts to match the colors exactly when they mix a batch of new dye," he explained, "the dye lots are always just slightly different. It isn't noticeable until you put the two carpets side by side."

My experience with the carpets reminded me of how children in the same family can also be different. They are born to the same parents, reared in the same home and fed the same food, yet no two children—including identical twins—are completely alike.

The biological, neurological and metabolic makeup of each child is unique. The intellectual potential of each is different. Why? Because the combination of physical characteristics inherited from each parent is a bit different for each child. Furthermore, the family environment is different for each succeeding child born to the same parents. The first child is born into a family of two members: mother and father. The second child is born into a family of three: mother, father and older brother or sister. The family dynamics change with each new member.

Successive children in the same family are also different because the parents are continually changing. In addition, each child is stamped with God's unique design, making him or her different from every other child ever born.

To understand your children better, appreciate them more and communicate with them effectively, it is very important that you discover each child's uniqueness. As parents affirm each child's uniqueness, the children will find it easier to believe that God accepts them just as they are.

It takes a tremendous amount of time, wisdom and prayer to recognize and affirm the uniqueness of each child and help each one develop unique traits and abilities. Many parents don't realize how vital this process is to the child! A 20-year study of the behavioral development of 231 infants by Drs. Chess and Thomas emphasizes the importance. The study revealed that the interaction between parent and child affects how the child's unique abilities develop and how much tension exists between them. In her book *Your Child Is a Person*, Dr. Stella Chess reveals the key factor to a successful parent-child relationship is:

The goodness of fit between the parents and child. If the parent's expectations and demands were in accord with the child's own capacities and style of behavior, then the child enjoyed optimal development. If the parents didn't understand or appreciate a child's special qualities, problems did occur. Surprisingly, even divorce or the death of a parent was not as important as this basic "fit."[1]

How can you discover your child's uniqueness? The best response I can give is wait, watch and listen and keep track of your observations and discoveries. Ask yourself questions about your child, especially in the following discussed categories.

Discover What Motivates Your Child

What causes your child to move into action? Is he pushed from the inside or pulled from the outside? Does his energy come from within himself or from other persons and situations? Some children are pushed into action by their own ideas; they don't need any outside assistance. Other children are pulled into action by other people or some other outside factors. If you are going to understand your child's uniqueness and communicate with him effectively, you must learn what motivates him.

SELF-MOTIVATED
If your child is self-motivated, what forces are at work within him to move him to action? Explore the following possibilities:

- Logical ideas pressing to be executed;
- Intuitive perceptions that can be applied;
- Convictions to be expressed;
- Other?

Communicating with a self-motivated child is an art. It requires that you frame your statements as possibilities and suggestions instead of telling. This child responds better to subtle, indirect guidance than to direct information and instruction. Plant ideas in his mind with comments such as: "Could it be that you...?"; "Have you considered...?"; "Did you see the article that suggested...?" You will be surprised what your self-motivated child can do with a few well-placed hints.

PERSON-MOTIVATED

If your child is pulled into action by other people, under which of the following conditions does she most readily respond:

- A leader (teacher, friend, parent, peer) presents an opportunity;
- A leader presents conditions to be met;
- An authority or expert invites response;
- An inspiring person calls for commitment;
- A mentor provides guidance;
- A team provides guidance;
- A team provides a place;
- Peers provide support;
- Others will pay attention;
- Others will follow or give allegiance or loyalty;
- Other?

Perhaps your primary role as parent to a person-motivated child will be to teach her to discern the positive from the negative in other people. Your child may tend to respond to outsiders without thinking through their influence on her life. Your carefully stated questions will help the child consider the implications of her involvement with others.

MOTIVATED BY CIRCUMSTANCES

If your child is pulled into action by circumstances, which of the following conditions seem to influence her most strongly:

- There is opportunity to do better than someone else;
- A difficult task or feat beckons;
- Excellence can be demonstrated;

· Conflict can be engaged;
· Something can be collected;
· Money can be made;
· Abilities or skills can be developed;
· There is a possibility of winning;
· An adventure opens up;
· Something new can be built or developed;
· Changes can be made;
· Conflicts can be resolved;
· A discovery can be made;
· Order can be established;
· Some form of expression can take place;
· Performance is possible;
· Other?

Discussing your child's interests with her can help her become more aware of what motivates her. Giving her choices between activities will be important for her growth. As you discover what motivates her and you create these conditions, you may find that your child is more responsive to you.

MOTIVATED BY AN INNER TIMEPIECE

We all go through life at different speeds in response to our own inner clocks. Some of us race through life as if tuned to an inner stopwatch. Others of us plod through life carefully and methodically, following an inner calendar more than a clock. Our children also have their own unique pace of life. To understand your child's uniqueness and adjust to his pace, you need to find out what kind of timepiece governs his behavior.

A child who operates by an *inner stopwatch* doesn't waste much time. This child:

· Likes to finish a task at one sitting;
· Wants a project finished by the time the day is done;

· Can produce a lot in a short period of time;
· Likes immediate results and feedback;
· Can do things spontaneously.

A child who has an "average" *inner clock* uses a moderate amount of time for tasks. This child:

· Wants to take the "proper" amount of time;
· Takes adequate time to complete a task;
· Shows care and concern in performing a task;
· Prefers short-range tasks and goals.

A child who is tuned to an *inner calendar* requires a lot of time to complete his tasks. This child:

· Is careful and meticulous about his work;
· Processes and thinks through details;
· Cannot or will not allow himself to be rushed;
· Enjoys being precise;
· Is very thorough in covering every point;
· Wants to enjoy everything completely.[2]

The Right Ways to Approach a Child

When you are approaching a trout stream, the way you come up to it can make or break your day. If you stand upright, so the sun casts your shadow on the water, and if you make noise—don't expect much from the fish. You have spooked them. If you come up slowly, quietly, carefully and out of the sun, however, you have a chance. It is all in your approach.

If you go rushing up to a large dog in its territory, it may think you are an intruder and respond accordingly. If you stand still, let the dog come to you and sniff you, however, it will probably welcome you into its territory. Again, it is all in the approach.

In the same way, how you approach any child will make a difference. The author of *The Influential Parent* said:

> Your approach is like a passport. It allows you to travel outside of your personal world. Once inside someone else's world, you have an opportunity to introduce yourself with an appropriate role and message.[3]

The way you approach your child, above all else, needs to be positive, so your child feels positive about him- or herself, and why not? Any child is an object of God's love and created in God's image.

David Domico suggests four approaches:

BE TRUTHFUL

Any approach needs to be truthful. At times, a person may not appreciate the truth, but there is really no other option in which to build trust. The way truth is expressed, though, is important. Scripture has much to say about it:

> Instead, speaking the truth in love, we will in all things grow up into him who is the Head, that is, Christ (Eph. 4:15).

> Therefore each of you must put off falsehood and speak truthfully to his neighbor, for we are all members of one body (Eph. 4:25).

> Do not lie to each other, since you have taken off your old self with its practices (Col. 3:9).

The passage in Ephesians 4:15 means that when the truth is spoken, your relationship is cemented together better than it was beforehand.

BE TENDER

The second approach is to be tender. Others hear a soft concern statement. It reflects sensitivity and tolerance, as well as nurturing.

BE UNARMED

Have you ever considered approaching your child unarmed? Strange question, but consider it for a moment. We all have our arsenal of weapons we employ in relationships. Often we approach our child with our weapons ready to fire as if we were daring him or her to react in a certain way we won't like. Sometimes our expectations are a self-fulfilling prophecy because the child picks up on the fact that our arsenal is armed and our finger is on the hair trigger.

If you approach unarmed, you are open to hear and consider what is said. By keeping the communication flowing in a positive way, you will probably disarm your child as well. Remember this: You will have more influence and control when you approach unarmed rather than armed. If a child responds in an attacking manner, where did he or she learn this approach? If a child is defensive, where did he or she learn this?

Who is the one in your family who approaches others with the biggest arsenal of weapons? What does this accomplish? How do others respond to this? It is something to think about.

BE REASONABLE

The last one is the reasonable approach. Has your child or teen ever said, "Mom. Dad. Come on. Be reasonable." What are they asking for? Could it be fairness? Calmness? Openness? When your child is angry or upset, the tender approach is better than the reasonable. When emotional energy subsides, the reasonable works better.[4] This approach is best described by the author of *The Influential Parent*:

> Being reasonable does not mean being so objective that you eliminate empathy or a caring attitude. In this approach, you are working to stay open-minded to issues that may trigger

strong feelings of resistance. This may involve extra work on your part. At times a parent using this approach might say, "My initial reaction is to say no. That's because what you want to do makes me feel afraid for your safety. I need some time to sort out my feelings before we talk about this rationally. Otherwise I'm likely to say no without hearing you out completely." You may have to postpone a decision on something at a time when your child wants an immediate response. You may have to collect your thoughts before engaging your child in an emotional conversation. You may have to talk with someone else in order to sort out your feelings. You may have to listen to all of what they have to say before drawing a conclusion. A reasonable approach is one in which you are informed by your feelings but not controlled by them to the point that you become rigid and unyielding. In this approach there is always room for an appeal.[5]

The Oppositional Child

Children vary in many other ways as well. Some of their tendencies may alarm, frustrate, anger, disappoint, amaze or puzzle you. We all have our dream of the ideal child who should emerge from our unique gene pool. Some children, however, wind up being oppositional, anxious, sensitive, self-centered, depressed, deceitful, compliant, strong-willed, dreamers, etc. Many of you wonder why they are this way. You also wonder what is the best way to respond to this uniqueness! How do you encourage them to become more like Jesus? Let's consider one of these ways. The best description was given by Dr. William Lee Carter in *Child Think*.

UNCOOPERATIVE
One of the problems that emerges with parents and children is a power struggle each one wants to win. This can happen between

any parent and child, but it is especially likely to happen when you have an *oppositional child*. This is a child who seems to be in constant conflict with adults, and the word "cooperation" is not in her vocabulary. She also tends to be consistent in her behavior.

This child enjoys being in control, so *she challenges authority* figures. She sees adults as standing in the way.

NEGATIVE

She also tends to *remain negative even though the negativism serves no purpose.* She seems to hold on to her right to be negative or upset forever, even after everyone else has settled down. The reality is the child's emotional reaction serves little purpose other than to demonstrate her ability to be stubborn. Does this describe anyone you know? Your efforts to get your child to calm down are seen as invading her right to do what she wants. When their emotions arise most children express them and then they diminish. The oppositional child is an emotion keeper.

COMPETITIVE

This child would rather compete than cooperate. It's almost as though she's an adrenaline addict. She craves and loves the excitement, the conflict that competition generates. She enjoys frustrating others and enjoys the power, the feel, in controlling others. Even negative attention is acceptable because it generates conflicts. This child fears losing so she provokes to keep problems alive. She doesn't know where the line of competitiveness and aggression begins. The results she receives from her interaction just serve to feed her competitive drive. Cooperation and working together doesn't appeal because others slow her down or block what she wants.

RIGHT AND WRONG ARE RELATIVE

In an oppositional child, right and wrong are somewhat relative. They seem to be *determined by the consequences of his or her behavior.*

For this child, if he's caught doing something wrong, then *perhaps* what he did was wrong. If no one saw him, it wasn't wrong. When a child thinks this way, it frees him from experiencing guilt. If this belief is really ingrained within the child, I would suspect inadequate conscience development.

This child is frustrating because he doesn't respond to normal discipline techniques or approaches. What you try may not work because the value you place on what you do or offer doesn't have the same value for your child.

If you try to use a reward system he probably couldn't care less. A strong punishment is "no big deal."

He may see more value in intimidation, fighting, a "bad" reputation or making others ill at ease.

Punishment to this child may be your refusing to argue, to debate, to get upset, or even to stay around talking to him. When you withdraw, he loses control, you don't.

This child is not dumb. Early on, he discovers that others don't understand him and he enjoys this. If he is punished, but his parents are upset, it is worth the punishment.

Why is a child like this? Is there one cause or a multitude of them?

Children are born with many behavioral characteristics, and being oppositional is one of them. Often you can identify this characteristic in the child as a toddler. It's just part of his natural temperament. Remember, though, that oppositional can be reinforced. Dr. William Lee Carter describes the child this way:

> The oppositional child tends to want to take charge of all his own decisions sooner than he is able to responsibly do so. When parents place barriers before him to prevent the harm that would inevitably arise from the child's lack of judgment, the child looks for other ways to satisfy the desire to be in control. In most cases, parents end up reinforcing this child's behavior.[6]

CONTROLLING

Even an argument leaves this child with the feeling he won. Why? This kind of child relies upon control to give him his sense of security. Rather than rely upon Mom or Dad for their sense of security, he tries to take over control of himself too quickly. He would rather do it himself. He tries to wrestle it away from them. He wants to make his own decisions way sooner than he is capable of handling.

> IF WE AS PARENTS ENGAGE IN A POWER STRUGGLE,
> IT MAY ENCOURAGE THE CONTINUATION OF
> OPPOSITIONAL BEHAVIOR.

How do we reinforce and reward him? By letting him draw us into a power struggle and get us emotionally upset. He is actually able to take charge of the emotions of his parents. *When he feels emotionally in charge of an adult, he is being rewarded.* It is as simple as that! We as parents have (or should have) more control over our emotions than a child, even an irritating child.

MAY IMITATE OPPOSITIONAL BEHAVIOR

In some cases, a child may *imitate* oppositional behavior—all too often from adults.

If we as parents engage in a power struggle, it may encourage the continuation of oppositional behavior. Often these struggles can become intense and ugly. It is easy for a parent to look for some punishment that will do the job, and be strong enough to control the child and convince him to give it up and behave as he should. The child, however, realizes what the parent is doing and won't budge. So the parent intensifies his or her efforts to stay in control, as does the child, and it continues.

Remember that when the child has taken charge of your emotions, he has won. You can't resolve this problem by forcing a solution. If you override and dominate the child, he will go underground like a mole that is out of sight beneath the surface of your yard.

How Parents Can Respond

What is the best way for a parent not only to respond to the oppositional child, but also to aid in his character development?

CONTROL YOUR EMOTIONS
The first step is in controlling the emotions—your own. These are your child's finest tools to control you—your emotions. You will need to disengage emotionally. If you can detach yourself from the problem behaviors of your child, you will respond better. It is not necessarily hiding your emotions from your child, but perhaps just stating them. The fact is that you don't want to feel that way and you are going to take the necessary steps to release them. State in a calm voice, "This problem is really yours. If you want to argue about it, that's fine. In fact, I'd encourage you to argue. If you would like to become upset over this, that's all right. I'd recommend you be upset. You need to figure out a solution about what to do. It's your choice and you have the capability to find it."

DON'T ARGUE
Stay out of arguments. You will lose. Remember what the Word of God has to say:

> A fool gives full vent to his anger, but a wise man keeps himself under control (Prov. 29:11).

> It is to a man's honor to avoid strife, but every fool is quick to quarrel (20:3).

> When arguing with a rebel, don't use foolish arguments as he does, or you will become as foolish as he is! Prick his conceit with silly replies! (26:4,5, *TLB*).

How can a parent stay calm enough to accomplish this? It is possible. I have seen it. You really don't want your child to be opposing you, do you? No. Have you been able to get her to stop what she is doing or the way she is responding to you? If not, quit fighting her head on. Do the opposite. In your heart and mind give her permission to be the way she is at this time in her life. Tell yourself you can han-

> ALLOWING CHILDREN TO EXPERIENCE THE LOGICAL AND NATURAL CONSEQUENCES OF THEIR ACTIONS PROVIDES AN HONEST AND REAL LEARNING SITUATION.

dle it. Remind yourself that your child covers up her insecurities by responding in this way. By doing this, you will take pressure off yourself, be able to disengage emotionally and respond differently. For a while you may not be changing the child, but you can change yourself.

SET BOUNDARIES THAT TEACH CONSEQUENCES

The oppositional child needs boundaries. You cannot force them upon her, because she needs to make her own conclusions about the wisdom of what she does. One of the best ways to respond is to give her choices that have consequences, but also create boundaries.

The child has to accept the consequences for what she does. Allowing children to experience the logical and natural consequences of their actions provides an honest and real learning situation. (This does not include situations that would be dangerous or injurious to the child.)

A child who continually forgets to take his lunch to school will quickly learn if he has to go without a lunch one day and Mother does not bring his lunch to him. A child who leaves his football outside (and has been warned against doing this), and finds it stolen one morning, must learn to do without or to use his own allowance to replace the ball.

A girl frequently gets up late for school and, to preserve her perfect record of not being tardy, demands that her mother drive her. If her mother lets her walk to school and experience the consequences of being late, the girl may realize she has a responsibility to get up on time. If she doesn't, she will just have to be late. Giving the girl her own alarm clock and letting her be responsible would help in this situation too.

HELP THE CHILD MAKE CHOICES

Let the child make choices. Set up situations or give instructions in which the child is able to make a choice between two or three alternatives. This allows you to continue to control the situation and suggest the possible choices. It lets the child know he has some voice and choice in the matter. It also teaches him that he must accept the consequences of his choice.

"John, you will have to make a decision. You can go to Jim's house this evening to work on your car and fix the garage door tomorrow night, or you can fix the door tonight and go to the game with Jim tomorrow night. You make the choice and I'll go along with it." Or, "Mary, you can wear the brown or the green dress today. You choose."

A child can be given a choice about when he does his homework. If he chooses to earn poor grades, then homework is done immediately after school. If he chooses to earn good grades, he can choose what he wants to do in the afternoon, but it is his choice.

When I was a youth pastor for seven years, I didn't have just one oppositional teen in my group—I had several! Approximately 100 to 150 kids attended the youth meetings. I learned an approach then that worked well. I simply told them it was a privilege for them to be able to be in this meeting. If they chose to listen and pay attention, they were choosing to stay. If they chose to talk and be disruptive, they would be making the choice of being asked to leave. That was all I said. I waited for the first one to be disruptive and then escorted him or her out. The others knew the rule would be enforced if they made that choice. It worked. Be sure you use the phrase "you have a choice."

PROVIDE POSITIVE INPUT

The way you communicate with this child is critical. What he needs rather than lectures and arguing (neither works) is positive input. The information you believe he needs (and he does) he will reject. He wants to learn about life his way. The familiar song "My way, I did it my way" is his theme song.

Three principles can help.

Listen. The first is found in James 1:19 *(Amp.)*: "Be...[a ready listener]"; and in Proverbs 18:13 *(Amp.)*: "He who answers a matter before he hears all the facts—it is folly and shame to him."

Listen to this child. Dr. William Lee Carter says:

Listening involves more than merely hearing the words that another person has spoken. The most vital function of listening is to accurately interpret the message being expressed. Listening accurately to an oppositional child can be difficult because of the aggressive way he communicates with others.[7]

Reflect on what is said. It also helps to reflect back what you think the other person is saying. You can use phrases such as:

"Kind of feeling..."
"Sort of feeling..."
"I'm picking up that you..."
"If I'm hearing you correctly..."
"To me it's almost like you are saying, 'I...'"
"Kind of made (makes) you feel..."
"The thing you feel most right now is sort of like..."
"So, as you see it..."
"I'm not sure I'm with you, but..."

"I somehow sense that maybe you feel..."

"I wonder if you're expressing a concern that..."

"It sounds as if you're indicating you..."

"You place a high value on..."

"It seems to you..."

"It appears to you..."

"So, from where you sit..."

"Sometimes you..."

"Very much feeling..."

"Your message seems to be, 'I...'"

"You appear..."

"Listening to you, it seems as if..."

"I gather..."

"So your world is a place where you..."

"You communicate (convey) a sense of..."

Use proper timing. When you have to focus on a problem, use timing, emphasize behavior and present the consequences. Scripture says, "A word aptly spoken is like apples of gold in settings of silver" (Prov. 25:11). Pick your communication times. Sometimes it helps to state the problem and then let some time elapse before you state the consequences. Stating the situation, rather than discussing the pros and cons with this child, works better. You don't want a war of words, because you will lose.

It is best to point out what went wrong factually. "You said you would clean up your room by 3 o'clock. You didn't. You and I had agreed on that together." Later on the father said, "I understand that you wanted to play, but this is not acceptable. I know you are capable of following through on this the next time. For now you will not be able to play the next two afternoons. After that you can because I know you will follow through with our agreement."

In responding this way you are not debating, you are pointing out the facts of what happened, what you expect and your belief in your child's capabilities.

Responding in this way helps a child feel understood. Hopefully, in the future your child will move from competition to cooperation.[8]

Notes

1. Ann Crittendon, *Babies Are Born Different* (Sept. 1986), adapted from pp. 107, 149, 150, 151, quoted in Barbara Sullivan, *No Two Look Alike* (Grand Rapids: Fleming H. Revell, 1987), p. 35.

2. Ralph Mattson and Thom Block, *Discovering Your Child's Design* (Colorado Springs: David C. Cook Publishers, 1989), pp. 108-112, adapted.

3. David Domico, *The Influential Parent* (Wheaton, Ill.: Shaw Publishers, 1997), p. 143.

4. Ibid., pp. 145-151, adapted.

5. Ibid., p. 152.

6. Dr. William Lee Carter, *Child Think* (Dallas, Tex.: Word Publishing, 1991), pp. 11, 12.

7. Ibid., p. 15.

8. Ibid., pp. 1-31, adapted.

IS YOUR CHILD REALLY STRONG WILLED OR JUST A DREAMER?

By H. Norman Wright

God gave them knowledge and skill in all literature and wisdom; and...understanding in all visions and dreams.

—DANIEL 1:17 (NKJV)

Strong willed: The label strikes fear into the heart of the strongest parent. You end up butting heads with a child who causes you to wonder where her head *is* at times. You may ask God: "Why me? What did I do to deserve this situation?" You may also wonder how you can help this child become more like Jesus, or if it is really possible. Perhaps you had hoped for a compliant child, one of those who just goes along with every suggestion and conforms. If you didn't get one of these children, don't fret. You may have a child who is neither strong willed *nor* compliant.

A Profile of the Dreamer Child

A third option is the dreamer. The dreamer child thinks, feels, acts and reacts in a different way from the strong willed or compliant child. He can be difficult to guide and parent because his way of thinking can be very different from his parents. He is a source of puzzlement for many parents. You may see this child as stubborn, moody, unique and compassionate. A dreamer child is the most imaginative, sensitive and idealistic of all other children. One of the authors of the book *Strong-Willed Child or Dreamer?* Ron Braund, said:

> When parents make a commitment to enter the world of the dreamer child, there can be many rewards. When a dreamer is cultivated properly and pruned responsibly, a balanced environment is created to equip him to respond to the challenges he will face.[1]

If this kind of care doesn't occur, the child won't reach his potential, misunderstandings will abound, pain and conflict could be constant and a long-lasting gulf between parent and child could exist.

The nurturing approach used with a compliant child doesn't work here. The assertive task-oriented approach used with a strong-willed child doesn't work either.

Your approach needs to be highly creative and innovative.

It is easy to label an obstinate child as strong willed. When you are dealing with this child who doesn't respond well, remember that a willfully defiant child doesn't see his or her behavior as defiant—not according to his or her logic. A dreamer child is sensitive, emotional and compassionate, but all too often these traits are overlooked because parents get hung up on other problems.

One of the best descriptions of this dilemma was written by Edgar Allan Poe in *Eleanora:*

> Those who dream by day are cognizant of many things that escape those who dream by night.

NEEDS FREEDOM

Some parents mislabel their dreamer child as strong willed, stubborn or even obstinate. When a dreamer child is threatened or restricted, his or her reaction can be intense. Remember this: a dreamer child doesn't feel secure with specific limits as do some children. He is like a wild horse that has been put into a small corral and enclosed by a high fence. His fear is he will be destroyed if the limits are too rigid. As a parent, you may be thinking: *But a child needs rules. He needs limits and absolutes.* That may be true, but which absolutes? A clean room and homework finished at a specific time? Not for the dreamer. He loves the more generalized absolutes of mercy, justice and obedience to spiritual ideals. He needs freedom rather than confinement of the emotions and imagination. He needs room to roam on the plains of life.

WANTS POWER

Some children are into power. They want it and you know they want it. You spend hours trying to disengage yourself from the power struggles. Other children are into peace. Whatever it takes, they will work toward a harmonious relationship.

A dreamer child works toward a "purpose at all costs." It is the child, not the parent, who decides whether an activity or event has any purpose or not. If a chore seems purposeless to the dreamer, guess what? It will be resisted. If she sees a purpose in something that doesn't make sense to you or even horrifies you, however, just be aware—*she's doing it.*

Dreamer children are enjoyable to be around because they do things other children wouldn't think of doing. My daughter, Sheryl, is a dreamer, but when she was younger I didn't know anything about a dreamer child, so more or less I saw her as strong willed. It wasn't until reading the book *Strong-Willed Child or Dreamer?* that the light bulb came on!

As a young child, Sheryl found purpose in things that made sense to her rather than to us. Artistically, she was very creative and, fortunately, she used the gift to rise to the top of her profession as a creative nail technician and artist. She would develop an idea, think *that's never been done*, and then say, "I'll give it a try.

I think I can do it," and then did it. Watch out for the dreamer child's creativity.

COMPASSIONATE

The compassion and sensitivity of a dreamer child comes out when she unintentionally hurts another person. She has a high degree of remorse. Inwardly, this child is fragile. She may not look it, but getting beyond the mask and the depth of compassion is something that can be used greatly for the Kingdom.

If at times you are confused by your dreamer child, don't despair. All the other parents are just as confused. You may not understand her dream world, mood changes, sensitivity or overreactions. It is especially difficult if you are a Sensor or Sensor-Judger on the Myers-Briggs personality scale.

IDEALISTIC

Do you know what dreamers want most? They want to change the world. They influence others in one way or another. They are just full of ideas. Sometimes you think they have hyper minds! They are also often misunderstood; but this reminds you of Jesus, doesn't it? He was misunderstood in many ways.

A dreamer is misunderstood because his logic differs from others. He is idealistic and can imagine all sorts of possibilities of what life and the world could be. Because he can be too idealistic about people, he can be hurt easily, especially about the realities of life he can't control or change. As a parent, if you do something that hurts your child, his feeling is you did it on purpose. After all (so they believe), you knew what his feelings were and thus should have known that what you did was going to hurt him.

One of the mistakes this child makes again and again is assuming that others know how he is feeling from moment to moment. This child is not aware that his thinking style is different from others.

Because this child imagines so many possibilities, he can imagine the positive, but also the negative. His thought life is so rich and vivid it is as though he can visualize, hear, taste, touch and smell mentally. The ideas he generates aren't based on fact, but on hunches or ideas. If you are a linear-thinking parent, you may think something was left out of your child's brain.

You are asking: "Where are the facts? What is the basis for this?"

Your child is saying, "It's there. It's an idea in my head." Preoccupation with new ideas causes him to ignore or overlook some of the mundane details of life that are necessary to survive.

EMOTIONAL

Emotional? Dreamers are on a mood swing that can rival the wildest roller-coaster ride imaginable. They can swing from joy and elation to depression and despair. They expect you to be understanding of these mood swings even though they may not be understanding of others. Don't expect them to be aware of the effect their mood swings have on others either.

The emotional range and intensity of feelings that dreamers experience set them apart from other children. On a scale of 0 to 10, their responses tend to be closer to a 10 than a 0. They wonder what is wrong with children who only react in the 0 to 3 range. Dreamer children enjoy experiencing their emotions. If they are outgoing or extroverted, everyone else knows about it. If they are quiet or introverted, they are the only ones who know about it. They also change directions emotionally—like flicking a switch.

HIGH EXPECTATIONS OF OTHERS

Dreamers expect a lot of others, especially you as a parent. Do you know what they expect of you?

They expect you to be kind.

They expect you to respect them.

They expect you to *ask* them to do things.

They expect you not to *tell* them what to do.

They expect you not to raise your voice at them.

They expect you speak softly when disciplining.

They expect you to be fair.

They expect others to be treated fairly as well.[2]

This child may not be fully aware of how his moods and feelings not only affect others, but his decisions as well.

STUBBORN

You might equate the word "stubborn" with a dreamer. It is interesting that such a sensitive person can turn and become so rigid and tough about others. A dreamer will be hurt more by criticism, continual correction, being misunderstood or rejected.

SETS HIGH STANDARDS

Often they set themselves up for failure because they set such high standards. If they think they can't attain the ideal they have set as their standard, they won't try. They will find a lesser, more attainable goal. Dreamers tend to minister to other people. They have a need to be needed, and it is easy to connect with peers who are having problems. Ron Braund described the dilemma this way:

> Unfortunately, the dreamer is as likely to be pulled down into the despair of a friend as he is to pull the friend out of despair. Gaining satisfaction from believing that he is making a positive impact on someone's life, he may disregard outside opinion, which he perceives as criticism of his compassionate nature. The same dreamer who is such a good listener to those in need can refuse to hear sound advice because he is so emotionally involved with needy friends.[3]

SPIRITUALLY SENSITIVE

Dreamers are spiritually sensitive, but they experience doubts and raise questions. They need people and the church to be genuine and caring or they may reject them. They want meaningful involvement, but they may not follow through, and if this disappoints them they may leave an organization or ministry. (If you want to determine if your child is a dreamer, an evaluation form has been provided for you at the conclusion of this chapter.)[4]

EMOTIONALLY DEPENDENT

Is your child reactive? If so, when? Is it when his goals are blocked or when he feels others don't like him? If it is the first, he is probably more of a strong-willed child, whereas the latter is the way a dreamer responds. A dreamer has very thin skin and soaks up the feelings of others as well as misinterprets others' feelings. He doesn't know the meaning of the word "boundaries"! He will hear others, including parents, say, "Don't be so sensitive." Self-esteem seems attached to a yo-yo. One day it is up, a bit later it is dropped. Dreamers, unfortunately, are too emotionally dependent. It is as if they see others' perception of them as a mirror. What others see or say determines how they feel about themselves.

Responding to Dreamers

What is the best way to respond to dreamers? They don't react well to a strict, strong authoritative response—especially if they perceive it as unfeeling or uncaring. At the other extreme, if you take a laid-back, let-them-do-whatever approach, they will consider you uninterested and uncaring.

COMMUNICATE UNDERSTANDING

The key word in responding to this child is "understanding." When you talk with this child, communicate understanding and acceptance. Acceptance means you can accept how the child feels and perceives, but not necessarily all of her behavior.

How do you express understanding? Praise your child's character rather then his behavior. Of course, this is going counter culture, but it can help your child feel valued. Dreamers can end up feeling second best in a society that praises and emphasizes results and production. Dreamers want recognition of what goes on inside them. They like to hear you recognize if they are sensitive to the needs of others, generous, compassionate, etc. If they are creative, mention this and ask how they are able to do what they do or the unusual ideas they create.

Start a discussion with this child. If you don't allow this, the inward response of your child is much stronger than you could ever imagine. Your child (right or wrong) will tend to believe that not only has he disappointed you, but also that you don't like him. You can be firm but nurturing. That will work. To keep you from reacting to your dreamer's extreme statements or feelings prior to your interaction with him, in your heart and mind give him permission to make such statements. After all, you are going to hear those expressions, so instead of resisting them, plan for them in advance.

LISTEN

As with all children, but even more so with dreamers, they need to be listened to. Hear what they have to say, but do it just *once*. You can reflect and acknowledge what they feel and have said. If they need correction, though, they need to be corrected, and it may be best for them to experience the consequences of what they may have done.

A dreamer child may try to tell you the story again and again. Don't argue, but say, "I heard you. The consequences are still..." and then leave. Your tendency may be to argue or convince your child by using facts and logic. *It won't work with this child.* How could it? She doesn't use objective fact-based logic, but subjective feeling-based logic. There's a significant difference. What is most beneficial in helping the dreamer accept consequences is keeping an emotional balance. Her emotional response is neither a phase nor a genetic defect that needs to be surgically removed.

ENCOURAGE

Whenever you have to correct a dreamer, remember the person's concern, "You don't like me." Deflect this by saying, "I always care for you on the inside even when you do things that I don't understand or when you break the rules. Even when you have to experience the consequences, I love and accept you and know that you are capable of learning through this experience."

Remember what was said earlier about a dreamer? His goal is attention rather than power. So when you correct and guide him, ask yourself this question: Is my child getting more attention from misbehavior and the consequences or more from doing what is positive? Think about it. *For whatever he receives the greatest amount of attention he is likely to repeat!* When your child shows self-control and attention to follow through, does the child receive the positive recognition needed? If not, why not? Everyone needs encouragement and this child even more so.

Do you know what encouragement really means?

ENCOURAGEMENT...CAN INVOLVE NOTICING WHAT OTHERS TAKE FOR GRANTED AND AFFIRMING SOMETHING OTHERS NOTICE BUT MAY NEVER THINK OF MENTIONING.

The *American Heritage Dictionary* provides one of the better definitions of the word "encouragement." It is a "tendency or disposition to expect the best possible outcome, or to dwell on the most hopeful aspect of a situation." When this is your attitude or perspective, you will be able to encourage others. Encouragement is "to inspire; to continue on a chosen course; to impart courage or confidence."

Encouragement is sometimes thought of as praise and reinforcement, but it is also much more than that. Praise is limited. It is a verbal reward. It emphasizes competition, has to be earned and is often given for being the best. Encouragement is freely given. It can involve noticing what others take for granted and affirming something others notice but may never think of mentioning.

Time and time again we hear about the positive effect of an encouraging mother upon her son. I remember hearing an interview one day with Scott Hamilton, who has become a household name in professional ice skating. During the 1992 Winter Olympics, Scott served as a television commentator for the ice-skating events. He shared on TV about his special relationship with his mother, who died prior to his winning an Olympic gold medal.

He said, "The first time I skated in the U.S. Nationals, I fell five times. My mother gave me a big hug and said, 'It's only your first National. It's no big deal.' My mother always let me be me. Three years later I won my first National. She never said, 'You can do better' or 'Shape up.' She just encouraged me."

Look at what God's Word tells us to do.

In Acts 18:27, the word "encourage" means "to urge forward or persuade." In 1 Thessalonians 5:11 it means "to stimulate another person to the ordinary duties of life."

Consider the words found in 1 Thessalonians 5:14 *(Amp.)*:

And we earnestly beseech you, brethren, admonish (warn and seriously advise) those who are out of line [the loafers, the disorderly and the unruly]; encourage the timid and fainthearted, help and give your support to the weak souls, [and] be very patient with everybody [always keeping your temper].

Scripture uses a variety of words to describe both our involvement with others as well as the actual relationship. "Urge" *(parkaleo)* means "to beseech or exhort." It is intended to create an environment of urgency to listen and respond to a directive. It is a mildly active verb. Paul used it in Romans 12:1 and in 1 Corinthians 4:16 and 16:15.

The Greek word for "encourage" *(paramutheomai)* means "to console, comfort and cheer up." This process includes elements of understanding, redirecting of thoughts and a general shifting of focus from the negative to the positive. In the context of the verse, it refers to the timid ("fainthearted," *KJV*) individual who is discouraged and ready to give up. It's a matter of loaning your faith and hope to the person until his own develops.

"Help" (*anechomai*) primarily contains the idea of "taking interest in, being devoted to, rendering assistance, or holding up spiritually and emotionally." It is not so much an active involvement as a passive approach. It suggests the idea of coming alongside a person and supporting him. In the context of 1 Thessalonians 5:14, it seems to refer to those who are incapable of helping themselves.

First Thessalonians 5:11 states, "Therefore encourage one another and build each other up, just as in fact you are doing."

Hebrews 3:13 says we're to "encourage one another daily." In the setting of this verse, encouragement is associated with protecting the believer from callousness.

Hebrews 10:25 says, "Let us encourage one another." This time the word means to keep someone on his feet who, if left to himself, would collapse. Your encouragement serves like the concrete pilings of a structural support.

The Dreamer's Sensitive Personality

As you guide your child into learning and growing through the use of natural and logical consequences (which have been described elsewhere), keep in mind how sensitive a dreamer is. This means that any consequence shouldn't be based on humiliation. She needs to both hear and have kept in private your concern and dealings with her. If humiliation is a result of what she has done, then what you didn't appreciate will continue.

One other factor to consider that is not given significant attention is the concept of restitution and restoration. If a problem has occurred between your child and another, the consequence needs to involve a relationship restoration. Any logical consequence that helps a dreamer improve her relationship both teaches this child and helps her keep her emotional balance.[5]

The Dreamer's Stubbornness
(or Determination)

Many parents say their greatest challenge is their child's stubbornness. Are you ready for a radical suggestion? Here it is anyway. Have you thought of *giving up* fighting this tendency, accepting it, going along with it and even praising it? I know if I had made this suggestion to you in my office right now I would hear the strong sounds of silence as well as see a puzzled stare of disbelief! That is all right. I have experienced many of those over the years. Think about it.

What is another word for "stubborn"? What about "determination?" It fits. If you were to label your child's response as determination and say the following, your relationship could improve: "You know, I like it. Yes, I do. It's good you have such a strong degree of determination. You will need this in life. What I would like to do (because the Scripture says this is my job) is to help you shape the direction of your determination. So when there is something I want for you or want you to do, you may feel I'm blocking your strong desire. I'm not really. I want you to feel strongly. I want to hear your feelings. But my job may be to guide your determination in a different direction that will be best for both of us. It's something for you to think about."

This may surprise your child, but it will help him, and you really don't have any other options, do you? You need a balance in your response and so does your child.

If you are harsh and overprotective, your child thinks he is incapable of making decisions, learning and facing consequences. This builds stubbornness.

If you are passive, it forces your child to make too many decisions and he winds up feeling insecure and will act up to get your attention.

Nurturing and Supporting Dreamers

What is the best way for you to nurture and support a dreamer? You can take several practical steps, some of which have already been mentioned, but need to be reiterated.

ACCEPTANCE

First, accept dreamers for who they are and give up all attempts to change them. Thank God for creating them in the unique way in which He did.

HELP IN HANDLING UPS AND DOWNS OF LIFE

Second, you may need to determine what you can do to teach them to handle the ups and downs of life. Because they are concerned about being liked and accepted, teach them skills in getting along with others, how to handle rejection, and most of all share how much God loves and accepts them no matter what.

If they tend to worry about what others think, encourage them to memorize Psalm 37:1-10 and Philippians 4:6-9.

If they tend to respond impulsively, help them learn how to delay their response. Help them learn appropriate ways to express their anger. Often they become angry because they think they are not listened to or understood, or that others don't like them. They want others to like them or come closer to them.

A dreamer may respond better to guidance or suggestions in the form of a story rather than in direct instruction of "being told." Telling them that responding to others in anger when in fact they want them to come closer has just the opposite effect. It actually pushes them farther away. Parables or role playing are tools that work well with this child.

These are children who need an abundance of your confidence that they have the ability to handle a situation. More than other children, they need you to be a cheerleader, a believer in them and their innate qualities of compassion, creativity and determination.[6]

The Dreamer's Learning Ability

How do dreamers learn? Is there any basic difference between them and other children? Usually they have a strong desire to learn, but children learn in different ways than adults do.

Let's consider the difference in learning as it pertains to the brain. Dreamers *tend* to learn with the right side of the brain. The right-brain skills such as color and sensitivity, music, shapes and patterns, seeing images in their minds and emotional expressiveness may be their bent. A dreamer could also have a bent toward language and reading, which is a left-brain function. Note the following diagram of this process:

Left	Right
Factual	Experiential
Logical, rational	Intuitive, nonverbal, knowing
Mathematical/symbols	Focused on patterns
Sequential	Simultaneous
Language skills (reading, writing, spelling)	Dreaming (brainstorming ideas)
Directed	Spontaneous, unordered
Linear	Spatial
Objective	Subjective
Analysis	Synthesis
Explicit	Implicit
Stores practical information	Stores emotions (nostalgia)
Denotative/literal (Goal in language is to be precise)	Connotative/associative (Goal in language is to create rapport)
Remembers names	Remembers faces
Metaphorically: a computer	Metaphorically: a kaleidoscope

CONCEPTUAL AND GLOBAL LEARNERS

Another factor should be kept in mind. A child can be a conceptual or a global learner. A conceptional learner is more concrete and linear in how he approaches learning. He pulls his information together in a linear step-by-step fashion such as one, then two, then three and then the conclusion.

Not so with the global learner. He needs to see the overall big picture first, then he can get to the specifics. He is not that concrete in his learning style. He goes from one to four to three to five, to two and then "got it!" "It makes sense now."

IMAGINATIVE

One characteristic that abounds in dreamers is imagination. Their minds are filled with a creative imagination. Practical they may not be, but can they ever invent. They are the innovators. They seem to have no limit when it comes to generating "off the wall ideas." Sometimes they come so rapidly they don't have time to remember what they thought of before the next one intrudes.

Abstract ideas are more prevalent than facts. Dreamers seem to have more insights with people, and they prefer relating to people rather than things.

All children engage in a fantasy life and it ends somewhere in their childhood. For dreamers? It never ends.

They use their imagination to explore the aesthetic world. My daughter was designing clothes and drawing from early on. Her room? Cluttered because of one project after another. If your child has this bent, give her materials to foster it and books to expand its potential. If you are highly structured and organized, you will be uncomfortable with this child. She won't be a replica of you at all. She won't color within the lines; and who says every child has to?

You don't want to stifle creativity, although some may need to be redirected. Remember the passage in Colossians 3:21: "Fathers do not provoke or irritate or fret you children [do not be hard on them or harass them], lest they become discouraged and sullen and morose and feel inferior and frustrated. [Do not break their spirit]" (Col. 3:21, *Amp.*)[7]

It is essential to allow imaginative children the freedom to express themselves. One creative child described her feelings this way:

I'm different. At least that's what others tell me. I don't know what the *different* means. Is it because I don't do things the way others do? Is it because I don't do things the way others want me to do them? I like what I do. I like life. There's so much to explore, so much to learn and so much to create.

Mom wants me to follow her schedule. I'm not always sure what a schedule is! And I wonder why is it so important that we live our lives by a schedule? Oh, well.

I liked school last year. My teacher was different, sort of like me. She seemed to understand me better. She said I was like some famous people in history. I remember two of them. One had a funny name. It was something like Len. No, it was longer...Leonard? No, he was from another country...Leonardo, yeah, that's right. Leonardo di...something or another. He was real different. He was an inventor and drew all these weird pictures. People didn't always understand him. He had a big imagination. He drew pictures of helicopters and submarines way back then.

My teacher showed me a picture of another man. He was so funny looking. He had white frizzy hair and a white mustache. He looked like he had put his finger is a light bulb socket and had gotten a shock. His hair stuck out all over his head. His name was Albert. She said he created some things called theories. Some of his work helped create a bomb, too.

My teacher said it was good to be creative. She let me put on paper what was in my head. She liked my stories. Sometimes my teacher became a part of my stories. When I took my pictures and stories home my mother would look at them and either say, "That's nice" or "What in the world is that? What are they teaching you there?" Then she'd always say, "Well, put it away in your drawer so it doesn't clutter up your room. You have to live in the *real* world." I thought, *I am living in the real world.*

Mom gets real upset when I start talking to my dog or my little sister, too. Oh, I don't really have either one. Not really. But in my head I do. We talk and play and have a wonderful time. I even made up a movie with all of us in it. I told the teacher, the one who understands me, and she said, "Why, that's a wonderful idea." I told my dad about it and he had a funny look on his face. I didn't tell mom about it. I knew what she would say.

This year I have a new teacher. I don't think she likes me. She doesn't want me to be me. When the teacher tells me to do things like all the other children do, I tell her, "But that isn't me." She says it doesn't matter.

This is the plight of many creative children. They receive criticism for their creativity.

Remember the song "Flowers are Red" by Harry Chapin? It's the story of a little boy and his experience in school. The boy takes some paper and begins to draw pictures using a wide variety of colors. When the teacher inquires into his activity, the boy says he is painting flowers and the colors are what he sees. The teacher's response is emphatic: this isn't the time for art, flowers are green and red, and everything has to be done in a certain time and in a certain way.

The little boy replies that he sees many colors in the rainbow. The teacher, however, concludes the boy is sassy. When the boy tries to assert his identity and creative style, the teacher punishes him. The boy eventually conforms by painting his flowers in neat rows of red and green.

Later, the boy attends a new school with a new teacher who says painting is fun and an expression of who you are. "So let's use all the colors." Sadly, the little boy can only color red and green flowers in orderly rows.

The teacher asks the little boy why he can't draw anything else or in any other colors. The boy's response echoes what his last teacher had drilled into him:

Flowers have to be red and green leaves have to be green, the only way to see flowers is the way they've always been seen.[8]

Three Modalities for Learning

There is yet another dimension to the way not only a dreamer learns, but also the way we *all* learn. There are primarily three ways of remembering (sensory perception). We all use these in varying degrees. Sometimes we see them referred to as modalities. Usually one of these is a prominent way of learning.

THREE WAYS OF REMEMBERING (SENSORY PERCEPTION)

...ARE *AUDITORY, VISUAL* AND *KINESTHETIC.*

Some of us are *auditory.* This person learns by listening to verbal instructions and remembers by forming the sounds of the words.

Others are *visual.* They learn by seeing, watching and reading. They use strong visual associations.

Others are *kinesthetic.* They learn more by becoming physically involved. They like to do something with what's being learned. They tend to be more feeling oriented as well.

As you listen to a person talk, the words he uses often express his learning style.

THE VISUAL PERSON
The *visual* person uses terms such as:
I *see* what you're saying.
That *looks* good to me.
I'm not too *clear* on this right now.
This is still a bit *hazy* to me.
Boy, when they asked that question, I just went *blank.*
That sheds a new *light* on the problem.
Do you pick up my *perspective*?

THE AUDITORY PERSON

The *auditory* person uses terms such as:

>That *rings* a bell with me.
>
>It *sounds* real good to me.
>
>I *hear* you.
>
>I'm trying to *tune* in to what you're saying.
>
>*Listen* to this new idea.
>
>I had to *ask* myself.
>
>Now, that idea *clicks* with me.

THE KINESTHETIC PERSON

The *kinesthetic* person will use phrases such as these:

>I can't get a *handle* on this.
>
>I've got a good *feeling* about this project.
>
>Can you get in *touch* with what I'm saying?
>
>It's easy to *flow* with what they're saying.
>
>I don't *grasp* what you're trying to do.
>
>This is a *heavy* situation.

Words That Express Pictures

Some writers have an uncanny ability with words. Dr. Charles Swindoll is one of my favorite authors. I like what he says, but he also appeals to me because he gives such detail that I can construct pictures in my head. Here is one example:

>Blow that layer of dust off the book of Nahum in your Bible and catch a glimpse of the last part of verse 3, chapter 1. "The way of the Lord is in the whirlwind and in the storm..." (TLB).
>
>That's good to remember when you're in a rip-snortin', Texas frog-strangler as I was a few weeks back. I nudged myself to remember God's presence as the rain-heavy, charcoal clouds hemorrhaged in eerie, aerial explosions of saw-

toothed lightning and reverberating thunder. Witnessing that atmospheric drama, I reminded myself of its Director who was, once again, having His way in the whirlwind and the storm.[9]

A different emphasis is expressed in this brief excerpt from the same book:

Children. They express their feelings. Deep down in their fragile, inner wells are a multitude of needs, questions, hurts, and longings. Like a tiny bucket, their tongues splash out these things. The busy, insensitive, preoccupied parent, steamrolling through the day, misses many a cue and sails right past choice moments never to be repeated.[10]

Dr. Swindoll shows a sharp ability to visualize in his descriptive writing! You have no doubt that he *sees* things—he's a visual sort of person.

Advertising to Appeal to the Individual Sense

Here is an advertising example of making an appealing presentation of a house to prospective buyers. As you read the three descriptions below, which house appeals to you the most?

1. This house is quite picturesque, with a quaint look about it. You can see that a lot of focus has been put on the colorful patio and garden area. The house has a lot of window space so that you can enjoy the view. It is clearly a good buy.

2. This house is soundly constructed and well situated in such a quiet area that all you hear when you walk outside

are the sounds of the birds singing. Its storybook interior has so much character you'll probably be asking yourself how you could ever pass it by.

3. This house is not only solidly constructed, it has a special feel to it. It's not often that you come in contact with a place that touches on so many important features. It is spacious enough that you really feel you can move around freely, yet cozy enough that you won't wear yourself out taking care of it.[11]

Which home did you choose?

Perhaps you have figured it out—all three descriptions fit the same house. Each was written to appeal to a different sense. If you leaned toward the first house, you are probably more visually (sight) oriented. If you were more impressed with the second house, you are probably more sound oriented. If you preferred the third, you are most likely feeling oriented.

One teacher who had what she called a "mediocre" group of high school students in an intermediate composition class used this approach in helping them improve their vocabulary. She explained to the class the three different modalities, had them identify their learning styles through a simple checklist (following this example) and then for three days divided the class into study groups using this learning style.

Here were the guidelines: The auditory group drilled one another aloud. One would give the word and the other the definition. The visual group wrote flash cards for each word and illustrated them with an appropriate word or design. Then they quizzed one another.

The kinesthetic group (the restless ones) designed body movements for each vocabulary word that would help them remember the definition.

When the students took this test on 84 difficult words, 26 of the 29 students did not miss one word. No one missed more than five.

What does this information about learning style say about the way you teach your child about Jesus? His life? His teaching? This may help your child hear what you say, see what you present and sense the message. (Incidentally, the last sentence used all three of the learning styles.)[12]

Modality Checklist

Place a check mark by all the statements that strongly describe your preference:

AUDITORY

___ I need to hear myself say it in order to remember it.

___ I often need to talk through a problem aloud in order to solve it.

___ I memorize best by repeating the information aloud or to myself over and over.

___ I remember best when the information fits into a rhythmic or musical pattern.

___ I would rather listen to a recording of a book than sit and read it.

VISUAL

___ I need to see an illustration of what I'm being taught before I understand it.

___ I am drawn to flashy, colorful, visually stimulating objects.

___ I look like I'm "daydreaming" when I'm trying to get a mental picture of what's being said.

___ I usually remember better when I can actually see the person who's talking.

KINESTHETIC

___ I have difficulty sitting still for more than a few minutes at a time.

___ I usually learn best by physically participating in a task.

___ I almost always have some part of my body in motion.

___ I prefer to read books or hear stories that are full of action.[13]

Is Your Child a Dreamer?

You probably already have begun to discern whether your child exhibits the dreamer cognitive style. You can use the following checklist as a tool in determining whether or not a child has dreamer tendencies.

DREAMER/DOER DESCRIPTIVE CHECKLIST

Although this checklist is helpful for rating young children, it is most accurate when used for rating children age six and older.

Which term is *more* descriptive of the child? (Select one per line).

	A	or	B	
1.	sensitive	____	logical	____
2.	moody	____	even-keeled	____
3.	compassionate	____	detached	____
4.	dramatic	____	level	____
5.	imaginative	____	productive	____
6.	creative	____	practical	____
7.	thin-skinned	____	thick-skinned	____
8.	defensive	____	obedient	____
9.	affectionate	____	somewhat stiff with everyone	____
10.	scattered	____	focused on details	____
11.	imagined fears	____	realistic fears only	____
12.	disheveled	____	tidy	____
13.	careless	____	precise	____
14.	forgetful	____	dependable	____
15.	clever	____	sensible	____
16.	daydreamer	____	on-task	____
17.	emotional	____	dispassionate	____
18.	unusual	____	typical for age	____
19.	original	____	imitator	____
20.	playful	____	industrious	____

21. deep	____	realistic	____
22. intriguing	____	predictable	____
23. considerate	____	blunt	____
24. easily hurt	____	oblivious to teasing	____
25. feels rejected	____	feels confident	____
26. know-it-all	____	humble	____
27. blames others	____	accepts blame	____
28. self-critical	____	easygoing	____
29. relational	____	independent	____
30. articulate	____	inexpressive	____

Total this column   ____   Do not count X's in this
                                  column

A score of 24 or more indicates a definite dreamer; 20-23 likely a dreamer; 0-19 likely a doer. (Note: If your child is an introverted dreamer, some of these characteristics may not be overtly expressed. Scores may underestimate the "dreamerness" of an introvert.)[14]

Notes
1. Dr. Dana Scott Spears and Dr. Ron L. Braund, *Strong-Willed Child or Dreamer?* (Nashville: Thomas Nelson Publishers, 1996), p. 8.
2. Ibid., pp. 74-79, adapted.
3. Ibid., p. 32.
4. Ibid., pp. 4-36, adapted.
5. Ibid., pp. 11-48, adapted.
6. Ibid., pp. 85-88, adapted.
7. Ibid., pp. 60-62, adapted.
8. Harry Chapin, "Flowers Are Red" on Living Room Suite, Electra Records, 1978, adapted.
9. Charles Swindoll, *Growing Strong in the Seasons of Life* (Portland, Oreg.: Multnomah Press, 1983), p. 132.
10. Ibid., p. 61.
11. H. Norman Wright, *How to Speak Your Spouse's Language* (Grand Rapids: Fleming H. Revell, 1986), pp. 83-86, adapted.

12. Cynthia Ulrich Tobias, *The Way They Learn* (Colorado Springs: Focus on the Family Publishing, 1994), p. 95, adapted.
13. Ibid., p. 90.
14. Spears and Braund, *Strong-Willed Child or Dreamer?* pp. 34,35.

A WARNING

By H. Norman Wright

See that you do not look down on one of these little ones.
For I tell you that their angels in heaven always see the
face of my Father in heaven.

— MATTHEW 18:10

We have talked about a healthy family and the importance to have a model, but it is also important to know what to avoid. Several telltale traits of families can stray off course. I want to share 10 of them with you. How many of these exist in a family and how often they occur reflect how far the family has strayed from healthy family norms. Such families neglect to provide an atmosphere that contributes to a child learning to become like Jesus.

Ten Characteristics of an Unhealthy Family

1. ABUSE

Abuses that exist in a family can include physical, emotional or sexual injury or neglect. Abuse may be blatant, such as one family member striking or screaming at another. It can be subtle, as when one person ignores another. Abuse can also be vicarious, such as the inner pain you suffer when observing the abuse experienced by your mother, brother or sister.

One form of abuse often overlooked because it leaves no visible scars is emotional abuse. Here are some examples:

Giving a child choices that are only negative, such as saying, "Either eat every bite of your dinner or get a spanking."

Constantly projecting blame onto a child.

Distorting a child's sense of reality, such as saying, "Your father doesn't have a drinking problem, he just works too hard and he's tired."

Overprotecting a child.

Blaming others for the child's problem.

Communicating double messages to the child, such as saying, "Yes, I love you" while glaring hatefully at the child. The child will believe the nonverbal message and be confused by the words.

2. PERFECTIONISM

Are you surprised that perfectionism is a characteristic of an unhealthy family? It is rarely considered an unhealthy symptom, but it is a common source of many family problems, especially in Christian homes. After all, isn't the challenge of the Christian life to be perfect as God is perfect? Not really. We are called to live a life of excellence, which is attainable, not perfectionism, which is unattainable. Expecting perfect behavior from a spouse or children, even in a Christian family, is living in a world of unreality.

A perfectionistic father conveys his standards and expectations through verbal rebukes and corrections, frowns, penetrating glances, smirks, etc., which continually imply "It's not good enough." He lives and leads by "oughts," "shoulds" and "musts." These are "torture words" that elevate guilt and lower self-esteem. A father who constantly overfocuses on defects in a critical way erodes his child's self-esteem. The child begins to believe that he is hopelessly substandard, and he carries this poor self-esteem image with him into adulthood.

3. RIGIDITY

Unhealthy families are characterized by unbending rules and strict lifestyles and belief systems. Life is full of compulsions, routines, controlled situations and relationships, and unrealistic and unchallenged beliefs. Joy? There is none. Surprises? There are none. Spontaneity? There will be none—unless it is planned!

4. SILENCE

Unhealthy families operate by a gag rule: No talking outside these walls. Don't share family secrets with anyone. Don't ask anyone else for help if you are having a problem. Keep it in the family. After all, what would people think if they knew you didn't have it all together?

If parents invoke the gag rule at home, children can grow up thinking they have to handle all their problems by themselves. It is difficult to ask for assistance or advice. They may also be hesitant to ask others to pray for them or counsel them.

5. REPRESSION

Many have grown up in a family where emotions were controlled and repressed instead of identified and expressed. Emotional repression has been called the death sentence of a marriage. Anger, sadness, joy and pain that should be expressed among family members are buried. The name of the game is to express the feelings that are appropriate instead of what they really feel. Deny reality and disguise true identity by wearing a mask. When you bury true feelings alive, however, some day they will explode in your face.

Emotions are a very important part of life. Like a pressure valve, they help us interpret and respond to the joys and sorrows of life. Clogging the valve by repressing or denying feelings leads to physical problems such as ulcers, depression, high blood pressure, headaches and a susceptibility to many other physical ailments. Repressing feelings can trigger overeating, anorexia and bulimia, substance abuse and compulsions of all kinds.

People repress their feelings to make them go away; but, of course, they don't. They fester and grow, looking for a means of expression. Some people stay excessively busy, so they won't hear the screams of their feelings that are just waiting to burst through. Repressed feelings cause people to do things they don't intend to do, such as yelling at the children, abusing pets or bursting into tears at a party.

> HEALTHY FAMILIES IDENTIFY, EXPRESS AND DEAL WITH FEELINGS AS THEY OCCUR. UNHEALTHY FAMILIES BURY FEELINGS AND THEN BECOME THE VICTIMS OF ALL THE PRESSURES AND EXPLOSIVE PROBLEMS THAT RESULT.

Repressing your feelings is like putting a wastepaper basket in the hall closet, setting it on fire, closing the door and leaving the house. You don't know what the outcome will be. The fire could extinguish itself, or it could spread and burn down the house. By repressing your feelings, you are no longer in charge of them. You don't know when or where they will pop up. Healthy families identify, express and deal with feelings as they occur. Unhealthy families bury feelings and then become the victims of all the pressures and explosive problems that result.

Listen to what Tim Kimmel said:

God has given His children two precious but fragile gifts. Cupped within our emotions, these gifts bubble up or spill out as needed. Their names are laughter and tears. Both are wonderful friends to the poised person. They can be enjoyed privately or given as an investment in others.

But like everything else in life, they can be abused, squandered or employed at the wrong time. Tears can be manipulative. Laughter can be deceptive. Both can be shaped into destructive weapons.

Loving parents realize that it is important to train children on the proper use of laughter and tears. They must help their children make these dimensions of their emotions friends rather than enemies.

I've watched macho dads mislead their boys by telling them tears are for women and sissies. They aren't stopping the boys' tears with that kind of irresponsible advice, they're merely changing the direction that the tears are falling. Instead of falling from a boy's eyes, those little drops of emotion will splash on the floor of his soul—compressed, denied, and spoiled.

Tears are friends. Allies. Like the valve on top of a pressure cooker, they relieve the soul. Like laughter, they can soothe and medicate a broken heart. Denying their expression is cruel.

We parents can be equally guilty of wiping joy from our children's faces. Placing stoic expectations on souls that were tailormade for laughter is a crime. A loving home needs to be bathed in laughter with parents setting the pace.[1]

How does your family handle emotions? Use the following lists of feelings to help you identify how well your family expresses emotions.

Place your initials beside each feeling you express in the context of your family. Then do the same for the rest of your family:

embarrassed	loving	worried	jealous
accepted	disappointed	guilty	affectionate
fearful	apprehensive	sad	morose
hurt	inferior	inadequate	rejected
mistrusted	depressed	afraid	frustrated
joyful	lonely	defensive	happy
elated	shy	angry	disgusted
grumpy	cheerful	jolly	glad
amazed	festive	edgy	shy

What did you learn about you, yourself and other family members? Is the expression of any of these feelings forbidden in your home? If so, who says so and why? Are any of the feelings difficult for you to identify and express at this time in your life?

6. TRIANGULATION

Triangulation relates to the communication process in the family. In triangulation, one family member uses another family member as a go-between. Father tells his daughter Sally, "Go see if your mother's still angry at me. Tell her I love her." Sally complies with his request. Mother retorts, "Tell your father to get lost!" How does Sally feel about getting caught in the middle? Perhaps she feels like a failure. She let her father down. Perhaps she fears that her mother is angry at her.

If triangulation is a regular pattern in a family, a child feels used and becomes involved in problems she should not be part of. She becomes a guilt collector, experiencing feelings she doesn't need and cannot handle.

7. DOUBLE MESSAGES

A wife asks her husband if he loves her. "Of course I do," he says as he gulps his food while reading the newspaper. Then he spends four hours in front of the TV and goes to bed without saying one more word to her. His words say, "I love you," but his actions say, "I don't care about you at all." It is a double message.

A young son puts his arms around his mother and feels her back stiffen as she tries to pull away. Both say, "I love you," but he also hears her body language saying she doesn't like being close to him. It is a double message.

Double messages abound: "I love you."/"Don't bother me now." "I love you."/"Get lost." "I need you."/"You're in my way." "Yes, I accept you."/"Why can't you be more like Susan?" Double messages are confusing, especially for the child. Do you hear any of them in your family at the present time?

8. LACK OF FUN

Unhealthy families are typically unable to loosen up, let go, play and have fun. They are overbalanced to the serious side of life. Their mottoes are: "Be serious." "Work hard." "You are what you do." "Play is a waste of time." When members of this family engage in play, usually someone gets hurt. They don't know when to stop. Humor is used as much to hurt as to have fun.

9. MARTYRDOM

Unhealthy families display a high tolerance for personal abuse and pain. Children hear their parents preaching that others come first, no matter what the personal cost. Children see their parents punish themselves through excessive behaviors such as drinking too much, overworking, overeating or exercising too hard. Children are challenged: "Tough it out, son; big boys don't cry." "You aren't hurt, Jane, so quit that whimpering—or else!" They see themselves as victims, pleasers or martyrs.

As adults, these people learn to steel themselves against weakness by denying themselves pleasure or advantage, and by suppressing their true feelings. Some martyrs actually pride themselves on how much they can bear before the pain becomes intolerable. Some, in the name of Christian humility, endure destructive responses from others that deny their value as children of God. God never asked us to live that way. Being a martyr is not a spiritual gift! It is a distortion of self-denial.

10. ENTANGLEMENT

The members of an unhealthy family are emotionally and relationally entangled in each other's lives. Individual identities are enmeshed. There are no clear-cut boundaries between each member. Everybody is poking his or her nose into everybody else's business. Mom makes Dad's problems her problems, Dad makes the kids' problems his problems and so on. If one family member is unhappy, the whole family is blue, and everybody blames everybody else for the state they are in. It's as though the whole family is sitting together on a giant swing. When one goes up, the others go up.

When one goes down, the others go down. Nobody thinks or feels for himself.[2]

ONE QUALITY HOUR [TOGETHER] IS MUCH BETTER
THAN 10 EMPTY HOURS.

Creating Quantity and Quality Time

Building a healthy family requires both quantity and quality time. Quantity time without quality is empty. I have seen families who spend an abundance of time together at home, but the hours mostly boil down to five individuals going about their separate lives.

Times of playing, sharing, working, traveling, learning and worshiping together are vital. One quality hour is much better than 10 empty hours. Sometimes we just need the knowledge that our family members are available if we need them.

A friend of mine made it a priority to give each of his four children one hour each week, exclusively, to do as they wanted and he followed their lead. Needless to say, this father found himself doing things he never anticipated doing as an adult. Another friend took each child out for lunch or breakfast (yes, even McDonald's counts) once a month and continued this commitment until each child left for college.

Nothing can take the place of one-on-one times between parent and child. I have a storehouse of memories of my many fishing adventures with my daughter, Sheryl. Josh McDowell shares one of his wife's projects with their children:

> Dottie enters into the world of her own children by keeping a record of each child's life on monthly calendars. I'm talking about those calendars that have at least a one inch square for each day of the month and into those squares

Dottie puts brief but special notations about what happened that day and what it meant to the child and the rest of the family.

Every year Dottie buys four calendars, one for each of our children. She tries to pick out photographic themes that fit each child. For example, one year Sean was into biking so she bought a calendar with pictures of ten-speed bike events. Because Sean's current big interest is basketball, this year he has a basketball calendar.

Kelly, Sean's older sister seems to be into everything, so Dottie wound up buying her a calendar that has a lot of pictures depicting shopping—a favorite sport of most teenagers. Katie, our ten year old, loves horses, so you know what is featured on her calendar.

Little Heather, only four years old, loves cats and, naturally, every month of her calendar has another picture of cats or kittens.

As each month unfolds, Dottie tries to fill in each day with a brief synopsis of what the child has done, what happened of note, and other brief remembrances. She doesn't always manage to cover each day, but she fills in an amazing number of days every month for all our kids.

The notations are simple ones—sometimes they even sound a bit mundane—but they're very meaningful to the children and to us their parents. For example here are some entries from last fall:

Heather—you went to school today. Daddy picked you up after school and you went to the drugstore for an ice cream Sundae.

Then the next day's entry reads:

You helped Dad and me at our family garage sale. Then you and I watched Boston lose the second playoff game with the Oakland A's. Sean—you got voted president of your freshman class today. I am sooooooo proud of you!

Luke came home with you to spend the night. He killed a scorpion that we found.

Along with making the notations on the squares for the day of the month, Dottie collects snapshots, certificates, news clippings, ribbons, and any other items that help record what the children accomplished or happened to them during the month. All of this memorabilia gets clipped, taped, or pasted on the photo/ picture page that appears above the days of the given month.

As each month passes, the scenes of cats, horses, basketball players, or shopping slowly disappear as Dottie adds a record of what has happened in the lives of our kids. You could say her calendar serves the same purpose as a scrapbook, but there is something intriguing about recording things day by day. It helps remind all of us of the value and meaning of time and how even the simplest things make up what life is really all about.

Like the notations, the photos and other memorabilia are often simple—but priceless. For example:

Sean is pictured with two different basketball teams he was playing on at the time. And along with those photos are some illustrations he drew for the science fair where he won a first-place ribbon.

On Kelly's calendar is a picture of Kelly with her "new car"—a 1957 Chevy that she got for a steal. If you're into cars at all you know that '57 Chevys are something of a "classic," but what's more important is that this photo records a classic time in Kelly's life—when she got her license and her own wheels and started using new freedoms and responsibilities.

Tucked in the back of every calendar are photos and other items that Dottie hasn't had time to record yet. But she works on her project every day—for at least ten minutes, when she makes her notations and tries to sort out photos and other items to display in their proper places. Dottie says that the calendars aren't a chore but something she really enjoys. I asked her what she might say for this book regarding the calendars and their value and she told me:

I would say the calendars are one of my biggest priorities because they're something that give us and the kids an invaluable record. I've often thought about when I would give these calendars to the children. When they get married? No, I don't think so. I believe I'll give them the calendars when they have children of their own. When they get married they'll be so busy getting their homes together the calendars might be lost in the shuffle, but when they have children then they'll realize the incredible value of a record like this.

The reason I got started was because I was given a baby shower gift when Heather came—a calendar with the stickers that said, "The first time I sat up," "The first time I smiled," and so on. I got such a kick out of filling out those stickers for Heather I decided to start making calendar records for all the other children, and that's what I've been doing ever since.

I admit the calendars are a lot of work, but they are also a lot of fun. As I collect the different years, I can see month by month how the children grow, what they are into, what their interests were, what they left behind and what they continued on to do. There's tremendous satisfaction in that.[3]

THE BEST OF TIMES

What is the criteria you use to measure whether or not you are succeeding in your family life? A couple named Jerry and Rita were asked the question, "What were the best times in your parenting?"

"We are still in the midst of the best of times," said Jerry. "Talking to my children like adults and watching them begin college are the best of times. My daughter called the other night from college and said, 'Dad, you talk to me like a parent, but you write letters like a friend.' What a feeling! I am experiencing adulthood with my children."

Rita likewise took a wide-open view of the best of times with her children. "The best of times as a parent is parenting. I tell people who don't have children, 'You can't know what you are giving up when you say you don't want to be a parent. There is no way you can sense what you would be missing unless you are a parent.' I am so glad this is what we've given our lives to—to raising our children and to loving each other."

When have they failed as parents? Rita: "The times I fail most are when I get angry. When I get angry, I cease to function. Feeling what the kids are feeling is the most important thing to me. When I'm angry, I don't listen. Then I am totally ineffective. All the things that make someone a good parent are gone when they are angry. At my angriest times, I try to go off privately, sometimes I cry, then come back and talk to everyone like I should have in the first place.

Jerry also sees his biggest parental failure as anger, not toward the children, but toward Rita. "If I am angry at Rita around the children, I feel I have not been in control as father of the household. I don't know how the kids see it, but I see it as a parental failure.[4]

This same couple was asked the question, "If you were to write a book on parenting, what would you include in it?" They suggested giving an abundance of praise and encouragement, consistently letting their kids know they are great kids, focusing on the positives and making the love relationship in the family the most important item. They said that relationships are the most important ingredients. Gift giving was essential—not material gifts, but the gifts of time, traditions, music lessons, travel and hobbies.[5]

SHARING FEELINGS

Another family told me what they especially valued in their family was openly sharing the entire range of feelings with one another. They could cry, hug, touch and be angry. When distance occurred between members, they would each take the initiative to return, talk about the issue, listen to one another, apologize when necessary and extend forgiveness. Each would conclude their part in the discussion by saying, "...and this is what I will do different the next time!" What an important and family-changing statement!

Criteria for Family Success

What are your criteria for family success? Use the space provided to list six to eight of the criteria you are using to measure success in your family.

1. _____

2. _____

3. _____

4. _____

5. _____

6. _____

7. _____

8. _____

Is each one consistent with Scripture? On a scale of 0 to 10, how realistic is each one? Most of us would like to see positive progress in our families. The following are some suggestions and ideas that individual parents have found helpful in spending individual time with their children:

Create for each child a never-ending story. Using him as the main character, each evening before bedtime weave a tale about him and his adventures. Ask him what things he'd like to do, see, explore, and learn about in his ongoing fantasy.

Whenever a young child shows you proudly what she did—a puzzle, a picture, a house of blocks—ask her if she'd like to do it again so you can watch.

While you are enjoying a hobby—gardening, woodworking, crafts, painting—invite a child to watch and introduce him to the basics. Provide him tools of the craft with which to copy you. One mother described herself as "an avid gardener. All my kids, even the two-year-old, know how to pull a carrot."

Use a tape recorder to produce a sound diary for each child. Record his earliest sounds—laughing, cooing, crying. Continue with his first words, songs, counting. In essence, create a permanent time capsule of his development through language. Set aside "recording sessions" for each child to tell his diary what he's learned recently.

Allow the child to select her own special day of the week. On that day, show or teach her how to do something; for instance, sing a song, write a poem, bake cookies, fry an egg, make toast, tie a ribbon, wrap a gift, sew on a button, sort laundry, pump her own gas, discriminate a weed from a flower, identify a tree by its leaves, bait a hook, read a road map, program the VCR, tie a tie, play tic-tac-toe. Said a youngster now in college, "Thursday was Dad's day off. He taught me how to tie my shoes on a Thursday."

Carry a camera with you or keep one nearby so as to catch a child in her own special moments with Mom and Dad.

Take a child to visit your workplace. If possible, let him spend time with you as you move through your day. Indeed, the chance to "see where Mom/Dad works" was ranked at or near the top of favorite parent-child activities by these children.

On a rotating basis, ask each of the children if she would like to go with you as you run errands, go to the store, visit a friend, or take a drive somewhere. The car is a prime vehicle for moments of privacy between parent and child. The destination of the trip is less important than the time taken getting there. Said a son about car trips with his father, "I loved my times *alone* with him, regardless of where we went."

Establish a weekly walk day during which you and one child take a leisurely walk. "I'll never forget how my dad would just let me stop and smell the flowers, look at the trees, pick up the stones," said one daughter. "Start young" is the advice of these parents. Introducing a walk day to a fifteen-year-old who fusses about taking the trash thirty feet to the end of the driveway may trigger a look that says, "Walk? I'll be ready to drive in six months."

Ask your daughter or son, depending on whether you're a mom or dad, for a "date." Agree on the day, set the time, and plan the evening to its completion. Said a seven-year-old daughter obviously in love with her daddy, "When my daddy gets me flowers and we go out is the best, because he loves me!"

Pick a day, say the third Monday of the month, as breakfast day, to spend with your son or daughter. Before school or work or athletic practice, you and your child go to breakfast together. Or let each child choose a lunch day or ice-cream day. Many of the children spoke enthusiastically of a parent coming to school to eat lunch with them or taking them out to lunch.

If your child practices a musical instrument, every so often quietly sit and listen. Your attention, punctuated by a complimentary word or two now and then, is a motivator and a display of pride. "If I had to choose one memory with my father, I'd say it was the time I came home from college on spring break and told him about the opera I was in at Indiana University. I remember relating to him the entire story of *Rigoletto* as we listened to the music. He'd never had any exposure to opera, but I was so pleased he shared with me this lovely discovery I'd made."

Step in occasionally and help your child with his chores—drying the dishes, raking leaves, shoveling snow, doing laundry, dusting, setting the table. In addition to giving a lesson in cooperation, you will stimulate some natural camaraderie. "Working in the garden or yard with my parents was a lot of fun for me. Other kids used to ask me why my parents made us work so much. If they only knew what fun we had at those times." It's not the chore that's fun, it's having you there, if only because you're not thinking up something else for the kids to do![6]

FAMILY TRADITIONS

Do you have any special family traditions? These can include what you do for holidays, birthdays, vacations, at mealtime, the way you greet one another or the way you say goodnight. For example, the Walton family on television would say goodnight to each other loud enough from each of their rooms so everyone could hear and respond. Come to think of it, watching this program together each week was one of our family traditions. We wouldn't miss it.

Some young children will call out to one of their parents after going to bed, "You forgot to say prayers with me tonight." That is a tradition. Family traditions can become so important that the members are quite upset when they are forgotten or neglected

Take a moment and respond to the following questions:

1. What were the family traditions you experienced in your family of origin?
2. Which family traditions did you bring with you into your current family?
3. Which new family traditions have you created?
4. What family tradition did your spouse bring with him or her?
5. What is the purpose and value of your family traditions?

The Tremaines were a family of five. Sunday dinner was a family affair that usually involved guests or some of the children's friends. All the plates were placed face down on the table. When everyone was seated, they would turn them over. One of the plates was labeled, "You are special today." Because the plates were put on the table randomly—including one on the floor for their Husky dog—no one knew in advance who would be that day's honoree. It was usually a wild time when "Blackie" was the special pooch for the day!

INVESTMENT OF TIME

Some of the most special family memories have nothing to do with traditions. They are built on relationships, experiences and the investment of time. Bart Campolo wrote this letter to his father, Tony, about his favorite family snapshots:

The times that I remember best, though, are the times I spent with you. I love those memories best of all, Dad, and they're a big part of who I am. That's the whole point of these letters for me. My childhood is gone, and I will never be able to be with you the way I was with you as a little boy. I will never be that small, and you will never seem that big again. But I have my stories, and they comfort me when I am overwhelmed by the world, when I am too old all of a sudden, when I lose my sense of wonder. They are all I have of my boyhood, and the reason I wish we had spent more time together is that I wish I had more of them now. It isn't that you didn't do enough, you see, for I would always want more. You were the king of the world back then, the imp of fun, the man with all the answers, the one who could always fix what was broken. You made life seem magical to me.

When you die, Dad, I will surely go to pieces for a while, because I still count on you more than anyone knows, but in the end I will be all right. I will have my stories, and in them I will always have part of you, the part that tells me who I am and where I came from. I only wish there was more because what there is means all the world to me.

Love,
Bart[7]

Notes
1. Tim Kimmel, *Legacy of Love* (Portland, Oreg.: Multnomah Press, 1989), pp. 90-91.
2. John Friel and Linda Friel, *Adult Children* (Hollywood, Fla.: Health Communications, Inc., 1988), pp. 77-79, adapted.
3. Josh McDowell and Dick Day, *How to Be a Hero to Your Kids* (Dallas, Tex.: Word Publishing, 1991), pp. 164-165.
4. Dr. Ray Guarendi, *Back to the Family* (New York: Villard Books, 1990), p. 13.
5. Ibid., p. 14, adapted.
6. Ibid., pp. 125-127.
7. Tony and Bart Campolo, *The Things We Wish We Had Said* (Dallas, Tex.: Word Publishing, 1989), pp. 213-214.